D0207600

Building Movement Bridges

Recent Titles in
Contributions in Sociology

Building Movement Bridges

The Coalition of Labor Union Women

Silke Roth

Contributions in Sociology, Number 138
Dan A. Chekki, Series Adviser

Westport, Connecticut
London

Library of Congress Cataloging-in-Publication Data

Roth, Silke.
  Building movement bridges : the Coalition of Labor Union Women / Silke Roth.
    p. cm.—(Contributions in sociology, ISSN 0084–9278 ; no. 138)
  Includes bibliographical references and index.
  ISBN 0–313–31632–5 (alk. paper)
    1. Coalition of Labor Women (U.S.)—History.   2. Women in the labor
  movement—United States—History.   3. Women labor union members—United
  States—History.   I. Title.   II. Series.
  HD6079.2.U5 R684 2003
  331.88′082′0973—dc21   2002029865

British Library Cataloguing in Publication Data is available.

Copyright © 2003 by Silke Roth

All rights reserved. No portion of this book may be
reproduced, by any process or technique, without the
express written consent of the publisher.

Library of Congress Catalog Card Number: 2002029865
ISBN: 0–313–31632–5
ISSN: 0084–9278

First published in 2003

Praeger Publishers, 88 Post Road West, Westport, CT 06881
An imprint of Greenwood Publishing Group, Inc.
www.praeger.com

Printed in the United States of America

The paper used in this book complies with the
Permanent Paper Standard issued by the National
Information Standards Organization (Z39.48–1984).

10 9 8 7 6 5 4 3 2 1

Copyright Acknowledgment

The author and publisher gratefully acknowledge permission to quote from the following:

Roth, Silke. Developing Working Class Feminism: A Biographical Approach to Social Movement Participation. In *Self, Identity and Social Movements*, ed. by Sheldon Stryker, Timothy Owens and Robert W. White. Minneapolis, MN. University of Minnesota Press, 2000, 300–323.

To

Maria Luz Samper

and

Myra Marx Ferree

Contents

Contents

Illustrations

Preface

This book is dedicated to two outstanding mentors: Maria Luz Samper and Myra Marx Ferree. The late Maria Luz Samper helped me to understand the American labor movement, opened countless doors for me, and cheered me up when I needed it. It saddens me that I could not present this book to her and I miss her very much. Myra Marx Ferree has supported this project from the earliest stages, reading virtually every draft. I could not have wished for a better, kinder, and more generous advisor. She is the teacher I had always been looking for.

There are many more people I am grateful to: First, I would like to thank the activists who took the time and answered my many questions. I am grateful for the support I received from the Coalition of Labor Union Women, especially national president Gloria Johnson, and Heather Hauck, director of the CLUW Center for Education and Research. I also would like to thank the CLUW staff—Chrystl Bridgeforth, Yvonne Cohen, and Samantha Burke—and the IUE staff, in particular Louise Smothers and Bill Gray—for their support, as well as Helene Shay and Lois O'Connor in Connecticut, and Helen Elkiss and Manny Tuteur in Chicago for their assistance and hospitality.

The dissertation research on which this book is based was supported through a dissertation fellowship of the Hans-Böckler-Stiftung of the German Trade Union Federation. I would like to thank Werner Fiedler for his assistance. The Hans-Böckler-Stiftung also supported a three-month-long internship at the CLUW Center for Education and Research, during which I conducted the membership survey. My research was supported through a Dissertation Fellowship and several summer fellowships from the Department of Sociology of the University of Connecticut. I greatly appreciate the help from Mike Smith and Toranda Spencer from the CLUW Archives at Wayne State University, who provided me numerous reference sources. I also would like to thank the staff of interlibrary loan of Homer Babbidge Library at the University of Connecticut for providing me with literature.

I owe the members of my advisory committee, Myra Marx Ferree, the late Maria Luz Samper, Gaye Tuchman, and Clint Sanders, many thanks for their support. Gaye Tuchman had always inspiring comments for me. I thank Clint Sanders for joining my advisory committee when this work was already well in progress and helping me to deal with my role(s) as qualitative researcher. Charles Kamen from the Department of Sociology at the University of Connecticut, now at the Census Bureau in Jerusalem, and Harald Künemund from the Department of Sociology of the Free University of Berlin helped me in designing the questionnaire. Ruth Milkman gave valuable advise and Barry Hirsch provided data on union membership. I also thank Margit Mayer from the J.F. Kennedy Institut of the Free University of Berlin for her continued support.

Portions of this work were presented at meetings of the American Sociological Association, the Eastern Sociological Society, the International Qualitative Analysis Conference, the Conference "The Relation of Social and Personal Identities and Self-Esteem: New Frontiers, New Implications" at Indiana University, colloquia at the Free University of Berlin, the Humboldt University of Berlin, and the University of Pennsylvania. The University of Pennsylvania was an excellent place for completing this manuscript. I am particularly grateful for the support of Demie Kurz, Robin Leidner, Doug Massey, Frank Trommler, and Herb Smith.

Francois Guesnet, Kathrin Zippel, Kimberly Morgan, Denise Anthony, Claudia Neusüß, Patricia Yancey Martin, and Ingrid Miethe read the manuscript and helped me tremendously with their critical and encouraging comments. Alison Anderson and Alice Goffman corrected my English and helped me make the book readable. Terri Jennings helped me through the formatting of the manuscript.

I am very grateful for the friendship and support of Denise Anthony, Ruth Arnold, Loretta Bass, Francois Guesnet, Elo Hüskes, Harald Künemund, Julia McQuillan, Ingrid Miethe, Claudia Neusüß, Naomi Reich, Kay Sauerteig, Diane Schaal, Friederike Tebbe, and Kathrin Zippel. Finally, thanks to my parents, Hermann and Liese Roth, for always being there for me.

Abbreviations

ACTWU	Amalgamated Clothing and Textile Workers Union
AFGE	American Federation of Government Employees
AFL	American Federation of Labor
AFL–CIO	American Federation of Labor–Congress of Industrial Organizations
AFSCME	American Federation of State, Municipal, and County Employees
AFT	American Federation of Teachers
ANA	American Nurses Association
APALA	Asian Pacific American Labor Alliance
APRI	A. Philip Randolph Institute
BWJ	Black Workers for Justice
CBTU	Coalition of Black Trade Unionists
CIO	Congress of Industrial Organizations
CLC	Canadian Labor Congress
CLUW	Coalition of Labor Union Women
CPUSA	Communist Party USA

CWA	Communication Workers of America
ERA	Equal Rights Amendment
HEREIU	Hotel and Restaurant Employees International Union
IAMAW	International Association of Machinists and Aerospace Workers
IBEW	International Brotherhood of Electrical Workers
IBT	International Brotherhood of Teamsters
ILGWU	International Ladies' Garments Workers Union
IUE	International Union of Electronic, Electrical, Salaried, Machine and Furniture Workers
NAACP	National Association for the Advancement of Colored People
NARAL	National Abortion Rights Action League
NEA	National Education Association
NOW	National Organization for Women
OPEIU	Office and Professional Employees International Union
RWSDU	Retail, Wholesale, and Department Store Union
SEIU	Service Employees International Union
SNCC	Student Nonviolent Coordinating Committee
TNG	The Newspaper Guild
UAW	United Autoworkers
UCLEA	University and College Labor Education Association
UFCW	United Food and Commercial Workers
UMA	United Mineworkers of America
UNITE	Union of Needletrades, Industrial, and Textile Employees
USWA	United Steelworkers of America

1

Introduction

In March 1974, a group of more than 3,000 women met in Chicago to form the Coalition of Labor Union Women. Organizers and participants were overwhelmed by the extent of interest in the convention and recalled the enthusiasm they experienced at the event. Catherine Conroy, who in 1975 would be the first woman elected to the Wisconsin State AFL–CIO executive board, was one of the participants. She recollected: "Of course, the famous big national meeting in Chicago. I was there for that. That was exciting. That particular convention made me think that I had been reborn and could see the beginning of the CIO, because everybody was so full of idealism and enthusiasm, but I think probably everybody realized the rough road was still ahead. The real problem is to coordinate these things, translate them into union action" (Conroy 1996: 252).

The last sentence hints at the massive struggles the newly formed organization experienced in its first few years because of the variety of backgrounds and experiences among its participants. Conroy, for example, had been active in labor organizing since the late 1930s and had been one of the few women staff representatives of the Communication Workers of America in the 1950s; she was also appointed to the Wisconsin Governor's Commission of the Status of Women, helped found the National Organization of Women, and was president of the first Chicago NOW chapter (O'Farrell and Kornbluh 1996). Conroy's involvement in the women's movement and the labor movement exemplifies what I call *social movement interaction*.

Social movements are neither internally homogeneous nor separate from one another. Instead they are connected, and the connections between movements are more often tense and conflicting than smooth. Furthermore, members do not necessarily participate in only one social movement. Activists often take part in several different movements and movement organizations (Mische 2003). Some members who are involved in various movements feel the need to form what I call *bridging organizations*, organizations that seek to make connections between different movements. This is especially important when the relationship between two movements (like the women's movement and the labor movement) is of vital importance to its constituency (working women) but strained. Bridging organizations seek to overcome the constraints and conflicts of the past in order to improve the relationship between those movements and thus enable broad coalitions. CLUW is such a bridging organization. Bridging processes change social movements because through their coalition and framing work new issues enter the agenda of movements and movement organizations. Internal differentiation, coalitions, organizations that pursue issues that concern more than one social movement, and overlapping individual memberships represent different forms of social movement interaction, which can be cooperative or conflicting, and even occur when movements attempt to ignore each other.

Social movements have typically been studied separately, and the focus has been on each movement's defining single issue and ideal-typical constituency rather than on how the movements challenge interlocking systems of domination like class, racial, and gender domination (Morris 1992). For example, the civil rights movement—or the issue of race—has been typified as a movement of African American men (Barnett 1993); the labor movement—or the issue of class—as a movement of white men (Roediger 1991); and the women's movement—or the issue of gender—as a movement of white women (Buechler 1990). The actual participation of women, especially women of color,[1] in all these movements points to the interrelatedness of race, class, and gender at both individual and movement levels, and calls for a framework that captures multiple forms of oppression and how they are addressed through social movements. In addition, social movements are heterogeneous in their organizational forms, constituencies, strategies, and agenda. Some theorists therefore suggest describing social movements as interactions (Tilly 1978; Melucci 1989; Mische 2003) to capture their emergence and ephemeral character.

I suggest the term "social movement interaction" to call attention to the interactions between different movements (for example, the women's movement and the peace movement, or the labor movement and the environmental movement), which can be analyzed in two respects. First, social movement interaction can be analyzed with respect to outcomes: the emergence and development of social movements or movement organizations. In other words, the appearance of a social movement organization or a change in a social movement can be explained as a result of conflict or cooperation with another movement. Second, the mechanisms of the interaction itself are of interest. Social movement interaction takes place in diffusion processes, coalition-building, and the sharing of personnel. The study of social movement interaction can build on knowledge about organizational linkages, networks and diffusion processes (Freeman 1975; Klandermans 1992; McAdam 1982; Morris 1984; McAdam and Rucht 1993; Mische 2003).

Social movement interaction has similarities with social movement spillover (Meyer and Whittier 1994). In both cases mechanisms of transmission include organizational coalitions, overlapping movement communities, shared personnel, and broader chances for social movements in the external environment (also known as political opportunity structures or cycles of protest) (Tarrow 1994). Mesomobilization processes involve the participation of movement organizations that belong to a number of different movements (Gerhards and Rucht 1992) and so constitute a form of social movement interaction. Social movement interaction differs from social movement spillover in that it addresses the exchange between social movements in both directions, analyzing how movements influence each other, rather than focusing on only one movement affecting the other. This means that, while "migration of personnel between issues and organizations is bounded by cultural and ideological constraints" (Meyer and Whittier 1994:292), these constraints are challenged through social movement interaction. The notion of social movement interaction thus takes into account that activists and organizations make decisions based on their biographies, histories, and identities. This suggests that feelings of accountability and loyalty might undermine the potential for coalition and collaboration, yet at the same time there might be attempts to reconcile or erase traditional conflicts, boundaries, or constraints.

The notion of social movement interaction is important for theoretical as well as political and pragmatic reasons. It goes beyond previous approaches to diffusion and allows us to address multiple and interlocking sets of oppressions such as sexism, racism, and economic inequality. It also allows us to better understand what is needed to form coalitions and alliances. I argue that bridging organizations provide crucial channels between movements and strengthen social movements by contributing to wider coalitions. Since the beginning of the 1990s, the American labor movement has experienced a revitalization (Clawson and Clawson 1999; Turner et al. 2001), putting special emphasis on organizing (Bronfenbrenner et al. 1998; Foerster 2001), acting like a social movement (Johnston 2001), and addressing particularly women and people of color (Adams 1998; Chen and Wong 1998; La Luz and Finn 1998; Needleman 1998). I contend that bridging organizations such as CLUW play an important role in this process.

Such social movement interaction, as this volume will show, can be analyzed at three interrelated levels. At the *individual* level, processes of political socialization must be addressed. A biographical perspective allows us to understand how activists develop political consciousness while participating in collective action. They gain experiences while participating in contentious politics and are confronted with having to prioritize or reconcile conflicting identities, for example, a feminist and a labor identity, if one or both of these movements demand exclusive solidarity (Ferree and Roth 1998). At the *organizational* level, bridging organizations serve as translators between different movements and seek to address issues that seem to "belong" to one movement. Bridging organizations need to position themselves. The structure and strategies of such an organization signal to whom it feels accountable. I argue that bridging organizations are founded by activists who seek to reconcile conflicting identities. Finally, at the *movement* level, social movement interaction provides a framework to understand how movements influence each other, how they form coalitions, and how movement agendas are broadened.

In this study, I show how political biographies or processes of political socialization at the individual level, and the formation and coalition work of bridging organizations at the organizational level, are interconnected and contribute to change in the organizations and their strategies, and broadening of the agenda of social movements. In processes of political socialization, activists develop a "taste for tactics" (Jasper 1997). They prefer certain organizational forms and strategies. Such preferences play a role when new organizations are founded. An organization's structure is an expression of its collective identity and will attract members who share its partiality for a bureaucratic or collectivist structure. Organizations thus must be seen as agents of socialization at the same time that they also result from earlier socialization processes. The analysis of bridging organizations is particularly interesting because their members seek to address goals that are usually addressed by different movements with different organizational cultures. Members of bridging organizations try to reconcile their loyalties to and resolve the tensions between the movements involved. The long, conflictual relationship between the women's movement and the labor movement makes CLUW an especially interesting case for the study of a bridging organization.

AN UNEASY RELATIONSHIP

The relationship between the women's movement and the labor movement has a long tradition of ambivalence and complexity. Women have been involved in the American labor movement as workers as well as supporters of working men since the first unions were formed in the United States. Though women workers have always benefited from unionization, unions have at times excluded women (and people of color) from their membership (Hartmann 1976; Milkman 1990). Labor shortages during wars or periods of economic growth opened the labor market and the unions to working women (Amott and Matthaei 1991; Foner 1980). The women's and civil rights movements of the 1960s and 1970s put women's and minority issues on the agenda of the labor movement (Bell 1985; Milkman 1985, 1990). On the one hand, the two movements cooperated with respect to improving the conditions of working women through lobbying for child and family care; on the other hand, they disagreed at times with respect to protective legislation and the Equal Rights Amendment (ERA). Protective legislation, which was hard won by the labor movement, emphasized the difference between men and women and led to the exclusion of women from certain jobs and work hours. The ERA, rather, sought to abolish legislation and practices that perpetuate the inequality of men and women (Mansbridge 1986).

Despite these obvious differences of interest, women of the labor movement have participated in the formation of women's movement organizations such as the National Organization for Women. Conversely, the diffusion of feminist consciousness (Klein 1987) resulting from the women's movement changed the expectations of women in the labor movement. Union feminism is at the intersection point, both historically and today. The founding of the Coalition of Labor Union Women in 1974 is embedded in the history of the American labor movement and marked by the conflicts between the labor movement and the women's movement, especially through the sixties and seventies.

THE COALITION OF LABOR UNION WOMEN

The Coalition of Labor Union Women (CLUW) was founded as one of the first national organizations of the second wave of feminism and serves a mediating role between the women's movement and the labor movement. The founders came from both communities. They agreed on the need to address working-class women's concerns as both class-based (hence part of the labor movement) and gender-based (hence part of the feminist agenda) and adopted four main goals: to bring women into union leadership, to organize unorganized women workers, to bring women's issues onto the labor agenda, and to involve women in political action. However, members differed regarding how to pursue these goals as well as how to structure the organization.

CLUW is a national organization with about 70 chapters distributed across most states of the United States. Members are active at the local level in chapters and at the national level as delegates to the National Executive Board (NEB), which meets about three times each year. State vice presidents and coordinators provide a link between the national, state, and chapter levels. Regular membership in the organization is limited to union members. Non-union members can hold associate membership, but they are excluded from the decision-making process. In 1994, CLUW had about 18,000 members. CLUW is an exceptionally diverse women's organization with a high proportion of "women of color," especially African American women, among the membership and the leadership. According to a 1994 survey of 524 members,[2] about one third of the respondents were minorities: 21% African American, 6% Hispanic American, 1% Asian American, 2% Native American, and 2% who indicated that they belonged to "other" racial/ethnic groups. CLUW reflects the higher unionization rate of "women of color" compared to white women: in 2001, 11% of the white, Hispanic, and Chinese women and 15% of the African American women were unionized (Bureau of the Census 2002).[3]

ACTIVISTS' BIOGRAPHIES AND POLITICAL SOCIALIZATION

This book analyzes social movement interaction at the movement, organizational, and individual level. At the individual level, we will be concerned with the biographies and political identities of social movement activists. Activists often move from one movement to another (Evans 1979; McAdam 1988) or participate in several movements simultaneously (Gerhards and Rucht 1992; Rose 2000; Meyer and Whittier 1994). This puts them in a position to reconcile various political identities (Roth 2000). Oppositional consciousness (Mansbridge and Morris 2001) is grounded in a variety of collective identities that may or may not be in tension with each other. The case study presented here focuses in particular on feminist consciousness, class consciousness and labor identity, and race and ethnic consciousness. But such interaction is also found between movements like the peace movement and the women's movement (Meyer and Whittier 1994) or the environmental movement and the labor movement (Rose 2000).

Members bring their experiences to bear on the movements in which they participate, while participation in the movement also changes their lives. The political (and other, like school, work, family) experiences activists bring to social movements and social movement organizations (Klandermans 1990) have an impact on the development of the movement, because members from different backgrounds may differ on the diagnosis of and potential solutions for social problems. The way members identify the purpose of an organization shapes their expectations regarding the issues the organization should pursue and the strategies that should be employed. The negotiation processes among members create the structure and collective identity of the organization. Depending on the experiences and preferences of the membership, the organizational structure may be bureaucratic or loosely structured; activities may range from insider tactics (Spalter-Roth and Schreiber 1995) like lobbying to civil disobedience. The decision for or against specific organizational forms and tactics is an expression of the collective identity of the organization (Downey 1986).

Tracing activists' biographies is one way to map social movements, in that the biographies tell about the emergence of political consciousness and collective action, recruitment processes and participation patterns, and networks (Diani 1992; Friedman and McAdam 1992; Klandermans 1990; Knoke and Wisely 1990; McAdam 1988b). The fact that movement activists often move from one movement or movement organization to another suggests that a biographical perspective will be especially useful for understanding social movement interaction (Miethe and Roth 2000). In general, participation in the social movements of the 1960s and 1970s changed the lives of activists (Whalen and Flacks 1989). White women's participation and experiences in the civil rights movement led to the emergence of the women's liberation movement (Evans 1979). Participation in movement actions like the Freedom Summer campaign (McAdam 1988a) had long-term effects on members' political convictions and professional and family lives.

The membership typology I develop is based on the evaluation of life-history and in-depth interviews with current and former members of the Coalition of Labor Union Women (see Appendix). I distinguish four membership types—founding mothers, rebellious daughters, political animals, and fighting victims. Activists became politicized in various contexts, moved from one social movement to another, and participated in several social movements or social movement organizations at the same time. Founding mothers and rebellious daughters created CLUW, and for them the organization became a place where they could reconcile their conflicting feminist and labor identities. The founding mothers emphasized their trade union identity, while the rebellious daughters criticized the sexism of the male-led labor movement. The political animals and the fighting victims joined CLUW later on. They learned about CLUW through the union, and CLUW became their avenue to the women's movement. The political animals were first active in community politics. The fighting victims were the only group that became active as a result of a discrimination experience.

The four types represent different versions of "union feminism,"[4] but they all saw the labor movement as an important ally for women and people of color. And for all four types it was important to address not only class and gender, but also race and any other source of inequality, discrimination, and oppression. They were aware that the labor movement had discriminated against women and people of color in the past and had only recently discovered the need to address the needs of these groups. Initially, I labeled this inclusive form of feminism, which is concerned with class, gender, race, and other systems of oppression, "working class feminism" (Roth 2000). However, CLUW as a labor organization included not only working-class women but also many professionals. Moreover, this is true not only for CLUW but also for the labor movement in general (Heckscher 1988). I also considered the term "social justice feminism" because CLUW members emphasize that they were against prioritizing any one form of discrimination and were convinced that all forms have to be addressed simultaneously.

CLUW was certainly concerned with social justice in a broad and inclusive sense, but it chose a specific social movement—the labor movement—in order to pursue social justice. As the membership typology shows, however, the four types differed regarding their relationship to the labor movement and what forms of action or criticism they found appropriate. These differences were grounded in different processes of political socialization. Thus one can see that the formation of CLUW was a result of processes of political socialization, namely the need of the founding members to reconcile conflicting feminist and union identities. The founding of CLUW was also a result of the cycle of protest in the late 1960s and early 1970s and diffusion of feminist consciousness, which led to a proliferation of feminist organizations.

Women in the four types differed regarding biographical continuity or the circumstances under which they became politically active and their recruitment into and participation in the labor movement, CLUW, and other social movements, political parties, and community activism. The union feminism of the founding mothers emphasized their trade union identity, while that of the rebellious daughters was anchored in a feminist critique of the labor movement and a critique of the racial and class biases of the women's movement. The union feminism of the political animals was issue-oriented, and valued the labor movement and the women's movement as equally important and mutually supportive. The union feminism of the fighting victims evolved from experiences of discrimination and the fight against discrimination in the context of the labor movement and CLUW. All four types of union feminism emphasized equality and justice regardless of race, class, and gender, and saw these as dimensions that needed to be addressed jointly. They also could be distinguished regarding the extent to which injustice—or experiences of unequal treatment and discrimination provided the motivation to get involved in political action.

The life histories thus show how experiences of discrimination at the individual level are resolved through participation in organizations. Sometimes these experiences could be quite ambivalent, for instance, if the union was perceived as an ally against economic discrimination but at the same time members experienced sexual harassment in the union. Furthermore, the members differed in terms of their feminist, class, or race consciousness. These identities were expressed in loyalty and accountability to social movements, in this case the labor movement and the women's movement. CLUW did not see its task as working on inequality based on race as such, but race issues were high in the organization's awareness.

BRIDGING ORGANIZATIONS

Coalitions of organizations and activists from various movements, overlapping membership, and bridging organizations constitute different forms of social movement interaction at the organizational level. They represent three levels (low to high) of movement integration. In each case, collaboration between social movements results in diffusion processes whereby ideas and repertoires of action are exchanged. Bridging organizations can be distinguished from coalitions and from mass-membership organizations with diverse constituencies. Participation in a temporary, issue-related coalition does not require that the partici-pating organizations change their organizations (though that might be an un-wanted and unanticipated effect). Organizations that have members who belong to a variety of other social movements like political parties or voluntary associa-tions do not seek to build ongoing relations with these movements. In contrast, a bridging organization attempts to synthesize the elements and goals of two movements, to establish itself as a link between movements, a task that can be difficult (and necessary) when relations between the two movements are strained. Bridging organizations contribute to and support coalition building and thus contribute to "mesomobilization" (Gerhards and Rucht 1992). They can be seen as nodes in a network. As Mische (2003) has pointed out, successful coali-tion building relies on strong ties (friendships) and weak ties (acquaintance-ships). A bridging organization provides both: on the one hand, members of the organization form close friendships; on the other, the organization provides in-formation and serves as an entry point.

Movement success builds on the ability to form coalitions—thus social movement interaction and bridging organizations are important concepts. While initial contact and mutual interests are the preconditions for the formation of social movements, bridging organizations institutionalize such contact. Bridge builders, individuals who belong to different social movements, for example the labor movement and the environmental movement (Rose 2000), or link social movements and the community, for example in the civil rights movement (Rob-nett 1997), are important. However, in contrast to these personal ties, bridging organizations provide an institutional connection between social movements and stand for the possibility to achieve long-standing compromises among varying actors.

Permanent collaboration in a bridging organization requires long-term agreement rather than the short-term compromises typical for coalitions. Mem-bers of any organization have to negotiate an organizational setting and strate-gies with which members can identify. Those who cannot agree with the negoti-ated structure will leave the organization sooner or later. The organizational form and strategies that inform about the collective identity and accountability of the organization also determine access to networks as organizational re-sources (Freeman 1973; 1975; Meyer and Whittier 1994). Success and failure of coalition building are closely related to the framing of social issues (Ferree and Roth 1998). Social movement interaction includes not only formation of coali-tions but also competition for resources (McCarthy and Zald 1977).

Bridging organizations address a diverse membership and intend to form a permanent coalition or alliance. Bridging work is a form of social movement interaction that focuses explicitly on efforts to overcome and negotiate conflicts that result from different collective identities that are rooted in and expressed by organizational and strategic repertoires. The organizational repertoires of the labor and the women's movement are quite different. Labor unions tend to be hierarchical, bureaucratic organizations. The women's movement, by contrast, encompasses a wide range of different organizations (Martin 1990; Ferree and Martin 1995). Some feminist organizations employ formal structures, but the movement in general emphasizes empowerment and direct democracy.

In a bridging organization like CLUW, members had to choose an organizational form. This choice communicated to the environment as well as to the members to which movement the organization felt accountable. CLUW is modeled after and is one of the support groups of the AFL–CIO. CLUW members participate in national conventions as union or chapter delegates. The labor federation provides financial and other resources (speakers, information material), while CLUW supports political and union action of union women. About a third of CLUW's budget comes from the AFL–CIO.[5] But CLUW also is a part of the women's movement in that it draws from community activism, it addresses gender as its key issue, and it has a largely female membership.

The collective identity of an organization reflects the logic and language of institutional sectors. The ambiguous and conflictual nature of CLUW's collective identity became most prominently visible in the negotiation processes of the founding members around the structure of the organization. In 1974, when CLUW was founded, women labor leaders and activists hoped they would gain more for women in unions within the framework of the labor movement than as an outsider organization. Those who argued for "union solidarity" prevailed and thus chose acknowledgment and support through the AFL–CIO over a critical position toward the discrimination that women experienced in the labor movement, but that was rarely addressed prior to the second wave of the women's movement.[6] Thus accountability toward the labor movement played a bigger role than accountability toward the women's movement. As Josh Gamson (1996, 1997) has argued, organizational structure is an expression of collective identity and represents an interpretation of the political and cultural opportunity structure in which an organization is situated. Based on the structure of the organization, CLUW presented itself more as a part of the labor movement than as a part of the women's movement.

This can be seen as a pragmatic response to the realities of the political opportunity structure. As Katzenstein (1998) has pointed out with respect to the Catholic Church and the U.S. military, sometimes the most efficient feminist strategies are "unobtrusive mobilization" and "discursive politics." Embeddedness and commitments set limits to the development of organizations. Bridging organizations, which are accountable to two social movements, are doubly constrained in finding a structure that reflects these commitments. As the quote from Catherine Conroy in the beginning of this chapter indicates, the structure of CLUW had to be negotiated. In the first two years after the founding of the organization, members argued over issues like the membership question, which was an expression of CLUW's collective identity. Some founding members did not identify with the results of the negotiation processes and were no longer involved in the organization.

BRINGING WOMEN INTO THE MAINSTREAM OF THE LABOR MOVEMENT

At the founding convention, CLUW adopted as its main goal to bring women "into the mainstream of the labor movement" and women's issues onto the labor agenda. Thus CLUW contributed from the beginning to gender mainstreaming.[7] How did CLUW pursue these goals?

The relationship between social movements includes drawing boundaries and cooperation between social movements, which are based on framing processes (Ferree and Roth 1998). Problem identification and resolution are also important framing processes (Snow and Benford 1992), especially when activists from various backgrounds develop a strategy. For example, differing ideological positions lead to conflicts over the structure of movement organizations and pose risks to coalitions (Arnold 1995). CLUW always chose tactics that were consistent with members' understanding of union solidarity and unity, even if that meant that the most efficient measures and allies were not the ones chosen.

CLUW contributed to broadening the agenda of the labor movement and the women's movement through adding issues of concern to working women to the agendas of these movements. The organization framed issues of relevance to working women, like child care, sexual harassment, and reproductive rights, as "labor issues" that had been neglected by the labor movement (and sometimes also by the women's movement). Bringing these issues into the labor agenda helped form coalitions and build bridges between the women's movement and the labor movement. Furthermore, CLUW brought economic issues of relevance to working women, like labor law reform, to the attention of women's organizations.

The analysis of CLUW thus contributes to our understanding of social movement interaction at all three levels. The investigation of processes of political socialization shows how individual members can reconcile conflicting political identities through the formation of and participation in bridging organizations. The study of a bridging organization like CLUW shows how diverse constituencies can (or cannot) be integrated and what the resulting organizational structure says about the accountability, loyalty, and collective identity of an organization. The analysis of bridging organizations shows how coalitions are formed within and among movements. Finally, because the labor movement has changed in the years since 1974, the case study of the Coalition of Labor Union women during this period contributes to an understanding of organizational development.

OVERVIEW OF THE BOOK

My study of CLUW combines qualitative and quantitative methods. Between 1991 and 1996, I conducted participant observation, life-history, and expert interviews with current and former CLUW members at the local and national level. This included a summer-long internship with the CLUW Center for Education and Research in 1994. During the internship I conducted a membership survey (N = 534, response rate 30%), compiled data on the development of women in union leadership, and contributed to a directory of women in union leadership positions. Furthermore, I draw on documents, in particular the newsletter of the organization. The Appendix to this book contains documentation of these studies.

Chapter 2 provides a short history of the American labor movement, highlighting the conflicts between the labor movement and the women's movement and describing the developments in the 1960s and 1970s that led to the decision to found CLUW. Chapter 3 focuses on the biographies of those who founded CLUW and those who joined later. These form the basis for the development of a typology of CLUW members. The chapter includes a brief characterization of the four membership types regarding race, education, and union affiliation. Chapter 4 explores the participation of women of color in CLUW, as well as diversity in gender, marital status, age, union affiliation, and union participation. I address how CLUW has achieved this diversity and the strategies it has developed to deal with diversity and conflict.

Chapter 5 describes the negotiation processes among the founding members around the organizational structure and strategies of CLUW. I analyze the outcome of three conflicts concerning the membership question, union democracy, and support of the farmworkers' union. The outcome of these conflicts reflects CLUW's identity as a labor organization. In Chapter 6, I argue that CLUW must be seen as a feminist organization because of its feminist goals—organizing the unorganized, bringing women into union leadership, supporting women's interest in the political process, and getting more women involved in the political process. In Chapter 7, I analyze CLUW as a bridging organization—introducing women's issues in the labor movement and labor issues in the women's movement as well as contributing to coalition building between the two movements.

I conclude with an assessment of CLUW's achievements and what other movement organizations can learn from the organization, as well as some predictions of CLUW's development.

NOTES

1. The participation of women in the labor movement has been studied by Foner (1979/1980), Fonow (2003), Kessler-Harris (1975), (1982), Milkman (1985a: 1990), and Wertheimer (1977). Collins (1990), Barnett (1995), Gilkes (1994), James (1993), and

Payne (1990) analyze the participation of African American women in the civil rights movement.

2. I conducted this survey during an internship with the CLUW Center of Education and Research (see Appendix).

3. In 1974, the year CLUW was founded, 22% of workers, but only 21% of women (compared to 31% of men), were organized (Bureau of Labor Statistics 1975). Since then the unionization rate of American workers has fallen, to 14% in 2001, but the proportion of women among unionized workers is increasing. In 2001, 13% of women workers compared to 15% of male workers were unionized. This development reflects structural change, the loss of workplaces in the industrial sector—a predominantly male sphere—and the increase of workplaces in the service sector, traditionally an area of women and minorities (Clawson and Clawson 1999).

4. Cobble (1994) terms the feminism among wage-earning women "working class feminism." She discusses in particular labor organizations in female-dominated sectors such as such food service, sales, and telecommunications. Milkman (1985) calls the resurgence of feminism among women workers in the 1970s "trade union feminism."

5. Interview which I conducted with Gloria Johnson in 1994; see Appendix.

6. The participation of women in the American labor movement will be discussed in the next chapter.

7. Gender mainstreaming refers to the systematic incorporation of gender into policymaking (Mazey 2001). The principle was introduced at the 1985 UN women's conference in Nairobi. Ten years later, at the Fourth World Conference of Women in Beijing in 1995, it was formally adopted. CLUW did not use the term "gender mainstreaming," but pursued it.

2

Sisterhood, Solidarity, and the Neglect of Working Women's Issues

Women have always participated in labor struggles, not only as union members but also in women's auxiliaries and community groups. To understand the significance of CLUW requires a perspective on the historical relationship between the women's movement and the labor movement. This chapter provides an overview of that relationship with a focus on how the two movements addressed working women's needs. "The" labor movement and "the" women's movement have been both allies and enemies from their beginnings. It would be a mistake, however, to perceive either movement as monolithic. Rather, both are highly complex and heterogeneous (Milkman 1990; Ferree and Hess 2000; Gluck et al. 1998).

WOMEN'S INVOLVEMENT IN THE LABOR MOVEMENT

The stance of the unions toward women's membership has changed over time and still differs among various unions. Milkman (1990) argues that to some extent, these differences reflect the gender segregation of the labor market at the time when the union was founded. She distinguishes four types of unionism: craft unionism, new unionism, industrial unionism, and public sector unionism. CLUW members belonged to unions of all four types, and the experiences they gained in the labor movement differed accordingly.

Craft unionism arose in the nineteenth century among skilled craft workers.

The American Federation of Labor, formed in 1886, was hostile to organizing unskilled workers, women, and people of color. The craft unions of printers, typesetters, and cigar makers initially excluded women (Hartmann 1976; Foner 1979). Later they extended admission to women workers and supported equal pay for equal work, largely to prevent (white) male skilled workers' pay from being undermined by a cheap, unorganized female labor force.

The *new unionism* that emerged in the early twentieth century was launched by the famous "Uprising of the 20,000" (New York garment workers) in 1909. In contrast to the craft unions, which restricted membership to skilled workers, the garment workers unions, like the International Ladies Garment Workers Union (ILGWU) and the Amalgamated Clothing Workers (ACW), organized skilled and unskilled workers alike. They were more open to organizing women and had some famous women organizers, like Rose Schneiderman, Pauline Newman, and Fannia Cohn. In fact, the majority of the members of the garment workers union were female, but the leadership was male, and the unions were characterized by a paternalistic attitude toward women members.

The unionization of women workers—both in craft unions and in the garment workers unions of the new unionism—was supported by women who belonged to organizations such as the Women's Trade Union League (WTUL) and the Consumer League (Dye 1980; Tax 1980; Skocpol 1992). But these organizations of middle-class reformers were also active on behalf of protective legislation: Protective legislation improved women's working conditions but excluded them from better-paying jobs; it emphasized women's needs as mothers and thus highlighted gender differences. This strategy represented a stark contrast to those who pursued women's equality, fighting for women's vote or for the Equal Rights Amendment. While working-class women found allies among "maternal" feminists, their needs were overlooked by elitist "equality" feminists.

The *industrial unionism* that emerged in the 1930s and 1940s represented a more egalitarian attitude than the previous two types. The New Deal brought significant and permanent growth in government programs, particularly in social welfare, and African American men and women obtained clerical and professional jobs in these programs (Amott and Matthaei 1991). Furthermore, the New Deal legislation was crucial for the unionization of white workers and workers of color. In 1935, the Wagner Act, guaranteeing workers the right to organize, was passed. In the same year the Congress of Industrial Organizations (CIO) was founded, which organized workers industry-wide across race and gender. Unionization expanded in the automobile, rubber, and electrical industries. The industrial unions of the CIO organized women alongside men. However, most of them failed to target women workers in their mass organizing. Due to the sex segregation of the labor market, the unionization of women did not increase as long as the organizing drives were focused on male-dominated jobs. One important exception to the CIO's general neglect to target women workers was the United Office and Professional Workers of America (UOPWA), established in

1937 (Strom 1985). In 1937 the unions affiliated with the CIO were expelled from the American Federation of Labor and formed the Congress of Industrial Unions. The two umbrella organizations merged in 1955 and formed the AFL–CIO, American Federation of Labor–Congress of Industrial Unions. Some unions, like the United Autoworkers and Teamsters were for a while not members of the AFL–CIO. The United Autoworkers disaffiliated from the AFL–CIO in 1968 and reaffiliated in 1981. The Teamsters affiliated in 1987.

The labor shortage of World War II created job opportunities for women of all racial-ethnic groups. White professional women moved into banking, insurance, civil service, education, and health services, and into the war industry. African Americans found jobs in factories and offices. In 1944, the United Auto Workers (UAW) formed a Women's Bureau in the War Policy Division and was thus the first American union to establish structures for women members as part of the war effort. The bureau was headed by Lillian Hatcher, an African American autoworker, and in 1946 was incorporated into the newly established Fair Practices and Anti-Discrimination Department. In the late 1940s regional women's committees were formed and in 1950 the National Advisory Committee to the Women's Bureau was established (Gabin 1985). The war economy also opened new job opportunities for Chinese American women, who were employed in the civil service, professional fields, factories, and office work outside Chinatown. Many found employment as sewing-machine operators in small sweatshops in Chinatown and became members of the International Ladies' Garment Workers Union (ILGWU).

In the 1940s and 1950s, anti-Communism and McCarthyism had a significant impact on social movements (Schrecker 1998). Unions as well as organizations such as the YWCA and the ACLU excluded members thought to be communists or sympathizers of the Communist Party–USA. Red-baiting was common among progressive organizations. Consequently, the growing concern of CPUSA with respect to gender and race lost its organizational base, although it was still pursued by individuals (Weigand 2001).

The fourth and most recent phase of union approach to gender came in the second half of the twentieth century. The economic shift from manufacturing to the service sector, the increase in women's participation in the paid labor force, and the women's and civil rights movements resulted in the unionization of service, public sector, and farm-workers, and an increase in women among the union membership (Bell 1985). *Public sector unionism* took on feminist issues such as affirmative action and pay equity (Blum 1991; Johnston 1994). A large number of CLUW members belong to unions of this type.

Labor in the 1960s and 1970s

The civil rights movement and the economic growth in the 1950s and 1960s brought important improvements in the economic status of African Americans through the mid-1970s. In the 1960s, as a consequence of McCarthyism, the economic prosperity of the postwar years, and the resulting emphasis on wage and benefit gains over political challenges to the status quo, organized labor no longer pursued an agenda of "social unionism" (Robinson 1993). African Americans continued to work in manufacturing and in the service sector. In 1958, Local 1199, a militant union representing mainly African American and Puerto Rican hospital workers, was founded in New York (Fink and Greenberg 1989). By the late 1960s the workforce in the lowest-paying jobs in the private sector were mainly Hispanic men and women already in the United States along with new immigrants from Latin America, the Caribbean, Asia, the Pacific Islands, and elsewhere (Amott and Matthaei 1991).

The public sector unions formed in the 1960s organized more women workers than the unions of the other three types. However, these unions did not target women workers as "women." The extensive organization of women can be seen as a historical by-product of the general project of organizing public workers, which began during the postwar period (Bell 1985). Still, the increase in female membership brought about changes in women's union participation and policy shifts in the unions. Once organized, women became increasingly active participants, succeeding in gaining leadership posts and in putting "women's issues" on their union agendas. Thus, they were able to advance the position of women, not only in the public sector unions, but in the labor movement as a whole (Bell 1985:280). Johnston (1994) refers to these organizing and bargaining efforts in the public sector as "social movement unionism." He points out that the organization of public sector workers—for instance, in the fight for pay equity in San Jose (Blum 1991)—bridged the labor movement and the women's movement.

But not only the service sector and public sector workers were organized at that time. In the 1960s and early 1970s, Jessi Lopez de La Cruz, Dolores Huerta, and Cesar Chavez organized Mexican farm-workers throughout the Southwest into the United Farmworkers (UFW). Employing tactics unusual for the labor movement, such as hunger strikes and a national consumer grape boycott, the UFW achieved extraordinary contract gains in pay and benefits and was instrumental in passing laws regarding working conditions, including regulations governing occupational safety and pesticide use. Furthermore, the mobilization of the UFW was important for the emerging Chicano movement as well as linking Asian American activists of the 1960s and 1970s with the labor movement (Chen and Wong 1998). It contributed to politicization and the creation of a collective identity. The conflict between the Farmworkers and the Teamsters played an important role in CLUW's founding.[1]

Due to the depolitization of the labor movement through McCarthyism, labor's responses to the anti-war, student, and environmental movements, and feminism tended to be conservative and hostile (Milkman 1985b:310). Red-baiting was common to discredit progressive movements. However, some social movements turned to the labor movements as a vehicle for social change and some unions—like 1199 and UAW—supported the claims of the civil rights movement.

The decline in traditionally organized blue-collar private-sector industries, the increase in women's labor force participation, and the organization of public and service sector workers contributed to the restructuring of the American labor movement. The organization of public and service sector unions was carried out by a few unions that organized drives during the 1960s. These unions included hospital workers, retail clerks, electrical workers, teachers, and government employees (Foner 1980:496). However, the increase in working women's unionization had not been accompanied by any corresponding increase in leadership positions within labor unions (Glassberg et al. 1980; Baden 1986).

Women's Participation in Labor Unions

Although the situation of women differed in the four types of unions, overall women were underrepresented in union leadership. From 1956 to 1976 the number of women in selected union offices[2] increased from 29 to 47, and in many cases women held more than one official position (Glassberg et al. 1980). Women represented a fifth of union membership in 1971, but held only 70 office posts in 47 of 208 unions (Bureau of Labor Statistics 1971), especially (but not only) in unions with a high percentage of women members, such as textile workers, communication workers, which organized telephone operators, and hotel and restaurant workers. Only one department head in the AFL–CIO—the librarian—was a woman. The 39-member AFL–CIO Executive Council, composed of union presidents, was all male. The 51 state federations reported only six women staff members and no woman held the position of regional director (Wertheimer and Nelson 1975).

In the labor movement successful and outspoken women leaders were exploited and marginalized rather than encouraged and appreciated. One of my interviewees recalled that when she started to work for the union as a business agent in the early 1970s she was told by the secretaries that "they would only type for the boys." She categorized the three roles for women in the labor movement as "secretary," "loyal bureaucrat," and "mistress." While women of color could align themselves with insurgent organizations such as the Farmworkers Union and the Coalition of Black Trade Unionists, white women in leadership positions were at risk of becoming "mascots of the old boys' network." "As long as you worked your butt off, the men in the union would praise you and say how wonderful you were and they would let you work really hard [laughs], they would give you lots and lots of work to do. . . . Now, if you were bad, if you were talented but assertive, then you would be fired."

Union women in staff, appointed, and elected leadership positions were often the only women on the executive board of their local or district council, or, rarely, in the national leadership. Furthermore, they did not necessarily know each other. One of CLUW's founding members compared CLUW to organizations of the civil rights movement. She explained "that women unionists by themselves were not able to make the strides they wanted to and therefore felt the need to get together."

In contrast to unions in other countries (for example, Germany; see Cook 1984), American unions in general did not have women's departments until the beginning of the 1970s. There were some exceptions. The war led to the emergence of a women's movement in the CIO unions (Milkman 1987). As noted above, UAW has maintained a Women's Bureau since 1944. Gloria Johnson—CLUW's national president in 2003—represented the International Union of Electrical, Radio & Machine Workers (IUE) on the National Equal Pay Committee in 1955. Later she became the Women's Representative of the IUE.[3] Johnson surveyed the membership in order to assess women's participation in her union. She found that women were underrepresented in policymaking positions, concerned about the implementation of the Equal Pay Act, and interested in leadership training. In 1957 the IUE held its first women's conference in order to respond to these needs (Johnson 1993). In 1972 a women's council was created, and since 1986 the women's council director has been represented on the Executive Board with voice and vote. Thus it took more than 30 years and the feminist movement until women's interests were represented in the highest decision-making body of the organization. Those women union leaders in unions with women's department were active in the founding of CLUW and provided resources.

THE WOMEN'S MOVEMENT IN THE 1960s AND 1970s

The media have often characterized the women's movement as a white-middle-class movement that was started by *The Feminine Mystique* (Friedan 1963). By now, a large body of research rejects this notion and documents the important role that women of color and working-class women have played in the women's movement (Cobble 1994; Gluck et al. 1998; B. Roth 2004; Weigand 2001). The misrepresentation nevertheless hints at the different priorities within the feminist movement and the tensions that arose from these differences. Class differences, as well as divisions along lines of sexual orientation, ethnicity, race, religion, and age, have created tensions, and lesbians and women of color have experienced exclusion. The "equality" feminism of the suffrage movement and the fight for the Equal Rights Amendment of the National Women's Party emphasized women's equality with men and disregarded class and race issues. Ironically, the emphasis on "equality" thus turned out to be elitist. Women of color and working-class women pursued women's interests and women's rights, but they did not identify with this branch of the movement, which did not address their needs and concerns.

Starting in the late nineteenth century, middle-class reformers, pursuing "maternal" feminism (Skocpol 1992; Giele 1995), emphasized women's difference in focusing on the needs of women and their children. They fought for protective legislation, social security, health care, and child care. Because of power differentials the relationship between (immigrant) working-class women and (white) middle-class reformers was not unproblematic. Coming from a charity and social work tradition, the reformers' pity for the poor was accompanied by social control based on the conviction that the poor needed moral and spiritual as well as economic help (e.g., Gordon 1993). Furthermore, they supported the norm of the male breadwinner, according to which men should earn a family wage that supports women and children. Race- and class-based assumptions resulted in distinctions between "deserving" and "undeserving" poor, compromising the position of the many in need who were single mothers.

In the progressive era, most U.S. states enacted new or tightened restrictions on women's hours of employment, and many states also passed minimum wage laws and special safety regulations for women. Such laws were premised on the idea that women workers needed extraordinary protection as actual or potential mothers (Skocpol 1992:317). By the mid-1920s, the capacity for further maternalist policies was exhausted and the women's movement experienced a backlash. Between the 1920s and the 1960s, the women's movement "survived in the doldrums" (Rupp and Taylor 1987). During this time, women were active in the National Women's Party, labor unions such as the UAW, emerging civil rights organizations, and progressive movements that lost more and more ground due to McCarthyism and anti-Communism.

The distance of women of color and working-class women from the second wave of the women's movement was expressed in statements such as "They did not have bras to burn" (hinting at the women's liberation movement's reputation as bra-burners). But women of color and women from the labor movement participated in the second wave from the beginning. For example, Caroline Davis and Dorothy Haener of the UAW women's department were among the founding members of NOW in 1966. Thus trade union women played an important role in the founding of the oldest of the new feminist organizations (Foner 1980; Rupp and Taylor 1987). African American women were also represented among the earliest leadership of feminist organizations like NOW (Davis 1991). Furthermore, there were a number of feminist organizations of women of color (Gluck et al. 1998; B. Roth 2004). Working-class women and women of color shared the emphasis that the women's movement put on employment. But these women were already part of the labor force. They were not only concerned with affirmative action and equal access to the labor market, but also with combining paid work with motherhood and family obligations. Therefore they were especially interested in child care and family leave options, but shared an interest in eliminating limitations to women's advancement.

African American women (Barnett 1995) and women in the labor unions

(Cobble 1994) were organizing for women's interests well before the emergence of the new women's movement. The legislation that resulted from the civil rights movement (Civil Rights Act, Title VII, Fair Pay Act), and the formation in 1961 of the President's Commission on the Status of Women contributed to networking and the context for "cognitive liberation" (Costain 1992; Ryan 1992). Esther Peterson, a former union organizer, and then director of the Women's Bureau, chaired the commission. State commissions were also established to do research at the state level. The activity of the federal and state commissions laid the groundwork for the future movement in three significant ways: it brought together a network of knowledgeable, politically active women, it provided evidence of women's unequal status, and it created a climate of expectation (Freeman 1975:52). In 1966 the National Organization for Women was formed during the third conference of the state Commissions on the Status of Women. Participants felt that it was time to fight and form an action organization.

The women who formed NOW and the "women's rights branch" of the new women's movement tended to come from the professions, labor, government, and the communications industry and were seasoned participants in lobbying, campaigning, and other aspects of the political process. Women who had been active in the Freedom Summer campaign (Evans 1979; McAdam 1988a) and the New Left formed the "women's liberation movement." They had experienced sexism in the civil rights, anti-war, and student movements and chose to organize separately after they realized that their voices were not being heard in the New Left. Socialist feminists formed women's liberation unions such as the Chicago Women's Liberation Union (Hansen 1986; Staggenborg 1988, 1989; Strobel 1995). Some of these unions, which combined feminism and socialism, were organized as umbrella organizations, while others functioned as membership organizations. The women's liberation unions suffered from a discrepancy between their ideology (serving working-class women) and their constituency (white, single, college-educated women). Formed during the end of the 1960s, they all dissolved in the middle of the 1970s (Hansen 1986).

In the 1970s a multitude of feminist organizations, including a battered women's movement and a women's health movement, emerged, thus further differentiating the women's movement (Davis 1991; Ferree and Hess 2000; Ferree and Martin 1995). Professional women formed organizations, and several think tanks such as the Center for Women's Policy Research and the Institute for Women's Policy Studies were formed to provide feminist lobbyists with data and fact sheets (Davis 1991; Spalter-Roth and Schreiber 1995).

The women's movement is of course much more diverse than this sketch would suggest. Branches of the women's movement concerned with culture, body, and sexuality like the radical, cultural, and lesbian women's movements also influenced union feminism. Sexual harassment, reproductive rights, and sexual orientation are workplace issues as well. But the brief overview of the participation of women in labor unions and the different branches of the women's movement should make clear that it would be misleading to conceive these movements as monolithic and separate from each other. Rather, within each movement, middle-class women, working-class women, white women, and women of color pursued women's interests, interpreting them differently and pursuing them with different strategies. This led to tensions and conflicts as well as to alliances and coalitions within and between the women's movement and the labor movement.

WORKING WOMEN'S ORGANIZATIONS

In the early 1970s, the women's movement and the labor unions still neglected working women's interests overall, despite the efforts I have already described. Several organizations of women workers were founded to fill this gap. Seifer and Wertheimer (1979) distinguish between "primary" groups (Women Employed, Nine-to-Five), whose members did not initially belong to unions, and "secondary" groups (Union WAGE, CLUW), which organize union women. Women Employed (WE), an organization of women office workers in Chicago, was founded in 1973. WE was successful in winning major back-pay suits, forcing large corporations to develop comprehensive affirmative action plans, pressuring the federal government to investigate discrimination in private industries, and bringing about an Illinois state regulation banning the sale of discriminatory insurance policies. The organization employed strategies such as public hearings, media exposes, and negotiations and confrontations with corporate and government officials. Women Employed was supported by membership dues, grass roots fund-raising, and foundation grants (Seifer and Wertheimer 1979:156–57).

Nine-to-Five, also founded in 1973, is an organization of women office workers in Boston. Nine-to-Five's achievements include a Massachusetts regulation denying licenses to insurance companies that discriminated against women and substantial equal pay, promotion, and training reforms in several companies. This organization utilizes a newsletter, public forums and hearings, demonstrations, petitions, leafleting, and in-company task forces to oversee enforcement of anti-discrimination laws and suits. Nine-to-Five obtained a charter from the Service Employees International Union, AFL–CIO, to establish Local 925 and negotiates bargaining contracts for women office workers. The membership of the organization includes women office workers and student and feminist movement activists. Nine-to-Five is supported by foundation grants, grass roots fund-raising, membership dues, newsletter subscriptions, literature sales, and fees for speakers and film showings about office workers. Nine-to-Five and Women Employed served as models for similar organizations in other American cities (Glick 1983; Seifer and Wertheimer 1979). Other examples for working women's collective action were the Willmar Eight, the J.P. Stevens boycott, and the Oneida Knitting Mills strike (Hoyman 1979).

In the early 1970s union women began to hold conferences to organize women workers into labor unions, and to urge labor unions to address the interests of women workers (Milkman 1985). In 1971 women unionists formed the Women's Alliance to Gain Equity—Union WAGE—in response to a conference of the National Organization for Women in California that did not address working women's issues (Foner 1980). This organization targeted women workers' interests in the unions, on the job, and in society. Its eleven-point program included support for free abortion on demand and the Equal Rights Amendment (ERA). The organization took the position that the ERA should be interpreted as extending labor standards to both sexes.

In this respect the demands of Union Wage were reminiscent of the Women's Charter that was introduced by the Communist Party and supported by some middle-class women's rights advocates belonging to the Women's Bureau of the Department of Labor, the Congress of American Women, the Russell Sage Foundation, the Consumer's League, the American Civil Liberties Union, and the National Federation of Business and Professional Women. The Women's Charter represented an alternative to the Equal Rights Amendment; its purpose was to secure equal rights for women while upholding protective legislation for women workers (Weigand 2001:31). The second wave of the women's movement was significantly influenced by women who had been active in the context of the Communist Party and progressive movements (Weigand 2001). Thus it is quite possible that those active in Union Wage were familiar with the Women's Charter or related activities.

Union WAGE included both women in unions and those not organized, and welcomed women who worked at home, even if they were not paid, and women who were unemployed, retired, or on welfare. The organization did not actively organize women into unions, but served as a resource for women who were interested in unions. Union WAGE published *Organize! A Working Women's Handbook* and a bimonthly newsletter that addressed sexism in unions and organizing campaigns.

Not only Union WAGE, but also AFL–CIO state federations (for example, in California), rank-and-file activists (for example, in Chicago), and labor educators (for example, in New York City) organized conferences for union women. In 1970 the National Rank and File Action Conference in Chicago adopted a Declaration of Rights of Women Workers that included demands for better working conditions and union representation of working women as well as health care, day care, family leave, and reproductive rights. It called for special attention for the interests of women of color (Foner 1980:498–99). These issues were later taken up by the Coalition of Labor Union Women. The formation of the National Coordinating Committee for Trade Union Action and Democracy also contributed to the formation of CLUW (Foner 1980).

In 1973, the California State Labor Federation held a women's conference that was attended by 300 delegates and 150 observers (including men), representing the entire state, a cross-section with respect to age and race, the majority rank-and-file union members, mostly shop stewards (Foner 1980). Union WAGE members were among the organizers of the conference. One of the panelists became a founding member and one of the national officers of the CLUW: Elinor Glenn, the general manager of Los Angeles County Employees Union, Local 434, SEIU. Conference participants recognized union membership as a means to improve working women's conditions. Therefore, the goals included organizing unorganized working women, bringing union women together through a national women's conference, establishing a committee to address women's issues, and extending protective legislation to men (Foner 1980).

The beginning of the 1970s thus saw a widespread proliferation of working women's organizations that pursued goals that had already been developed by women active in the context of the Popular Front, Congress of American Women, and Communist Party (Horowitz 1998; Weigand 2001). The constituency of these working women's organizations and conferences were predominately rank-and-file members and also included non-unionized women and women with connections to socialist organizations. Given the anti-Communist stance of the labor movement and the tendency to red-bait, this working women's movement posed a challenge to the labor movement.

THE DECISION TO ORGANIZE CLUW

Women labor leaders were aware of the women's conferences that had been held since 1970 and of the growing movement among women rank-and-file unionists for a national base from which to fight against sexism in the labor movement, organize unorganized women workers, upgrade women in the workplace, and achieve an effective role for women in union policymaking (Foner 1980). The formation of the Coalition of Labor Union Women was closely related to the controversy around the Equal Rights Amendment (ERA). In the 1960s and 1970s women in both the women's and the labor movement differed with respect to the ERA. Women from the UAW supported it, while most union women opposed it (Cobble 1994; Gabin 1985). In general, women who belonged to unions that organized women who worked alongside men tended to support the ERA, while women who represented women workers in highly segregated sections of the labor market were against it. Opposition was grounded in the fear that it would undermine protective legislation improving women's working conditions; supporters saw it as a means to end discrimination in the labor market.

The controversy around the ERA exemplifies the gender-class debate that contributed to tensions within and between the women's and the labor movements. Ironically, the AFL–CIO shared the rejection of the ERA with its arch-enemy the Communist Party. The Communist Party developed the Women's Charter to integrate class and gender interests (preserving protective legislation and demanding women's equality) (Weigand 2001); the AFL–CIO eventually endorsed the ERA in 1973.

CLUW is often credited for influencing the AFL–CIO in this regard, although CLUW's founding convention took place after the AFL–CIO changed its position on the ERA. This can be explained by the fact that preparations to form CLUW had already begun in 1973, and that CLUW had supported the ERA since its inception. In fact, one of the reasons to form CLUW was to overcome the different approaches of women to the ERA. Reflecting the different positions among labor union women, some prominent women labor leaders who were involved in the formation of CLUW were opposed to the ERA. Myra Wolfgang of the Hotel and Restaurant Workers Union had testified against the ERA in 1970. Olga Madar, a UAW staff member, testified in favor of the ERA. However, after CLUW supported the ERA, it was no longer a contested issue among the union women and did not lead to internal conflicts in the organization. Myra Wolfgang died shortly after CLUW was founded.

However, the ERA played an important role in getting the formation of CLUW started, as Olga Madar described:

We were working with [organizations of the women's movement], and [the] National Women's Political Caucus and [the] National Organization for Women. They were making remarks about our sister unionists about that they were not really for the women and so forth. And I said, "This is not so. [The ERA is] an issue that they differ on, but on other kinds of issues they are with us." So, it was from that to try to show them we could network with women's organizations on common cause.

Initially, Madar was involved in setting up networks for economic rights in various states when she learned from Addie Wyatt—another union leader and CLUW founder—that those already existed. She then suggested shifting the effort to organizing a network of union women. Later Madar met with union women in staff and officer positions in various parts of the country. She contacted women union leaders she already knew and asked them to invite other union leaders to small meetings. These meetings were neither publicly announced nor open to rank-and-file members. One interviewee recalled:

What happened was that Olga Madar from the Auto Workers knew some women in various parts of the country. She was a leader in the Auto Workers and she contacted somebody in [city], [name], who was active in women's affairs, trade unionist. And [name] got a hold of me and asked me if I was interested in meeting with Olga Madar at the airport with a few other women who were active in the unions who were women at some leadership level, to meet, to hear about this proposal to set up a feminist group in the trade union movement.

These women labor leaders sought to form an organization that would strengthen their position in the labor unions and convince the male union leadership that the organization of women workers would benefit not only working women but also the labor movement as a whole. Given the increasing number of women in the labor force, the failure to organize women workers might weaken the labor movement (cf. Foner 1980).

These women labor leaders believed that these goals could best be achieved within the existing trade union structure and expected the objectives to be supported by a number of male trade union leaders (Foner 1980). They rejected the notion of creating independent organizations or "dual unionism," which is consistent with long-standing international union practice and policy. They were afraid that attacks, like feminist criticism, might undermine the labor movement. Therefore they began building a national organization of union women within the framework of the labor movement in order to bring more women into union leadership and women's issues onto the agenda. They thus saw themselves as allies of the labor movement who sought more recognition and acknowledgment. Some have interpreted these actions as an attempt to create an organization that would advance women leaders in their unions rather than broadening the participation of women in unions (Foner 1980; Glick 1989; Milkman 1985).

As I will show in later chapters, the members differed in their visions of the organization. While some justified the prerequisite of being in a leadership position in one's union to take on a leadership role in CLUW, others wished for a higher turnover of CLUW membership.

In April 1973, eight women labor leaders[4] met in Chicago to discuss how union women, working together, could make the trade unions "responsible to the pressing needs of 4 million organized women and 30 million unorganized women in this country." They felt that there had long been a need "within the union movement for a consolidated and concerted approach by union women to deal with their special concerns as unionists and women in the labor force" (Foner 1980:505).

In June 1973, more than two hundred delegates from twenty international unions and eighteen Midwestern states met in Chicago for the Midwest Conference of Union Women and endorsed the calling of a national conference of trade union women and the establishment of an inter-union framework for continuing cooperative action to "confront male chauvinism and paternalism of male trade unionists" (Foner 1980:507). In the following months regional conferences were held in all parts of the country. The participants in these conferences decided to establish a continuing organization. One of the participants in the New York conference, which had been organized by members of Cornell University, recalled: "We had to turn people back because we would never have had enough room for them. It was more than 800 people because everybody was fed up. It was the need of the frustration of women felt."

This quote hints at the enormous interest and need of women in the labor movement to form an organization that represented their interests. This need was felt by women of different age groups, different unions, and different positions within the union. Mary Callahan attended a planning committee in Philadelphia. She recalled, "I went to the meeting. There were people that I had never met before. Young people, which made me very happy. I felt like a grandmother there, literally. We had the meeting down at the Amalgamated Clothing Workers hall, and four hundred women came to that from all walks of life, all unions, all the way from the teachers down through the laundry workers" (Callahan 1996:133). Despite this diversity, the women attending the meeting had similar concerns: they did not feel taken seriously in their movements. Coming together allowed them to exchange their experiences and to voice their demands. "All they wanted was that women get recognition in the union for their input. Over and above that, there were some people who thought, and probably rightfully so, that anytime they opened their mouths they got a put-down because they were women or because they were viewed as mouthy young women trying to upset the apple cart. So that's how CLUW started" (Callahan 1996:133).

Another founding member of CLUW explained that women unionists sought to create a space in which they could come together.

Women, union women worked in different shops across the country but we had nothing that brought us together, . . . We decided, you know we are talking about 1974, that there ought to be an organization where women can come together and discuss what concerns us as trade union women, to air out our grievances, to pool our resources, . . . to be a voice for ourselves in our own unions. We were dedicated trade unionists and we certainly were concerned with building our unions, because we know that in spite of the conditions from which we worked within our unions we were still better off than non-union women.

Here the emphasis is on inclusive solidarity, creating a space for union women is not meant as an attack on unions.

In February 1974, a National Conference Planning Committee of forty-four women representing twenty-two unions and all regions of the United States met in a two-day session to plan a national conference, to establish the structure for a national organization of union women, and "to bring women union members and retirees of bona fide collective bargaining organizations to deal with our special concerns as unionists and women in the labor force" (Foner 1980:495). The committee decided to hold a convention for the formation of a new national organization to be called the Coalition of Labor Union Women (CLUW) in March 1974, in Chicago. Committees in several unions began preparing resolutions to be sent to the CLUW Conference Arrangements Committee (Foner 1980).

Women who were involved in the labor movement and the women's movement knew about the convention, especially those who were active in both movements. However, that does not mean that all the women in the labor movement got involved in the formation of the organization. Some current members heard about CLUW but did not join the organization at that point; others were invited to the founding convention but were not interested in attending. Participants came either as delegates from their unions or as individual trade union members. More than fifty unions from more than forty states were represented.[5] One participant reported: "It was probably the largest labor convention ever held, in all history. . . . The arrangements committee was in shock. There was no place to seat, let alone sleep, so many people. On the convention's opening morning the conveners (torn between joy and terror) announced that 2,100 delegates had registered. By afternoon the figure had risen to more than 3,200! Even the UAW, whose conventions are probably bigger than any other union's draws only 2,500, tops!" (Sexton 1974:381)

Over half of the delegates were attending an event like this for the first time. Most participants were white, but 20 to 25% were African American and a few were Asian, Hispanic, or other minority women. Another participant stated: "It was just like any other big labor union convention. Standards dotted the floor marking the places where Machinists, Steelworkers, Clothing Workers, Teachers and Teamsters and Auto Workers were sitting—well, not quite like any union convention in recent years. The delegates were different too—most of whom had paid their own way to attend the founding conventions of the Coalition of Labor Union Women" (Jordan 1974).

The founding convention thus attracted not only women who already held leadership positions but also many rank-and-file members and women who were involved in primary socialist and feminist organizations. Furthermore, it got extensive coverage in the labor, left, and mainstream press, which indicates the broad interest in the formation of a labor union women's organization.[6] The large number of women who attended the founding conference shows that these activists saw the need for a working women's movement that addressed the social and economic needs of women. They were dissatisfied by a labor movement that focused on the needs of male workers and a women's movement that ignored the needs of working-class women, working mothers, and women of color. They looked for an organization that would address gender-, class-, and race-related issues. However, what they wanted the organization to become depended in part on their varied expectations and needs. The following chapters show the effort to shape an organization that reflected such a diverse constituency.

NOTES

1. This will be discussed in Chapter 5.

2. Glassberg et al. (1980) surveyed female representation in unions and associations with over 100,000 women members.

3. IUE later affiliated with CWA.

4. The eight women were Addie Wyatt of the Amalgamated Meat Cutters and

Butcher Workmen, Ola Kennedy of the United Steelworkers, Olga Madar and Edith Van Horn of the United Auto Workers, Alice Weatherwax and Jean Thurmond of the American Federation of Teachers, Joyce Miller of the Amalgamated Clothing Workers, and Helga Nesbitt of the Communication Workers of America (Foner 1980:505).

   5. UE, IUE, UAW, Teamsters, Retail Clerks, ILGWU, ACWA, Meat Cutters, AFT, IAM, Department Store Employees, CWA, Flight Attendants, Grain Millers, AFSCME, AFTRA, Hotel and Restaurant Employees, SEIU, Steelworkers, District 1199, District 65, and Newspaper Guild were represented (1980).

   6. See CLUW press clippings.

3

Developing Union Feminism

Although we were formed on the basis of getting our unions . . . to subscribe to those feminist issues, which we consider not just to be women's issues in that they relate to women, but which relate to the family and the total community. And what we also said, we are talking about equity and therefore there is no question where we stand on racism and any of the other things, gay-baiting, anti-Semitism, we have to feel the same way on that as we do in terms of women being treated correctly.

Olivia Magyar, founding mother

A number of different groups were involved in the formation of the Coalition of Labor Union Women: union leaders and rank-and-file activists, socialist feminists, and participants in the movements of the 1960s and 1970s. Some of the founding members had been active in the labor movement since the 1930s and had participated in the organization of the industrial unions. They had witnessed the purging of Communists from labor unions during the McCarthy era. Furthermore, as labor unionists they had supported for the civil rights movement and the women's movement. Other early members of the organization were politicized in the New Left and the social movements of the 1960s and 1970s. They were primarily interested in empowering the powerless and getting as many people as possible involved in political action. Still others became union members when the public sector was unionized toward the end of the 1960s. These members were not familiar with any of the earlier movements. Public sector unionism and the Coalition of Labor Union Women represented their avenue to political participation.

In this chapter I examine the processes of political socialization of CLUW members who were either involved in the founding of the organization or joined it later. Understanding the differences between the needs of these groups helps us understand why people stayed in the organization, why they left, and what consequences this had for organizational development. Using a life-course perspective, I identify four membership types, representing different versions of union feminism, which are based on different processes of political socialization and which result in different preferences for strategies and different patterns of participation in CLUW, the labor movement, and other political movements and organizations. As Jasper (1997:244) points out, "there is an interplay between pre-existing tastes and their transformation during protest. The more prior political experience the new recruits have had, in all likelihood, the stronger their tastes in tactics when they join a new movement." This holds true not only for involvement in protest, but also for formation of movement organization, as we shall see in the chapter on the organizational structure of CLUW.

A LIFE-COURSE PERSPECTIVE ON POLITICAL SOCIALIZATION

Processes of political socialization have both personal and organizational consequences. Social movements can be seen as sources as well as results of political socialization and the formation of collective identities. For example, the women's movement functions as an agent of socialization in a variety of contexts: consciousness-raising groups and other all-women's organizations, media and education, as well as through demonstrations and other forms of collective action (Sapiro 1990). Similarly, movements and protest activities in the civil rights movement "have been central to black political socialization and behavior. . . . Political socialization is a process rooted in a group's history and shaped by available options" (Morris et al. 1989: 281).

Political socialization is a lifelong process (Andrews 1991; Braungart and Braungart 1985; Sapiro 1994; Wasburn 1994). It includes not only traditional areas of formal political participation such as voting and membership in political elites, but also participation in social movements and community activism (Ackelsberg and Diamond 1987; Blumberg 1990; Bookman and Morgan 1988). Political socialization encompasses relationships of power and inequality in everyday life—everyday processes at home, school, and work as well as in marriage and other relationships, that are translated into political consciousness and political participation. This fact is reflected in the phrase "the personal is political," coined during the social movements of the 1960s and 1970s (Breines 1982; Evans 1979). Earlier, C. Wright Mills (1959) pointed out that "personal troubles and public issues" are intertwined. This statement does not mean that every action is political, but it does emphasize that politicization processes are grounded in the daily experience of power and inequality, and that political participation is not restricted to participation in elections.

Furthermore, adult political behavior is influenced not only by the cohort-generational experience of one's youth, but also by life-cycle changes and the current societal context (Braungart and Braungart 1985:280). A life-course model offers a view of the political socialization process over the course of an individual's lifetime. Since every individual is, to a greater or lesser extent, an active agent in his or her own political socialization (Wasburn 1994:10), political socialization can be conceptualized as individual political development, rather than as the transmission of dominant norms (Sapiro 1994). Such socialization processes can best be captured within a biographical perspective using life-course interviews (Della Porta 1992; Jasper 1997; Miethe 1999; Miethe and Roth 2000). As Jasper (1997:216) puts it,

We can search for patterns in the careers and life histories of individual activists. We can compare their moral visions and values with the requirements imposed on them by formal organizations: sometimes organizations serve their purposes; at other times they clash with them. We can contrast individuals' careers of protest with their membership, even leadership, of formal organizations. Tracing individuals might allow us to see many sources and activities of protest that are not organized by formal groups and leaders, as well as the cultural and biographical materials out of which new organizations arise.

Social movement activism has long-lasting "biographical consequences" (McAdam 1988a; 1989; 1992; Evans 1979; Taylor and Whittier 1992; Whalen and Flacks 1989). McAdam's (1988a; 1989) research on Freedom Summer reveals that social movement participation has roots in previous relationships and activities, and indicates the impact of social movement participation on the life-course of participants.

Political Biographies and Social Movement Development

To return to the notion of social movement interaction introduced earlier, the analysis of it at the individual level concerns how previous or parallel memberships shape activists' expectations of social movements and social movement organizations. If someone is active in several different movements, at the same time or successively, experiences can be transferred from one movement to the other (Meyer and Whittier 1994; Rose 2000). But activists may also pursue different issues in different contexts. Furthermore, the way members identify the purpose of an organization shapes their expectations regarding the issues the organization should pursue and the strategies it should employ. The negotiation processes among members result in the structure and collective identity of the organization.

Members bring their experiences to bear on the movements in which they participate, while participation in the movement also changes their lives. For example, "bridge builders" connect the labor movement and the environmental movement (Rose 2000). Activists bring political (and other) experiences to social movements and social movement organizations (Klandermans 1990) that have an impact on the development of the movement, because members from different backgrounds may differ with respect to the diagnosis and potential solutions of social problems. Tracing activists' biographies is one way to map social movements in that the biographies tell about the emergence of political consciousness and collective action, recruitment processes, and participation patterns.

FOUR PATHS TO UNION FEMINISM

The membership typology I present encompasses four groups: the founding mothers and the rebellious daughters who were involved in the formation of the Coalition of Labor Union Women, and the political animals and fighting victims who joined the organization later. Between 1991 and 1995 I conducted interviews with 68 formerly or at the time of the interview active CLUW members from all regions of the United States.[1] The typology resulted from comparing and contrasting biographies with respect to the involvement in political and social activities prior and parallel to participation in CLUW, identity, access to resources, and experiences of injustice and discrimination. Here and throughout, I use real names in the cases of the national presidents (Olga Madar, Joyce Miller, and Gloria Johnson) when I refer to published material. All other names are pseudonyms, and identifying information has been omitted. In this chapter, I particularly focus on the white women in the organization; in the next chapter, I will discuss the participation of women of color.

Founding Mothers

The founding mothers were already leaders in the labor movement and familiar with the women's movement before they came together to form the Coalition of Labor Union Women. They were born in the 1920s and 1930s and look back on long-standing involvement in the labor movement—some of them participated in the organization of the CIO unions in the 1940s. They came to the labor movement along different paths: from the assembly line, from graduate school, from progressive movements, from the Jewish community, from Roman Catholic or Protestant churches. Some joined the union as rank-and-file members, volunteer organizers, and staff members. What unites the founding mothers across these differences is that they were pioneers in the labor movement, the first women, white, African American, or Latina, to hold offices or staff positions. Most women of color started out as rank-and-file members. Others obtained a college education and were influenced by progressive movements. Religious affiliation was also meaningful. Some founding members were still active in CLUW at the national level as officers and as members of the National

Executive Board after retirement. Some had been active in the civil rights and women's movements and sought to integrate women's and civil rights issues into the labor movement.

Martha Winter and Ethel Gilman referred to their Jewish background and their parents' political and social commitments. They both were initially active in progressive male dominated CIO unions. Gilman described her mother as a suffragist and her father as a dedicated trade unionist and "mild socialist." "My mother . . . told the four of us, 'You are not vegetables . . . Our purpose in occupying space is to make the world better, because we are here.' And that's what I heard. That's part of my background. My ethnic background, I am Jewish. . . . I drank it in with the mother's milk, your duty is to make the world better. . . . So coming from this background it was not unusual that I became active in unions." After graduating from college, Gilman worked as a teacher and volunteered to organize women workers in a CIO union. She described her involvement in the labor movement as a "natural progression." Later she became a full-time organizer and eventually a district manager in a service sector union.

Winter's parents were active in the Jewish community and involved with the Jewish People's Institute. She worked as a secretary for a CIO union that organized farm equipment workers; she became radicalized during the Memorial Day Massacre in 1937 when she saw the police shoot into the crowd of picketers and kill several people. "That is the main part of an experience that really absolutely not only radicalized me, but made me the greatest defender and loyalist of the labor movement which subsequently led into the other work that I was doing. . . . So these were the beginnings of my education in the history and the understanding of classes of the workers and the bosses and who is for the workers and who is against the workers. And that was a segment of some movements, radical movements, who were for class collaboration." In Winter's case, political consciousness meant class consciousness. Winter worked as a printer and participated in her union as a rank-and-file activist and a delegate of her union.

Whether the founding mothers belonged to craft, industrial, service sector, or public sector unions, they were invariably the first women officers in their locals or international unions. Many had male mentors who helped them, but they also had to overcome prejudice and discrimination. The formation of CLUW answered their need to come together with other women union leaders and increase the role of women in union leadership.

Most founding mothers had been active in the labor movement for a long time before they became involved in the formation of CLUW. Some were also involved in the civil rights and women's movements. They provided a considerable proportion of the officers and activists at the national and the local level. Most of them stayed active in CLUW.

The founding mothers identified first and foremost with the labor movement, which they saw as the best means to overcome injustice and inequality. They were also critical of the labor movement with respect to gender issues. Their motivation to found CLUW was to reform and improve the labor movement and bring it in line with their race and feminist consciousness.

Rebellious Daughters

The rebellious daughters were a more homogeneous group with respect to their recruitment into the labor movement. They were born in the 1940s and 1950s and were active in the social movements of the 1960s and 1970s before they became active in the labor movement. Some came from working-class backgrounds; some were clerical workers or had jobs in university libraries. Their political involvement started when they were in college. For a number of rebellious daughters, the farmworkers' union represented their first contact with the labor movement; others were members of feminist organizations like Nine-to-Five or Union WAGE.

Supporting McAdam's (1988b) findings on the long-time consequences of activism, after they had been involved in the anti–Vietnam War, student, and civil rights movements, they remained activists. While some never finished their degrees, others completed college or graduate school before they joined unions as organizers and business agents. Some returned to graduate school after some years in the labor movement in order to get a degree in industrial relations or law.

The rebellious daughters tended to be staff members of unions at the regional level, as organizers, business agents, district managers, and union lawyers; rank-and-file members were an exception. They were likely to work for unions that represented women workers, especially office and health care workers. These were the unions with a higher proportion of women among the union leadership, unions that were pro-choice and supported pay equity and sexual harassment prevention.

Mildred Sequira came from a working-class background and had been active in the Democratic Party since high-school. In college she joined Students for a Democratic Society (SDS) and became involved in anti-Vietnam protests. She became involved in the labor movement when she started to organize university employees. She recalled: "I just became hooked. I found that I enjoyed all the union work much more than my academic work. I did finally finish and get my degree in political science but stayed with union work rather than going into teaching, which is what I thought I would do. It just became addictive, I could not get it out of my blood."[2] Sequira participated in the CLUW founding convention but was temporarily denied participation because she was not a member of a collective bargaining organization. She later became a staff member of a union and remained active in CLUW at the national and chapter level.

Margitta Guirard typifies the multiple memberships of the rebellious daughters. In the 1960s she was involved in a feminist health care collective that performed abortions, the Black Panthers, and the farmworkers. In the 1970s she started to organize day care workers as a volunteer organizer. As the result of a successful organizing drive she was fired from her job as a day care worker and started working as a business agent for the union.

Geena Watson, one of CLUW's national officers, completed an industrial relations graduate program and became a staff member of a union that organized clerical and professional employees. She became involved in the civil rights and women's movements in college. She explained her involvement in various social movements as due to a "need for collective action to make change." Like Sequira, she emphasized the satisfaction she gained from participating in collective action. "The truth is that I've always been involved in one movement or another, you know, the anti-war movement, the women's movement, the environmental movement. I mean I have been involved in all of them." This indicates very clearly that she did not prioritize one issue, but saw them as supplementing each other.

Overall, rebellious daughters were activists in a broad range of movements who were especially aware of the need to fight for women in low-paying jobs. They perceived CLUW as an instrument to reach out and organize non-unionized women workers. While some were active on the chapter level and national level, others had left the organization because the development of CLUW did not match their expectations. At the time of the interviews, several rebellious daughters were still active in the labor movement and were dues-paying members of CLUW, but they were no longer active in the organization. They felt a need for a feminist organization, but disagreed with CLUW's approach.

Political Animals

Many political animals were born in the 1920s and 1930s, some were born in the 1940s and 1950s. Some of this group attended business school or teacher's college. After graduating from school, marriage and motherhood was the next step in their biographies. Some met their husbands in high-school or college, others at work. Their educational careers were more strongly shaped by gender norms than were those of the founding mothers and rebellious daughters. The political animals wanted to work outside the home; marriage and motherhood were not enough for a fulfilled life. They often became telephone operators, clerical workers in the public sector, or teachers, entering workplaces that were already unionized. Both the workplaces and the unions representing them were female-dominated. The political animals attended a union meeting after being invited by co-workers or because they wanted to see how the union dues were put to use. Several found that the union meeting was not run properly and spoke up against violations of Robert's Rules of Order. Subsequently, they were asked to become active in the union. They did not participate in the founding convention of CLUW but joined the organization later. This means that some were already close to retirement when they joined CLUW.

Heather Stone explained that she did not use the college scholarship she had been awarded because her income was needed to support her family. Stone met her husband at work and suspended work only briefly when she had her four children. She indicated that she had to work as a young women in order to support the family, but she denied that she was working for financial reasons after she got married: "No, no, no. It wasn't financial reasons at all. It was very definitely that I needed to work. I just had the drive that said that I had to work and that I had to accomplish something. . . . I worked for the satisfaction of working and I guess I worked to get other things that I wanted, too. I worked to take vacations with my children and with my family and everything." She was the only working mother in her neighborhood and was criticized by neighbors who claimed she would neglect her children. Stone reported that her husband also faced disapproval because he shared household chores and childrearing with his wife, thus violating gender norms.

Evelyn Smith never considered going to college. Prior to her marriage she worked as a waitress; later she became a telephone operator. Like Stone, Smith met her husband at work. She justified her desire to go to work with earning money to buy a house. She convinced her husband that their daughter would not suffer when she returned to work. She and her husband both worked shifts and alternated so that they never needed a baby sitter. "And I wanted to get a house, I wanted to get out. . . . Under the pretext, . . . 'I am going to work, I want to save my salary, and we put it away so we can buy a house.' Well, that kind of softened him up a little bit. You know, he was always mad when I went back to work. He did not want me to go to work. And so I said, 'I am not neglecting you, I am not neglecting my child, or anything else.' But I went." Through her successful negotiations, Smith disrupted contemporary gender norms that required married women and mothers to stay home if there was not financial need; on the other hand, she maintained the gender order by maintaining the conventional division of labor at home and assuming full responsibility for household and child care.

Smith recalled how she first attended a union meeting: "A couple of the girls said, 'We are going to a union meeting tonight, Evelyn, do you want to come?' And I said, 'What are you going to do there?' 'Well, they listen to troubles and talk about things they are going to do and stuff like that.' And I said, 'All right, I'll go.' I went, and the first thing I do is I open my mouth, because I did not like [how the meetings were being run]." Smith voiced her concerns and was approached afterward and asked if she wanted to become a shop steward. After assuring her husband that she would not attend union meetings every night, she agreed. Four years later, after her husband died and her daughter started college, Smith became more involved in the union and became a business agent. The union assigned Smith to attend meetings of the Coalition of Labor Union Women and "check CLUW out." She found that CLUW was a "very valuable organization" and convinced the union to support it. Her union paid for her participation in national CLUW meetings and conventions.

For Smith there was clearly a relationship between union involvement and family life. On the one hand, the union to some extent replaced the family; on the other, her family obligations no longer constrained her involvement in the union.

Annie Fisher represents another case in which family life and union activity were closely intertwined, but in a quite different way. She and her husband met at teacher's college. They married after graduating and started working as teachers. Both joined the union. Fisher had three children in four years and returned to work after her third child was born. She became very active in the union after her husband moved up in the union hierarchy. He became an international representative, and began to travel frequently. While she was raising the children on her own, Fisher filled the positions in the union local and labor council that her husband had previously held. She maintained her marriage and family (her son later also became a representative of the same union) through her involvement in the labor movement. Her family became a part of the union and the union part of her family. Fisher felt that her husband and children supported her union activity and perceived her husband as her mentor. "I guess I would have to call him my mentor. . . . I would watch him, and listened to the various problems that we were having here. So, how he proceeded in negotiations and kinds of things that he was driving to achieve, the struggle that he went through, and I think that was what perked my interest." She explained that she felt that her husband had contributed a lot to the local labor movement, and she wanted to maintain his legacy.

In this narrative, the nuclear family was expanded through the union, which provided a connection between the family members. "My husband and my son [are] working in the union [and are] certainly very supportive in that area. I think they are very happy to see me still involved in the union movement. And it is not . . . taking a lot of time away from family. . . . My husband is on the road all the time, so he is pretty much away. And [my] children are all grown. . . . So I am able to devote a lot of my time to CLUW and labor council and some of the other groups that I belong to." As one of the women leaders in her state, Fisher was invited to become a charter member of a CLUW chapter in formation. Her involvement in CLUW gave her the opportunity to meet women from other unions. Prior to joining CLUW, Fisher had no connection to the women's movement and feminist issues.

Lara O'Neill met her husband in high-school and was active in the community and the Democratic Party. She returned to work after her children went to high-school and college and she did not feel needed any more. She described the transition from community politics to involvement in the labor movement as a natural progression. "You finished with one thing and you went to work and you became involved in things that were more work oriented. So as I transferred to the union, I gave up the political stuff. Now, obviously as a union member we are very concerned as state employees. We are concerned with the legislature, so I am up there [at the state Capitol] when I can be. And I interact a lot with the legislators, but not with the same activity within the political party. With other words, the Democratic Women's Club now has become CLUW and the Democratic Party is the Labor Council. And I think that's the way it is." O'Neill thus stated very clearly that the focus and organizational context of her political participation changed due to changes in her personal life. She saw a continuity in her political action and framed CLUW as a women's organization in the labor movement.

Like O'Neill, Myrtle Jessop was also involved in community organizing prior to returning to work. She had been active in a union and progressive politics before she married. After becoming active in an interracial group that primarily focused on socializing, Jessop helped organize a neighborhood council. Jessop's and O'Neill's involvement in civic groups and local politics were connected to their motherhood and their lives in the neighborhood. Due to their involvement in the community, O'Neill and Jessop were involved in labor organizing prior to becoming union members themselves.

The political animals were not involved in the founding of the organization, but joined CLUW later. They perceived their union participation as an extension and natural progression of their political involvement in community politics and the Democratic Party. They belonged to the executive boards of their local unions, the labor council, and committees of the state AFL–CIO and were outspoken rank-and-file activists. The political animals worked in female-dominated occupations represented by public sector and other unions that had a high proportion of women members and supported women's leadership at the local level. These unions also promoted the participation of their women members in CLUW. The political animals came into contact with the women's movement through CLUW.

The political animals had been active in community politics and neighborhood associations before they became active in the labor movement. CLUW was their avenue to the women's movement. For some the union represented a family extension and substitute. Overall, they were ambitious and work-oriented women who combined work and family and enjoyed organizing. They learned about CLUW through their union and perceived CLUW as a women's movement in the labor movement. They did not see a need to change CLUW. Together with the founding mothers they were the strongest supporters of CLUW and involved at every level of the organization.

Fighting Victims

The fighting victims differed with respect to age, race, and nationality. Some married shortly after graduating from high-school and started working outside the home after getting divorced. Many came from poor and working-class backgrounds, and upward mobility was a major personal issue for them. All started their careers in low-paying jobs that were open to women, minorities, immigrants, and those with little education. Unionized workplaces provided them benefits, job security, and an opportunity for upward mobility within the union. They realized that unionization and college education were ways out of bleak job prospects. The union became instrumental in offering them a chance to become involved in collective action and improve their own and others' life situations. They joined CLUW to meet other union women and acquire leadership skills; they left if the organization no longer offered them anything.

In contrast to the previous three groups, who had been politicized in social movements and community politics, and emphasized that they were active on behalf of others who were less resourceful and articulate, the fighting victims became politically active after they personally had been discriminated against. This does not mean that the other three types had not been discriminated against or that they did not talk about such experiences (as I will discuss later in this chapter); it means that they did not frame these experiences as a catalyst for their political participation and involvement in the women's movement or other social movements. The participation of the fighting victims in the labor movement and CLUW was grounded in the experience of being treated unfairly. They became politicized through their union activity, for instance in the fight for comparable worth, or against sexual harassment.

Karen Shils married when she was 19 years old after graduating from nursing school. Ten years later she divorced her husband when their children were five and seven years old. After her divorce Shils resumed working for a community health care plan, first part-time and then full-time. She became an active union member, shop steward, volunteer organizer, and later a business agent of her union. According to Shils' experience, people became shop stewards due to discrimination experience. "I think there are some individuals that either at some point in their life experience or because of combinations of their personality and their life experience become individuals who may have experienced dissimilar treatment or may have experienced something negative by their employer, decided that they want to be a spokesperson, they want to be an advocate. They felt the pain and they therefore want to participate in the cure. . . . And I decided I am one of them." Here the experience of discrimination clearly played an important role.

Jody Hunter left college after her freshman year and married her high-school sweetheart. She started to work and helped him through college, planning to return to college after he graduated and found a job. Hunter was 19 when she got married; when she was 23 she had "a baby, a house, and a husband with a decent job." When the baby was a year old, her husband left her. Hunter looked for a job that would allow her to earn enough money to live and have time to spend with the baby. She chose a bricklayer's apprenticeship, which she obtained through an affirmative action hiring process, because the pay was good and there was time off due to bad weather and layoffs. She completed the apprenticeship and became a journeyman in spite of the hostility of her male colleagues, who resented that women and minorities "took away their sons' jobs." She remarried and had a second baby. A former business agent helped her to find employment with the state AFL–CIO.

Dottie Jones' father died when she was a teenager. She had to start working while she was in high-school to contribute to the family income. Her mother received welfare checks and worked menial jobs "under the table." Jones also noticed that her mother had to lie about her age in order to get the job and was denied loans. Furthermore, she realized that women's work pays less than men's work and that her mother suffered gender discrimination. Jones decided that this should not happen to herself and set out to obtain a college degree. She attended junior college because she could not afford to attend school full-time, and looked for an employer who would support her college education. While working in a supermarket she found out that the male employees were better paid, even though she was their supervisor. She changed to factory work when she heard that the employer might be willing to pay for college costs. After a while she realized that she might have to wait for this forever. Eventually, she found a job in a unionized factory in the defense industry. "I just did not want the same situations that happened before to happen again, and I felt that women, because of my experience in the small shop, that women were really underpaid and really getting a second class status in the working place. And I felt that the union, any union by its philosophy, maintains equality for all its members, no matter what." She joined the union and became active as a shop steward. The union supported her college education as well as a master's degree in industrial relations. Jones became a trustee of the local and an employee assistance coordinator.

Overall, the fighting victims were women who had experienced discrimination. They turned to the union to fight against discrimination in the workplace and became active in the fight for pay equity and against sexual harassment, racism, and anti-immigration policies. They saw the union as a tool for supporting women's interests. Often they moved up in the union from rank-and-file activists to officers and staff members; in some cases they achieved a college education, empowerment and upward mobility through their participation in the union and CLUW. They joined CLUW in order to acquire leadership skills and tended to leave CLUW when they found that the organization did not offer them training or other support.

VARIETIES OF UNION FEMINISM

The membership typology reveals a variety of union feminisms that were formed in political socialization processes over women's life-courses. The union feminism of the founding mothers emphasized their trade union identity. The union feminism of the rebellious daughters was anchored in a feminist critique of the labor movement and a critique of the racial and class biases of the women's movement. The union feminism of the political animals was issue-oriented and valued the labor movement and the women's movement as equally important and mutually supportive. The union feminism of the fighting victims evolved from discrimination experiences and the fight against discrimination in the context of the labor movement and CLUW. All four types emphasized equality and justice regardless of race, class, and gender, and saw these as dimensions that needed to be addressed jointly in order to pursue inclusive solidarity.

The contrast between the rebellious daughters and founding mothers suggests an interpretation of the types in terms of generational units (Mannheim 1952; Whittier 1995). Mannheim distinguishes between generation location—being born in the same historical and social region—and generation as an actuality—"where a concrete bond is created between members of a generation by being exposed to the social and intellectual symptoms of a process of dynamic destabilization" (1952:303). Furthermore, within a given generation, Mannheim identifies separate generation units that respond to their common experience in different specific ways (304). Whittier (1995) introduces the term "microcohorts" in order to account for variations within political generations. However, although there are certain affinities with my groupings, none of these concepts fully corresponds with my typology. First, only one of the types—the rebellious daughters—represented generation as an actuality. The rebellious daughters experienced the emergence of the social movements of the 1960s and 1970s when they attended college. But these movements also represented an important context for the political socialization for the other types.

The founding mothers developed class consciousness and a trade union identity, while the rebellious daughters were socialized in an anti-hierarchical style. For both types their political identity was related to their preference for organizational structure. The founding mothers participated not only in the labor movement but also in the women's and civil rights movement, while the rebellious daughters joined the labor movement after initially participating in the social movements of the 1960s and 1970s. Thus both types participated in multiple movements and were confronted with different organizational styles. In contrast, most political animals and fighting victims became involved in unions that supported women's issues and were less aware of tensions between the women's movement and the labor movement.

Second, the founding mothers, political animals, and fighting victims encompassed more than one generation. Mannheim's concept of generational units and Whittier's concept of micro-cohorts emphasize the differences within generations, whereas I observed similarities and differences across generations. For instance, the founding mothers and some of the political animals were born in the 1920s and 1930s. The founding mothers have been involved in the labor movement much longer than the political animals, and vividly remember McCarthyism and conflicts between the women's movement and the labor movement around the Equal Rights Amendment. The political animals joined the labor movement much later. They were not aware of these tensions, and therefore had a different perspective on the relationship between the women's movement and the labor movement, even though they were in part of the same generation as the founding mothers.

The four types came to CLUW for different reasons and with different experiences and expectations, and their hopes affected what they did with and for the organization. Where did their interest in CLUW come from, and how did their goals differ? In order to answer these questions, I compare the four types with respect to injustice (empowerment, overcoming discrimination), identity (feminist consciousness, class consciousness), and resources. These three dimensions are crucial for mobilization into social movements and have repercussions for the development of a social movement organization. The belief that prevailing social arrangements are unjust is one condition for the mobilization of collective action (Gamson et al. 1982; McAdam 1982; Piven and Cloward 1979). Collective identity and political consciousness are crucial preconditions for social movement participation (Gamson 1992) as well as results of collective action (Fantasia 1988). Finally, resources like education, and especially organizational affiliation, matter because different backgrounds mean different experiences, expectations, and access to networks.

EXPERIENCING AND OVERCOMING INJUSTICE

The experience of injustice is an important motivating factor for involvement in contentious and conventional politics. Injustice is a core category of the social psychology of social movements (Gamson 1992; Klandermans 1997) and political socialization. Something (for example racism, sexism, economic inequality) is wrong, someone caused it, and someone has to do something about stopping it. The notion of injustice thus informs tactics and strategies. All four types experienced injustice and addressed it in their activism, but they framed it in different ways according to their socialization. A sense of injustice can stem from a variety of sources: from their personal experience with discrimination, to a religious and moral upbringing that emphasized responsibility to end injustice. The context of the life-course clarifies how experiences of discrimination are linked to feelings of solidarity with other oppressed groups: prejudice and discrimination can be experienced in the family and at the workplace, in the union and other social movements. How and in what contexts did CLUW members perceive and experience injustice, and how was it related to their political consciousness and political participation?

All four types were sensitive to all forms of oppression and discrimination, with respect to gender, age, race, class, as well as religion, sexual orientation, and so on. All saw the labor movement as a vehicle for social change and overcoming inequality and all had experienced discrimination or harassment within their unions. They differed, however, in their assessment of the labor movement. Furthermore, they could be distinguished according to their emphasis on fighting for others or on combating personal experiences of discrimination.

Standing Up for Others

Founding mothers, rebellious daughters, and political animals emphasized that they were active on behalf of others. A sense for injustice and inequality was part of the social consciousness of the founding mothers, grounded in involvement in the Jewish community, progressive movements, or the civil rights movement. The founding mothers grew up with the obligation to make the world a better place.

The rebellious daughters developed a sense for injustice during their participation in social movements. They presented their involvement in collective action not as a way to improve their own personal situation but as a tool to contribute to the empowerment of low-wage working women. They criticized the women's movement for overlooking the needs of women of color and working-class women. Like the founding mothers and political animals, the rebellious daughters put more emphasis on fighting for the rights of women than for themselves.

Similarly, the political animals presented themselves as advocates for the powerless, and described their opposition to improper behavior of authority figures such as parents, bosses, and union leadership. The political animals initially were active in community politics to stand up "for the underdog." Evelyn Smith described herself as a "a very positive person. I just look. I look at the underdog all the time and I always want to help, I always want to be that one to help the underdog. . . . I have been a fighter, I've been a fighter all my life. And when I see that something is wrong I want to try to right it." Another CLUW member said that she "always had this feeling, a sense of equality for people, that nobody should be so exploited—they should have a decent standard of living. And I worked for the [welfare department] for a number of years, doing case work, working with people who were living a month of welfare."

Some political animals became involved in the union after they attended union meetings in which they spoke up against the political positions the local leadership took. Consequently they were asked to become active in the union. One CLUW member perceived her involvement in CLUW as a "calling"; she said that "in the church world they look upon that as missionaries or evangelists administering to people that are hurting or what-have-you. And in the labor movement, essentially, that's what you're speaking out for those that cannot speak for themselves. So I guess that's the thing that has become innate to some extent." However, while many CLUW members emphasized that they felt the obligation or need to become active on behalf of others, they also experienced discrimination themselves.

Discrimination and Inequality in the Workplace

The fighting victims described how they had been discriminated against in the workplace and how they found support from the union and CLUW. In contrast to the other three types, who became politically active in order to help others, for the fighting victims the personal experience of discrimination and being treated unjustly led to their union involvement. They entered the labor force with little formal education and job training, and had to earn a living for themselves and their children after a divorce. They became aware of the low-wage level in women's jobs or experienced discrimination in the workplace, and became active in the campaign for comparable worth. When Samantha Torrell started to work in the public sector after having worked in the private sector, she was outraged by her low pay and felt that she had never been treated so unfairly. "When there's somebody who's an illiterate who can make more money than you, doing something that you do at home for free—carry boxes around and scrape dishes—I mean that was his job. Was my job more valuable to the state while I was a secretary, or was his job more valuable? Pointswise I knew that mine was, and I also knew if I was working for a director in private industry, I would have been making a lot more money." After realizing that female-typed jobs were lower in pay than male-typed ones, some fighting victims sought employment in so-called nontraditional jobs to avoid the wage differential. Susan Carter had been working in a clerical position for years before she started to work in the defense industry, where she "earned the same like the man working next to me." The fighting victims found an ally against workplace discrimination in the union. They turned to the union to file grievances and improve their work situation. In CLUW they learned about strategies to address women's issues such as comparable worth, child care, and sexual harassment. Initially they were active in the union in order to improve their own situation. As shop stewards and business agents, they became active for others.

Discrimination and Harassment in the Union

Regardless of whether they had experienced discrimination in the workplace or not, all four types had experienced discrimination in the union. However, they differed in their evaluation of this harassment. The founding mothers attributed it to the unions' lack of knowledge and experience with women. The rebellious daughters perceived it as proof of the deep-rooted sexism of the labor movement. The political animals and fighting victims downplayed the gender dimen-

sion of the inequality and presented it as an inconsistency with union philosophy.

Several of the founding mothers experienced gender discrimination in their
union prior to the formation of CLUW. The founding mothers were aware of
gender discrimination in the labor movement and presented their discrimination
experiences as examples for their success in influencing the male union leadership. Ethel Gilman, for example, described an argument she had with a male
union leader when she applied for the position as organizer. She was told:
"'Based on women's issues, yes, you are the president of the union, et cetera,'
the leader said, 'But we can't hire you as an organizer, even if you are doing
organizing on your own [and] you are a wonderful organizer. And why? Because you are a woman.' And my response was, 'Because I am a woman for 30
years, what's so strange about that?' 'Well you can't go out at night to go to the
hospitals.' I said, 'I go out at night, I am a married woman, and I go out at
night.'" Gilman responded to this discrimination with the suggestion that she be
hired for a 60 day probation period. After this time the members should decide
whether she should be appointed organizer. The leadership agreed and after 60-
days the members voted for Gilman's appointment. The founding mothers
pointed out that they were able to convince the male leadership that women
were a valuable resource for the union. They gained leadership positions in their
unions and the support of their union for their participation in CLUW.

The founding mothers presented gender discrimination as singular incidents
that could be overcome individually. After living with gender discrimination for
a long time, they felt that collective action in the form of founding CLUW was
needed. For example, one of the founding mothers realized that the union leaders were against the unionization of the female office workers when she started
to organize them. "And I started a little committee to help organize the office
workers. And the thing that also impacted itself on me, is that the leaders of the
unions who were my bosses, did not like the office workers to organize. They
did not want us to organize and that also had an important impression on me.
Because here they acted like the bosses, what the hell was the difference between them and the other guys?" She was confronted by the contradiction of the
union.

Furthermore, the civil rights movement and the women's movement made it
clear for them that the labor movement did not live up to its ideal of representing
workers' rights equally. They acknowledged that gender discrimination was a
structural problem in the labor movement. The founding mothers were aware of
racism, sexism, and other forms of oppression. They presented the union, as well
as CLUW, as means to overcome these forms of injustice and discrimination
using methods like contracts that cover pay equity and sexual harassment.

For the rebellious daughters the fight against sexism, racism, economic ex-
ploitation, and homophobia constituted a continuum. Geena Watson spoke about
racism and sexism in the civil rights, the anti-war, and labor movements that

made it necessary to form "caucuses and other movements to install changes within." Each of these movements addressed injustice and fought against discrimination. However, the rebellious daughters emphasized sexism in the labor movement and the neglect of race and class issues in the women's movement. One of the respondents recalled that women delegates were called "braless brainless broads" when they addressed women's issues at a labor convention. In contrast to the founding mothers, the rebellious daughters were explicit regarding the sexism in the labor movement. Miriam Miller remarked: "You can't overstate that there is still a lot of sexism in the labor movement." Angie Harrington also found that the labor movement was heavily male dominated: "Talk about male chauvinism, I can tell that unions can be the worst places to work. . . . I believe the trade unions in this country are still heavily male run and very chauvinist."

The rebellious daughters were mostly concerned with organizing low-wage women workers; they realized that CLUW excluded unorganized women workers from regular membership and contributed to their organization only indirectly through training programs and through the support of organizing drives upon request from unions. Therefore, many of the rebellious daughters lost interest in CLUW, instead turning directly to unions that were targeting low-wage women workers. Some became active in organizations that tried to reach these women.

In addition, some of the rebellious daughters experienced discrimination due to their union activity. Margitta Guirard and Eleanor Junker, who were rank-and-file activists, were fired after they had successfully organized day care workers. Junker consequently went to law school in order to learn labor law, while Guirard became a full-time union organizer, only to face sexism and racism later in the labor movement. Rebellious daughters experienced that women, including themselves, were exploited and sexually harassed in the labor movement. Guirard expected that CLUW would provide a support group for women in the labor movement, while another rebellious daughter, Angie Harrington, never considered the local CLUW chapter as an ally against her union harassers.

The political animals did not experience discrimination in the labor movement as personal; they were concerned with structural discrimination. When Evelyn Smith read the union contract to find out more about her duties as shop steward, she realized that men and women were treated differently in the bargaining contract. "The very first thing I spotted [was] that the men in the plant department got paid the first day they were out sick and the women got paid the second day. This is one contract!" She was shocked about this inconsistency.

Compared to the founding mothers, who downplayed gender discrimination in the labor movement, the political animals (like the rebellious daughters) emphasized it. The difference between the founding mothers and the political animals can be explained by the fact that the founding mothers were already involved in the labor movement when they encountered injustice there, while this injustice marked the beginning of involvement for the political animals. In contrast to the rebellious daughters, who had been active in feminist issues prior to CLUW, for the political animals CLUW presented the "springboard" or the access to the women's movement.

Evelyn Smith realized that she needed to become a member of her union's bargaining committee in order to be able to end the unequal treatment of women in the contract. Another form of discrimination noted by the political animals was that men attended conventions of international unions (even if they belonged to an independent local), but that the participation of women in CLUW conventions was not supported. Heather Stone observed that women staff members of the union she belonged to participated in CLUW and the summer school, but "did not think it was necessary for the members to participate in CLUW." Stone "put an end to that," running for office in the union and joining CLUW, paying her own travel expenses to the first CLUW convention she attended. Later she became a staff member of a public sector union who paid the travel expenses of delegates to CLUW conventions.

Although the fighting victims experienced the union as an ally against unfair treatment, for them being a union member was an ambivalent experience as well. They experienced the union as a supporter in the fight against unequal treatment, but they also were discriminated against in the union. For instance, Jody Hunter as an apprentice in a bricklayers' union found that her co-workers and union members, all white men, resented the fact that she received an apprenticeship as a woman, while their sons (presumably) could not get apprenticeships. Hunter recalled: "You're working all week and then you went to class on Saturdays and learned about unionism and maybe go on a picket line even. . . . But within your own union people hated you and resented you, because they figured you had a job just because you are a woman." Hunter experienced a discrepancy between the ideal of solidarity and the actual feelings of exclusion and being resented.

Dottie Jones also realized discrepancies between the ideal and the reality of union solidarity. She said she knew "that the philosophy is idealistic, and reality sometimes is not the same way." While Jones saw in the labor movement a "prime vehicle" to secure economic rights and achieve pay equity, she also perceived differences between the "union philosophy and the reality of the labor movement. As much as you don't like to admit it, there is still that patriarchy will sit in the unions as well." Even the unions that predominantly represented women were run by men, not women. Nevertheless, Jones decided "that the union really provided the philosophy, the means, and the support that women needed to achieve and maintain some decent economic status." In addition, some fighting victims had to file grievances against their supervisors on discrimination for union activities; thus they also experienced discrimination due to their union activity.

In their emphasis on justice and equality, some fighting victims rejected affirmative action and perceived it as reverse discrimination. In this way the fighting victims put an emphasis on the solidarity of workers, rather than on the differences of interests between workers. However, fair treatment included recognition of special needs for them, like respecting the religious holidays of all religious groups.

In conclusion, the founding mothers, rebellious daughters, and political animals were active in the labor movement, other social movements, and the community due to their social consciousness. They were concerned with gender discrimination as well as other forms of discrimination. Some personally experienced discrimination, but they did not present their involvement as a response to such an experience. Rather, they identified with "workers," "low-paid women workers," and "the underdog." They tried to help other women workers and bring women into leadership positions. The founding mothers and the rebellious daughters emphasized inequality and injustice in the workplace. They experienced gender discrimination in the labor movement but interpreted it differently. The founding mothers framed it as an inconsistency of the labor movement that could be overcome, while the rebellious daughters described it as typical. Like the political animals who got satisfaction from helping others, the rebellious daughters addressed the help that others needed but not their own needs. In contrast to the other three types, the fighting victims became politically active in order to improve their own situation. After they turned to the union to do something about being treated unfairly, they became involved in the labor movement and political action in order to fight for the rights of other women and workers.

CONSTRUCTING POLITICAL IDENTITIES

The way injustice was experienced and framed was closely related to the political identities of the four types. Through interaction with different occupational, racial, political, and age groups, feminist, racial, ethnic, class, generational, and other forms of political consciousness are reconstructed and contested. How did CLUW members identify with their union, the labor movement, and the women's movement? How did they describe their feminist consciousness, class consciousness, and racial and ethnic consciousness?

As already noted, the union feminism of CLUW members encompassed multiple and interrelated systems of oppression. However, due to the differences in political socialization, the types differed as to whether they stressed class, gender, or race as most important for their identity. Some CLUW members had difficulties with the term "feminist" and spent considerable time explaining what feminism means to them. Their identification with the women's movement and the labor movement was related to their perception of CLUW as part of the women's movement, and part of the labor movement.

Labor Union Identity and Class Consciousness

The founding mothers emphasized their "trade union identity." Since some founding mothers came from middle-class backgrounds and joined the labor movement at the staff level after graduating from college, their class consciousness was obviously independent from their class position.

Some of the founding mothers had been involved in the National Organization for Women and other organizations of the liberal women's movement, and they emphasized two things about this involvement. First, they stressed that the liberal women's movement had neglected working-class women and women of color. They wanted to "sell" unionism to the women's movement. Second, they asserted that labor union women needed their own organization and should be members of CLUW before they joined women's movement organizations. Olivia Magyar put it this way: "Together we will make feminists unionists and we will make unionists feminists."

While some rebellious daughters found ways to reconcile feminism, unionism, and anti-racism in the labor movement, others found this difficult. Margitta Guirard recalled how she was perceived by union members with whom she worked as a labor educator: "They [union members] thought that your first loyalty was to the labor movement and then if you want to be a feminist and a fighter against racism. But your first loyalty was to the union. . . . and they considered that I was this raving. . . . I was a feminist, . . . they thought that I was going to bring up gay rights, they thought I was going to bring up workers' control. They thought that I was going to alienate everybody with my . . . feminism."

Political animal Evelyn Smith did not support reproductive rights due to her religious beliefs, but considered herself feminist and described herself as a union person. Karen Shils initially rejected the label feminist and explained that in her role as business agent she did not discriminate between women's rights and men's rights, but fought for "employee rights." She criticized the efforts of her union to address diversity of the union membership. Rather than singling out minority groups, Shils wanted to see everybody treated equally.

Founding mothers, political animals, and fighting victims were much more inclined to adopt a union identity. Some enthusiastically declared themselves a union person. The rebellious daughters were least likely to identify with the labor movement. They had a more distanced (and critical) relationship to the unions, but saw them also as vehicles for social change.

Feminist Identity

Compared to the other three types, the rebellious daughters were significantly more likely to perceive themselves as "feminist." Over 70% of the rebellious daughters, less than half of the founding mothers, and about a third of the political animals and fighting victims considered themselves feminists (CLUW membership survey). The difference was much more pronounced than the differences regarding participation in the women's movement. Thus members distinguished between the women's movement and feminism (Ferree and Subramaniam 2001). Feminism constitutes only one version of women's movements; it addresses gender power relations, while women's movements encompass political or social engagement of women as women. There were significant differences among the different types of members with respect to the affiliation with social movements. Over 80% of the founding mothers and rebellious daughters said that they were involved in the women's movement; less than half of the political animals and about half of the fighting victims said that they belonged to it. More than a third of the female respondents indicated that they were involved in the National Organization for Women. More than half of the rebellious daughters and almost half of the founding mothers belonged to NOW, but only a quarter of the political animals and less than a third of the fighting victims did (CLUW membership survey). These figures show that CLUW activists were involved in the women's movement to a much higher extent than American women in general. But they also indicate that there were significant differences between the types, suggesting that not every CLUW member saw her participation in CLUW as involvement in the women's movement.

Although the rebellious daughters were most likely to define themselves as feminists and had been involved in the women's movement prior to the labor movement, they had an ambivalent relationship to the women's movement. The concern of the rebellious daughters was how far the women's movement was willing and able to go beyond gender issues. June Hoffman said: "I have always been a feminist. And when I started working in the labor movement my class consciousness became much more uncovered. I learned about my own class background. . . . So my class consciousness got really developed. Much more. I had a political consciousness. I was part of the socialist movement in this country. But CLUW was a place where I could merge the two, I could be a feminist and I could be a class conscious working woman."

In spite of their involvement in the women's movement and their feminist perspective on the labor movement, some rebellious daughters were reluctant to call themselves feminists. Whether they accepted or rejected the label "feminist," they pointed out that worker, community, and family issues needed to be part of the agenda of a working women's movement.

The other three types had even more trouble with the label "feminist." Martha Winter's statement typified how the founding mothers felt about the label. "What's a feminist? Give me a good definition of a feminist. If a feminist means protecting and fighting for women's rights? Absolutely, 100%. But if a feminist means all the silly things that they attribute, burning their bras, or doing all those ridiculous things, no, I am not. I don't go along with nonsense. I go along with that which is going to help women achieve equal status in society, to work, to get good jobs, and union wages. To have proper care for their children. Get health care."

Winter thus distinguished between issues worth fighting for and "feminist nonsense" like bra-burning. She thus accepted the image the media had constructed of a white-middle-class women's movement (Tuchman 1978) and distanced herself from it. This does not mean that feminist issues were not relevant to her. For instance, she described that she introduced herself as "brother Martha" at a union convention because the speakers only addressed male delegates. She found that this was an effective way to make her point, and she was henceforth known in the union as "brother Martha."

Some of the political animals described themselves as feminists, while others expressed gender consciousness (Rinehart 1992). For instance Evelyn Smith, a white political animal, said, "So I felt that being a woman I could fight for what women needed in their contract and it worked fairly well."

The political animals, Evelyn Smith, Heather Stone, and Lara O'Neill, labeled themselves feminist. For Stone and O'Neill, being a feminist meant supporting a pro-choice position even though such a position contradicted their religious beliefs. O'Neill said that she was not a radical feminist, which for her meant being against men. Other political animals were more reluctant to accept the label feminist and distinguished between supporting women's rights and being a feminist. Annie Fisher answered my question "Would you say that you are a feminist?" very evasively. "Certainly, I believe in—, I don't—. See that kind of has a conno—, I don't, you know feminist, really what do you mean with feminist?" First, she accepted the label ("certainly"), but then she demanded to know how I defined feminism and referred to connotations of the term. Then she gave her own definition for being a feminist. "I certainly do believe in women's rights and women's issues. So in that respect, yes. Equality for women, definitely. But I believe in rights for everyone and not just women certainly, you know. I think any of the minority groups. I would certainly be willing to give equal attention to any groups that I thought were having problems. I would not just single out women, in other words." Fisher defined women as one among other minority groups; she did not want to single out women, or any other group. While she supports women's rights, she emphasized that the interests of other minority groups are just as important to her.

Only a few fighting victims accepted the label "feminist." Samantha Torrell became a feminist based on the gender discrimination she experienced. She explained:

The civil rights movement had a lot to do with it and getting divorced had a lot to do with my becoming more of a feminist because I had to do a man's job in order to earn a living. Then I went to [work to the hospital] and it was rammed down my throat again that I was in a women's job. . . . So it just grew. You know, it wasn't my saying: 'I'm going to be a feminist.' It just kind of grew like Topsy, that's all. Things like that happen to you, I guess. I don't know. It wasn't a conscious thing, my saying 'I'm going to become a feminist.' It was deciding what was right and going in that direction.

Torrell was not active in the civil rights movement, but she referred to the events during the Freedom Summer campaign as opening her eyes to injustice. The civil rights movement thus provided an injustice frame (Gamson 1992) within which she interpreted her experience at work.

Some fighting victims participated in NOW before they joined CLUW; some learned about CLUW in NOW. Many fighting victims accepted the label "feminist" only after they had defined it or rejected it altogether. For instance, Tracy Dallas stated that she was "definitely not a feminist." However, she could not explain what she meant by that statement. "I don't know. How do you explain you're not a feminist? I'm not a non-feminist. I kind of like to do my own thing. . . . I don't even know how to categorize a feminist anymore. I'm not even sure what that really means. . . . Women's issues are basically—workers' issues are usually women's issues. Some women's issues may not be some workers' issues, I guess, but I think a woman in the work force deals with a lot more than just being in the work force. There's a lot of things externally that they're dealing with, more so than their male counterpart." Dallas argued that workers' issues reached beyond the workplace. As long as women are responsible for unpaid labor at home, issues of combining work and family are women's issues. But these issues are also workers' issues because they are related to work hours and flexibility. She concluded that one should not talk about women's issues or workers' issues but about family issues. Dallas found it divisive and exclusive to address women's issues rather than workers' or family issues, which address both women and men.[3]

The founding mothers and rebellious daughters were aware of the tensions between the women's movement and the labor movement. The founding mothers emphasized their trade union identity and some of them identified as feminists. For them, racial consciousness, class consciousness, and feminist consciousness were not competitive or mutually exclusive but complementary and reinforcing. The rebellious daughters identified with neither the white middle-class women's movement nor the white male labor movement, but they presented themselves as feminist and class-conscious. The rebellious daughters were very excited about the formation of CLUW, where they hoped to reconcile feminism and unionism. The political animals and the fighting victims saw the women's movement and the labor movement as natural allies and emphasized that both movements stand for justice and equality. The political animals described themselves as feminists and labor persons.

RESOURCES: QUALIFICATIONS AND CONNECTIONS

The differences in biographies and processes of socialization result not only in experiences of injustice and the development of political identities but also in resources such as education and experience gained in political action and organizational affiliations that members bring to the organization.

Overall, the rebellious daughters were better educated than the other three types. Almost a third of the rebellious daughters had a master's degree; only about a sixth of the founding mothers and political animals and less than a tenth of the fighting victims held such a degree. Over 40% of the fighting victims had a high-school diploma or less (CLUW membership survey). Some founding mothers were college graduates or had graduate degrees. The rebellious daughters attended college; several returned to graduate school after some years of union activism and obtained degrees from law schools or labor education programs in order to be better prepared for their role in the labor movement. Some mentioned that they came from a working-class background. Most political animals had a high-school degree, and some had graduated from college. The fighting victims graduated from high-school and worked in administrative jobs in the public sector, service sector, and crafts before they started working full-time for the union as staff representatives, full-time officers, or staff of the state labor federation. CLUW was diverse not only with respect to race and ethnicity, but also to socioeconomic status (income and education): 37% of the members considered themselves middle-class while 52% perceived themselves as working class; 11% had a household income of less than $25,000, 35% $25,000 and $49.999, and 48% more than $50,000 (CLUW membership survey).

Movement Participation

The four types also differed with respect to their political experiences and affiliations prior to joining CLUW. Over 80% of the members were involved in the Democratic Party. The founding mothers had been active in a variety of social movements and political organizations prior to their involvement in CLUW and remained active on behalf of multiple causes. They had a variety of skills and network connections and brought these resources to the organization.

The rebellious daughters were comparable to the founding mothers regarding their networks with social movements other than the labor movement. They were active in the women's movement and other social movements of the 1960s and 1970s. They participated in SDS, SNCC, WREE, WAGE, Nine-to-Five, and more recently formed organizations such as the Asian Pacific Labor Alliance (APALA) or Black Workers for Justice (BWFJ). Women of color were active in their communities (Table 3.1).

The political animals were immersed in local politics, were active in the Democratic Party, labor council, and state AFL–CIO, and interacted frequently with male leadership. They knew Robert's Rules of Order and were familiar with parliamentary procedure. Some of the political animals first came into contact with the women's movement through CLUW and never participated in other organizations of the women's movement. In addition, many political animals belonged to public sector unions that supported feminist issues such as pay equity, family and medical leave, and addressing sexual harassment.

Few of the political animals were in the women's movement prior to their involvement in CLUW. Heather Stone called CLUW a "springboard for women's issues." Evelyn Smith said about CLUW that "it keeps me abreast of the things that are going on that concern women." She was not interested in women's issues before she returned to work and became involved in the union.

Table 3.1
Involvement of CLUW Members in Various Social Movements and Social Movement Organizations

	Founding mothers	Rebellious daughters	Political animals	Fighting victims
Women's movement	86%	83%	47%	58%
Civil rights movement	78%	72%	38%	48%
Peace movement	36%	76%	27%	24%
NOW	46%	60%	25%	31%
NARAL	22%	42%	12%	16%

Source: CLUW Membership Survey; N = 320.

Torrell, one of the fighting victims, attended NOW meetings. She said that these meetings raised her consciousness, but that she left the organization because it did not solve her problems. "I wasn't really that active because at the time most of them were all married and they were all dissatisfied with their lives, and trying to find themselves. I was by this time divorced, self-supporting and it didn't answer my needs." Torrell emphasized the differences between the other NOW members and herself: she had material needs rather than "identity needs." At NOW Torrell met two women who encouraged her to become active in the fight for Objective Job Evaluation.

Union Affiliation and Position in Unions

The four types also differed with respect to union affiliation. More than half of the founding mothers belonged to unions that organized professional workers (AFT, OPEIU) and service sector workers and female-dominated industries (CWA, SEIU, UFCW, UNITE); only 10% belonged to the public sector union AFSCME. Most of these unions are characterized by a high proportion of women members, women in union leadership, and support of women's issues. Among the four types, the fighting victims were most likely not to belong to these unions but to male-dominated unions (CLUW membership survey).

Almost half of the rebellious daughters belonged to unions that organized service sector workers and female-dominated industries, which was consistent with their goal to organize the female work force. More than half of the political animals were members of the female-dominated industrial unions and AFSCME; in addition, almost one fifth belonged to the male-dominated auto-workers union (UAW) in which women were involved in women's committees and political action committees. Only 11% of the fighting victims belonged to unions that organized professional workers; more than two fifths were members of male-dominated unions. In addition, a fourth of the fighting victims belonged to AFSCME, a public sector union (CLUW membership survey).

Participation in CLUW was closely related to the positions members had in their union. About two thirds of CLUW members held a union office (66% of the founding mothers, 58% of the rebellious daughters, 64% of the political animals, and 69% of the fighting victims held a union office), but not all of these positions were paid. Almost three fourths of the founding mothers held paid officer or staff positions in their unions, while almost two thirds of the political animals were volunteers or rank-and-file union members. More than half of the rebellious daughters and almost half of the fighting victims were paid by their unions. More than two thirds of the political animals and fighting victims did not hold an officer or staff position in their unions. One fifth of the founding mothers, but only one tenth of the rebellious daughters, held positions at the national level (CLUW membership survey).

Some of the rebellious daughters were in staff positions in their unions and shared support from and loyalty to their unions. Like the founding mothers, they drew on these resources in order to participate in CLUW. Some rebellious daughters found mentors in the founding mothers and in some cases replaced them. They found that the other officers and founding mothers were very supportive.

The political animals mentioned that they had learned about CLUW through their union, or that the formation of a CLUW chapter came about through the labor council. Like the political animals, the fighting victims learned about CLUW after they became active in the union, some through the union or labor council, others through NOW or Nine-to-Five. CLUW provided them with leadership skills and support and helped them to achieve leadership positions in their unions. CLUW was a resource to the "fighting victims." They acquired knowledge, skills, and connections in CLUW that led to their full-time positions in their unions.

CLUW members differed with respect to their perception of CLUW as being more part of the labor movement or part of the women's movement. In part, these different perceptions can be explained by their political socialization, in particular with their involvement and participation in these movements, as well as with the time they joined the labor movement and to which union they belonged. Although the majority thought that CLUW was more of a labor organization than a women's organization, more political animals and fighting victims found that CLUW was more of a women's organizations (see Table 3.2)

This reflects the fact that the founding mothers and the rebellious daughters were more familiar with the women's movement, while CLUW constituted the venue to the women's movement for the political animals and fighting victims.

Table 3.2
Perception of CLUW by Membership Type

	Founding mothers	Rebellious daughters	Political animals	Fighting victims
More labor movement	58%	59%	39%	48%
Both equally	19%	21%	25%	18%
More women's movement	25%	21%	37%	35%
N = 293	45	68	117	63

Source: CLUW Membership Survey.

Aleeta Walker described the motivation of the founding mothers to form the Coalition of Labor Union Women: "There were networks building up in the political arena; religious women, women of other groups were building networks. And many of us who were in the organized labor movement were a part of these networks but we did not have our trade union identity and we thought that was most important. And then we sought then to call together women trade unionists wherever they were and we formed the Coalition of Labor Union Women."

The founding mothers emphasized that the organization worked within the framework of the labor movement. They sought the approval of the labor movement and perceived endorsement and support through the AFL–CIO or individual unions as success. Some referred to CLUW as the women's AFL–CIO. The founding mothers emphasized that unions stand for equal rights. For instance, founding member Cynthia Delgado observed that the unions and the civil rights movement were linked: "I say to people, when I am talking about the civil rights movement, I say the unions were the first civil rights movement because they were there building a contract that did not leave anybody out before Dr. King, who is the greatest civil rights leader, came along. . . . A trade union is a civil rights, a human rights organization."

The founding mothers argued that, as Gabrielle Jordan put it, CLUW was "seen as a viable organization in the labor movement not only by the labor community, the union community, but by the women's and civil rights community as well."

In contrast to the founding mothers, the rebellious daughters saw CLUW more as a working women's movement, a place where their feminist consciousness and class consciousness could be reconciled. For them CLUW represented a chance to bridge that involvement in various causes. Joan Hoffman said: "Before that [CLUW] I had really been involved in the women's movement and the labor movement pretty much as two separate things." Rather than seeking the approval of the AFL–CIO and the unions, the rebellious daughters were interested in organizing and empowering working women. The founding mothers came from the "old" labor movement, while the rebellious daughters came from the "new" social movements, in particular the New Left. Thus, the two types represented, to a certain extent, different styles of organizing and empowerment in these movements. One of the rebellious daughters described the national officers as very supportive. She also noticed generational differences between the older officers and the following generation:

Well, definitely a difference in style. Well, to some degree, I think, those women the founding members . . . they know the politics of the national much more and are more immersed in it than many of the younger [members]. They see much more of a need to play to the leadership of the AFL–CIO, for example, than a lot of the younger women who are . . . sick of seeing too many white men making speeches at conventions . . . and don't feel that they have to give those leaders such a place on our dias. . . . But probably [the difference between older and younger members is that the younger members are] just not as politically savvy. In some ways not as politically savvy, but in some ways just not really caring to be. . . . We know what we want and we know our own agenda and there is reason to pull the punches and I think they are more direct. A lot of the younger women are much more direct and a lot more willing to say things straight out and not be so diplomatic [laughs] should we say. And I mean, which is good and bad at the same time [laughs]. There is lot to be said for both. So its good that we kind of temper each other.

In pointing out the differences between older and younger CLUW members, this rebellious daughter was careful not to appear too critical of the founding mothers. But in her opinion, the founding mothers were overly concerned about the approval of the male leadership, while the rebellious daughters were not very interested in the approval of male union leadership. However, the differences were reconciled by pointing out that they complement each other.

Mildred Sequira, another national officer, believed that CLUW's choice to become an insider organization contributed to its success in bringing women's issues on the labor agenda. Watson and Sequira agreed that there were still not enough women in union leadership positions, but that the labor movement had changed. Other rebellious daughters pointed out that the labor movement was in such a desperate condition that it had to open up to women, regardless of CLUW's existence. However, they acknowledged that CLUW certainly contributed to the increase of women in union leadership and the inclusion of women's issues on the labor agenda.

Most of the political animals and the fighting victims joined CLUW later and were not involved in the founding of the organization; thus the conflicts between the labor movement and the New Left, and the women's movement and the labor movement, were less salient and less relevant to them. They came into contact with the women's movement through the Coalition of Labor Union Women. From their perspective, the distinction between the labor movement and the women's movement appeared much less pronounced or even blurry. They took the bureaucratic structures of the labor movement and of CLUW for granted and were primarily concerned that the organization was run properly and efficiently.

The political animals and fighting victims had difficulties situating CLUW with respect to the women's movement and the labor movement. Heather Stone, for instance, had difficulties with the question concerning whether or not she perceived CLUW more as a part of the women's movement or more as a part of the labor movement. "It's more a part of the women's movement or the labor movement? I don't think you can separate them. I don't think you can separate them and I think it's women who happen to be in labor who are pushing for issues." First, she argued that as far as the Coalition of Labor Union Women was concerned, the women's movement and the labor movement cannot be separated. CLUW represented women in the labor movement who were "pushing for all issues": issues of the women's movement and issues of the labor movement. But then she returned to the question and made another attempt to give one of the two movements priority. "The women's movement or the labor movement? I think it's because we're women in labor we're pushing for issues for women in the work force and trying to improve everything and by doing that we are also— maybe we're pushing for women in labor issues under a disguise of really women's issues. When you use the format of having the union as the backdrop, but it's really women's issues that we're pushing for, which will become secondary? Good question." Eventually she decided that CLUW was more a part of the women's movement, because even the labor issues that CLUW addressed were "really women's issues." Finally, she wondered if CLUW addressed workplace issues at all and came to the conclusion that CLUW was a women's rights organization. "Do we push for workplace issues? Maybe not. What issue do we push for in the workplace? Just sexual harassment, otherwise it's all women's issues and reproductive rights and rights for women. So it probably is women's rights."

Some fighting victims were not sure if CLUW was an organization that was formed by labor women or by women from the women's movement and saw CLUW equally as part of the women's movement and the labor movement. Dotty Jones explained, "by virtue of their philosophy they are more part of the labor movement. But I think it is very, very hard to separate those two. I think there is a very big integration with women's issues and the labor movement."

The perception of CLUW as part of the women's movement and the labor movement was related to the experiences members had with various social movements. One of the rebellious daughters had the impression that many union women supported the goals of the women's movement, but only a few of them actually participated in women's movement organizations. Therefore, she did not think that CLUW provided a bridge between the women's movement and the labor movement. "Well, you might think that CLUW would be a bridge between the women's movement and the labor movement, but I don't think that it always is. Most labor union women, in my experience, don't have experience in the women's movement. Most union women that I've met and worked with came out of labor unions and maybe were influenced by the women's movement's effects on greater society, but they haven't been leaders in or members very often of women's organizations."

CONCLUSION

The membership typology shows that union feminism varied and was built on specific perceptions of injustice and constructions of identity that were grounded in activists' biographies and processes of political participation. Although all four types emphasized the equal importance of race, class, gender, and other systems of oppression, they differed in their identification (or criticism) of the women's movement and the labor movement. These differences can be explained with the experiences in and attachments to various movements. Based on their participation in various movements, members felt at home in different movement cultures. All four membership types had experienced discrimination or harassment in the labor movement. The founding mothers who identified most strongly with the labor movement were least critical of it in this respect. In contrast, the rebellious daughters felt most alienated from the bureaucratic structures of the labor movement and thus were the strongest critics of the sexism in the labor movement.

The four types experienced the labor movement and the women's movement differently, not only because the movements themselves changed over time, but also because different branches needed to be distinguished within the movements. Thus women who joined the labor movement at the same time, but became members of different unions, experienced the labor movement differently. Furthermore, rank-and-file members had a different perspective on the labor movement than staff members and officers. All union members represent the union. However, officers and staff members held paid positions and represented the union toward membership and leadership. In order to remain in these positions they needed the support of the membership and other officers. The rank-and-file members had less to lose if they spoke up against the leadership.

The four types of members with their different union feminisms have shaped the collective identity of CLUW in different ways and have been in conflict on some points. The founding mothers and the rebellious daughters had both been involved in the founding convention. The formation of CLUW grew out of previous involvement of the founding mothers and the rebellious daughters in the labor movement and other social movements. The founding mothers represented the labor movement and thus the "Old Left"; the rebellious daughters had been involved in the women's movement and the "New Left." The two groups created CLUW to merge unionism and feminism. The rebellious daughters either became "labor bureaucrats" like the founding mothers or left CLUW and formed or joined outside organizations that focused on organizing low-wage women workers.

The political animals and fighting victims joined CLUW later. Prior to becoming union activists, they had been active in the community. CLUW represented for them an avenue to the women's movement. Participation in the labor movement and in CLUW was the logical step for the political animals who participated in community politics before they became union members. The fighting victims turned to the union to improve their lives and experienced empowerment through collective action. They became involved in the union after it provided them with help, and their union activity led to upward mobility. In contrast to the other three types, the fighting victims became involved after they had been discriminated against.

The four membership types related differently to CLUW's collective identity, as they expressed in varying forms of participation in CLUW. The typology thus represents different understandings of union feminisms, formed in the respective political socialization processes over the life-course. The organization was shaped by these types to different degrees. As we will see later, seniority and membership turnover play an important role in the development of social movements and social movement organizations (Whittier 1995; Klandermans 1990). In Chapter 5, I will discuss different visions for the organization and which structure was ultimately adopted. But first I will turn to the diversity of CLUW's membership.

NOTES

1. This chapter sketches the characteristics of the four groups; see Appendix for the methodology.
2. Here the "pleasures of protest" (Jasper 1997) were emphasized.
3. I will later return to the framing of women's issues as workers' issues.

4

Addressing and Achieving Diversity

The Coalition of Labor Union women was diverse not only with respect to class—education and occupation—but also with respect to gender, race, ethnicity, and sexual orientation. This chapter explores how this diversity has come about. How were CLUW members as individuals and CLUW as an organization able to integrate race, class, and gender in their notion of union feminism, and what strategies were used to do so? Did they prioritize one identity, and if so, which identity and under what circumstance? Was race individualized, or was it addressed in the structure of the organization, and if so, how? These are important questions for women's organizations and feminist organizations that are often dominated by white-middle-class women or have difficulties achieving diversity (Leidner 1993).

RACE AND ETHNICITY

Diversity with respect to race and ethnicity made CLUW a highly unusual women's organization. About one third (30%) of the membership were women of color. In 1994, more than 20% of the organization were African American, 6% were Hispanic and Latina, 1% were Asian American, 2% were Native American, and 2% considered themselves members of "other racial or ethnic groups" (CLUW membership survey)."[1]

The high proportion of women of color in CLUW reflected the high unionization rate of women of color, especially African American women. In 2001, their unionization rate (15%), was higher than those of white, Hispanic, and Asian (11%) women and as high as that of white men (15%) (Bureau of the

Census 2001). Unionization rates also reflected the racial segregation of the labor market. A higher proportion of members of unions that organize professional women (AFT, OPEIU) were white (CLUW membership survey). Unions organizing women in the service sector (SEIU, UFCW) and female-dominated sectors of the labor market (CWA, UNITE) had a high proportion of white, Hispanic, and Asian American women. The participation of African American women was especially high in the public sector (AFSCME) and in industrial unions (UAW). At national meetings and conventions, AFSCME was usually represented by a large number of African American members. The autoworkers union (UAW) and the postal workers union (APWU) also had many African American members. Hispanic and Chinese CLUW members tended to be members of the textile and garment workers and the food and commercial workers unions.

The founding members of CLUW—many of them women of color—from the beginning wished to include women of color and sought to create an organization that would be representative of all unionized women workers. Women of color were represented among all four membership types. The types differed somewhat, however, in racial and ethnic composition. A higher proportion of founding mothers and fighting victims were women of color, African American in particular, while the majority of the rebellious daughters and political animals were white.[2] The women of color differed somewhat from the white women in their family and occupational careers, a fact that reflected occupational segregation as well as cultural differences with respect to family life.

Founding Mothers

Aleeta Walker, an African American, was a vice president of her union when CLUW was founded. Walker started out on the assembly line and became a rank-and-file member of her international union in the 1940s. In the early 1950s she was the first woman in the union to be elected president of a union local; she was appointed as international representative responsible for organizing, negotiating contracts, and servicing members of local unions. She was also appointed to coordinate "anti-discrimination" programs on women's concerns and civil rights, working with Martin Luther King, Jr. She explained: "My involvement in the civil rights movement and in the women's movement and in the political movement came about as a result of our involvement in the organized labor movement. The training and the orientation and the involvement that we have from time to time in the labor movement has resulted in our being effective leaders in these other areas."

Gabrielle Jordan, also African American, had been a national officer of CLUW from the beginning. After obtaining a master's degree in economics, she started working for her union as a staff member in the 1950s. In her interview Jordan emphasized the continuity of being involved in the civil rights movement and the women's movement. "I saw it [my involvement in the labor movement] just as an extension of what I did with civil rights. I have great difficulties separating the two. I think that if you win one without focusing on the other there is no victory. And that we have to continue to fight for both." She emphasized that in order to achieve social change both race and class have to be taken into consideration.

Isabella Toledo was one of the few Latina women who participated in the founding convention. She began to work as office staff for a retail workers union in the early 1950s. In the mid-1960s she became an organizer and continued to work for the union full-time. She was convinced that she would not hold her current union position if CLUW had not been formed. "I am not doing anything different than I was doing in 1968. But I believe that if CLUW and the women's movement had not happened some man would be sitting where I am sitting. . . . Because the consciousness of society would not have been raised . . . because of the changes that have taken place as a result of CLUW and the women's movement." She emphasized that the position in her union she held at the time of the interview was not due to her personal achievement but reflected social change.

Like the white founding mothers, these women of color were pioneers in the labor movement. Often engaged in the labor movement since the 1950s, they entered through different paths—clerical and factory work or graduate school. Participating in both the civil rights movement and labor organizing, they emphasized the support the civil rights movement gained for unions. They were loyal trade unionists, but found it necessary that women and minorities join movements, organizations, and caucuses that addressed civil rights and gender issues.

Rebellious Daughters

Like the white rebellious daughters, women of color also went to college and were involved in the movements of the 1960s and 1970s. They also attended college, but not all of them graduated and some worked in female-typed low-wage and low-skill professions. The family played a greater role for these women of color than for the white rebellious daughters.

For My Chang, supporting the fight of the farmworkers in California was especially important, since many Asian workers were involved in this labor struggle and she saw it as related to her Asian American identity. After graduating from college Chang became active in community organizing in New York City's Chinatown. She became involved in the labor movement during the legendary 1982 strike (Milkman 1993), and afterward joined the garment workers union as a staff member. She learned about CLUW from one of the Hispanic founding mothers, Karmen Andes, who was active in the same union. Andes suggested that Chang and other Chinese women form a Chinese committee in CLUW after the model of the Hispanic caucus. Chang was active in CLUW at the national level on the National Executive Board and at the local level in the Chinese committee and the local CLUW chapter. She was involved in founding the Asian Pacific Labor Alliance, the support group of Asian American union members, and was active at the national level of this organization. Chang credited CLUW with making her feel welcome in the labor movement, a place she found alienating. CLUW and the women she met in the organization made her feel "like there is some hope for someone like me in the labor movement, because the labor movement seemed to be so hierarchical and structured and CLUW was successful in training women to know how to use the labor movement and access places that you need to access." In addition, she applauded CLUW for addressing the needs of immigrant women, who often had to combine family and work and thus were interested in issues like child care.

Tabitha Elton was born in the South in the mid-1940s. Her parents were both union members. Her mother worked as a nurse and was a union steward. Her father worked in various jobs. Tabitha left college after a year to become active in the Student Nonviolent Coordinating Committee (SNCC) and participated in voter registration projects for the Black Panther Party. She remembers this time as very exciting. "I mean, it was a great time for me. It was my introduction into activism, which I never forget, and I'm certainly active now." After SNCC disbanded, she started to work as a telephone operator, got married and eventually divorced. Although she had only planned to work temporarily for the telephone company, she stayed there for nineteen years. In the late 1960s, shortly after she started to work for the company, the workers went on strike. About ten years later she became active in the union. Early in the 1980s the employees again went on strike, and Tabitha became a picket captain. She got involved in Nine-to-Five and subsequently in CLUW. Furthermore, she initiated the formation of a women's committee in her union.

In the mid-1980s, Elton participated in a summer school for union women and was asked to become an organizer for a service sector union. She strongly wanted to organize women workers, so after some consideration she accepted the offer, although she was faced with a huge paycut as well as having to move to another state and—as traveling organizer—relocate frequently. She regretted that she has not been politically active continuously from the time of her participation in the civil rights movement. "If I had to do it over again, I wouldn't have that gap, because I think in terms of my political development, my understanding of things and where things are now, it would be better." The union activity for her thus meant resuming her political activism and closing the gap.

Political Animals

The political animals included few women of color, but Ella Turner was one of them. After graduating from high school in 1966, she started to work in an automobile plant. She became involved in a strike and then in the union. She was appointed alternate steward and then at age nineteen as chief steward. She lost the next election because she was running against the president of the union local, and returned to the assembly line. She remained active in the union, getting involved in the standing committee as well as the women's and education committee. She also started taking classes at the local junior college. Several years later, she ran for office again as part of an all–African American slate. She lost the election to the bargaining committee by five votes, but was happy that her slate won.

By that time she had saved enough money to take advantage of the educational leave the plant was offering. For eleven years she alternated between the plant and college, graduating with a degree in education. After graduation she ran for vice president and was overwhelmingly elected. In the early 1980s, recommended by the regional director of her union, she was asked to teach labor studies at the university and started teaching leadership training for women and minorities. She taught labor studies for twelve years. During this time she married and had four children. Although she did not participate in the founding of CLUW, she was aware of the organization early, and collaborated with CLUW on developing educational programs for women and by inviting CLUW leaders to speak on campus.

Turner was active not only in the union but in the community and local politics. When her neighborhood park was not renovated by the city, she went to the city council to demand that something be done about it. The next day, the park was fixed. Based on this experience of success, she decided to run for city council, was elected, and stayed on the council for ten years. She was the first African American woman to hold such a position in her state.

In 1991, her international union offered her a position as lobbyist in Washington, D.C. For Turner, who knew "everybody" in the state and had been a "big fish in a little pond," this meant a big change, and she was reluctant to move. Her husband encouraged her to take the position, telling her that this was what she had been striving for all her life. She moved with her family to Washington and loved her work. After becoming a lobbyist, she became active in CLUW regarding legislative issues, informing and educating other CLUW members. At the end of the interview, she told an anecdote in which she described how her nine-year-old son met then Vice President Al Gore the night of the vote on the Family and Medical Leave Act, on which Turner had been working. She thus managed to meet the "big fish in the big pond." Turner described herself as "a trade unionist in my heart, and a politician." Although she had participated in the feminist movement during college, she did not consider herself a feminist.

Fighting Victims

Like the white fighting victims, the women of color in this group started to work in factories or low-level administrative jobs, and some developed a strong career orientation. They attended college while working full-time and actively participating in the union. In some cases they were single parents and solely responsible for raising their children. In their accounts, their participation in the union was not an additional burden but a resource. They were mentored and encouraged to complete their college education, and mentor support led them to managerial positions in their unions.

Alison Itt was born in Hong Kong in 1949. At nineteen she married her husband in an arranged marriage. They moved to Holland two years later; in 1976 they came to the United States. Through the help of her sister, Itt found work in the garment industry. She spoke some English, and soon became a shop steward because she always helped her co-workers. "So, next day, when I arrive I go to work in the garment factory and then I was elected as a shop steward, chairlady in the shop. Everywhere I go, I was elected as chairlady. Because I am always willing to help people, the others. I speak a little English so people have the language problem, you know the Chinese come here in the United States most of them have language problem. Difficult for them."

Itt was active in the 1982 garment workers strike. Chinese workers were perceived as a docile work force, but they mobilized the community. "The union called the strike because the negotiations broke down, we tried for our best to negotiate but there was a lockout. . . . So they think they can frighten the workers. But it is not successful. They lock out, they close down for one day. And then we called the rally immediately. And we know that they would raise their voice but we have good preparation. We have the big rally, we don't sign the contract." Itt described how the strike was supported by the community. Old and young people supported the strike. The participation in the strike was an empowering experience for the Chinese workers. Through the strike, she learned about CLUW, which supported the garment workers strike. After the strike, she became first an organizer and later a business agent for the garment workers union. In 1986 she divorced her husband, who was a gambler and abused their children. She raised her three children by herself.

Feminist versus Ethnic and Worker Identity

Reflecting the overall segregation in the labor markets, the women of color differed somewhat from the white women in their occupational careers. Some went to college after they started to work and became active in the union. They were somewhat more reluctant to call themselves feminists and put a stronger emphasis on race and ethnicity than the white women.

Racial consciousness was as important as feminist consciousness to the founding mothers, who found that both were compatible with a trade union identity. The labor movement to them was a civil rights movement that encompassed the rights of workers, women, and minorities. Aleeta Walker described herself as a "strong advocate of women's equality and women's rights, and I was a strong advocate of civil rights for our workers, strong voice for women, strong voice for the non-white community and I was a strong voice for coalition building of all these groups . . . but it also was through the union that we were able to unite with other people, other workers, who had common concerns and common goals."

The rebellious daughters emphasized that minority women were often married and had children and felt alienated by the women's movement. For example, My Chang found it problematic that the "white feminist movement" rejected marriage and family. "We didn't view women's rights as one, as being against all men, or rejecting the whole question of families and children. So we looked at issues like child care, you know, or health care and all those issues were very important. And I think at different stages the feminist movement in the U[nited] S[tates] tended to just kind of ignore that or that was not an essential thing to them." Chang applauded CLUW's approach of "pushing the family agenda into the labor movement" and making such issues the concerns of the entire labor movement. CLUW represented to her a version of feminism that took the needs of working mothers, and thus immigrant women, into account.

Kathy Quen said that, for her and other members of CLUW's Chinese committee, ethnic identity was more important than feminist identity. She and other Chinese members supported women's issues (such as child care), but issues that concerned the Chinese community were more important to her: "And eventually we began to understand that this group could be a bridge between the women's movement and the labor movement and also the ethnic community." Quen supports the notion that CLUW was a bridging organization. In the early 1990s in New York, one of the textile workers unions with a high proportion of Chinese members supported the political struggle of Chinese immigrants and was active in the Chinese community. In turn, the Chinese community supported the garment workers strike. The success of the strike was quite unexpected. Often, in ethnically homogeneous occupations, the high proportion of recent immigrants with ethnic ties keeps workers from getting involved in the labor struggle. However, while illegal, undocumented immigrants are vulnerable to deportation and can be expected to be more fearful about the risks involved in union organizing, immigrants are often very militant (Milkman 2000).

Ella Turner perceived herself as unusual among African American women, who she said still believed the women's movement was a white-middle-class movement and rarely would call themselves feminists.[3] "I am not the norm of African American women, . . . I have a different perception of the women's movement, because I had dealings with the women's movement at [university]. And I was part of the women's movement. In 1978, as a matter of fact, I was here, marched for the ERA, dressed in white like everybody else was." Yet, although Turner described herself as part of the women's movement and different in this regard from other African American women, she rejected the label feminist: "I am a trade unionist in my heart and a politician, but I am not a feminist.

Like I said, a lot of things that the feminist community espoused, I do not necessarily agree with. And it puts me in a real awkward position because [they support] a lot of the causes and a lot of the things we fight for, as a coalition; but I don't consider myself as a feminist. . . . They are workers' issues for me, not feminist issues, but workers' issues."

Although she rejected the feminist label, Turner supported coalition-building between labor, women, and civil rights groups even when this included the support of issues of which she disapproved. For example, CLUW endorsed a pro-choice position (see Chapter 7), whereas Turner personally was against abortion. Turner nevertheless represented CLUW in coalitions of organizations of the women's, civil rights, and labor movements.

Susan Carter, an African American woman, found it unnecessary to frame women's political action as feminism. "I don't think that we have to be titled feminists in order to really be active in our communities or active in the women's issues. We're just women. You know what I'm saying? We're just women out there for a common cause and we are out there because we feel that there's a need for certain things to be addressed or certain issues to be brought to the attention of others." During the interview Carter sometimes identified her standpoint as "from a minority point of view," as a "minority woman," or as a "woman." Obviously the situation shaped the perspective she spoke from—gender, race, or both. With respect to CLUW, she stressed gender. "It wasn't whether you were a woman of American descent or whether you were a woman of foreign descent because you had women there from all over and we were just women there for a common cause. . . . They've stressed women's issues and women's issues encompass all women, all women! I haven't seen them address anything singly for any minority or whatever because I see them addressing it for all women, which is the thing to do as far as I'm concerned." She did not want special programs for women of color as long as the programs were addressed to all women, including women of color.

Tabitha Elton made a distinction between "feminists" and "womanists." She identified herself as womanist, which to her meant to "support women in having rightful roles in leadership and organizations and politics." Elton defined feminists as being focused on women's issues, but this was not her central focus: "I mean the central focus would be justice for workers, all workers, and that women can lead workers—male, female, regardless of race, ethnicity. . . . I guess, in terms of feminism, yes, it certainly lives within the labor movement and within the organization. I'm thinking about within the BWFJ [Black Workers for Justice] there's a Women's Commission. But I think most of the women would not identify themselves as feminists. That that's a central part of what they're doing, but more to deal with the question of basic respect and identification that women are leaders, too." Here she again rejected feminism while emphasizing workers' rights.

Women of color did not necessarily identify participation of women in leadership positions as feminist. Regarding her participation in CLUW and Nine-to-Five, Elton remarked: "And it's so funny, because I never thought of it as feminism in joining the Nine-to-Five or being a part of CLUW. I thought of it as women coming together for their rights. I never really put that label on. And I think there are among Southern black women a strong tradition of fighting and coming together for their rights, always having worked most of their lives."

The African American women thus saw themselves in a long tradition of strong women leaders who had little or nothing to do with the white feminist movement. Jacqueline Lanois, an African American woman, also had difficulties with the label feminist. She said that she supported women's rights, but she wanted to know how I defined feminism before she accepted the label. Lanois saw women's issues, worker's issues, and civil rights issues as interrelated and all relevant to women. "Our union here . . . represents both day care and head start workers and as you know that is a priority for CLUW. Is it a feminist issue only? I don't think so. It is a family issue. . . . I am the first one on the front of the line to do whatever I need to do, . . . for the good of the membership and for the good of the family unit. So if that makes me a feminist, then I guess I am."

Lanois very clearly equated women's issues with family issues. Here women workers were conceptualized as mothers or other family members and situated as "familied selves" (Ferree 2000), meaning a self that is conceptualized in relation to others across gender and generation. This notion of feminism is quite different from an individualizing liberal feminism.

The African American and white women who founded CLUW were involved in the civil rights movement and members of organizations of and for African American union members like the A. Philip Randolph Institute (APRI, the AFL–CIO support group of African American Union members) and the Coalition of Black Trade Unionists (CBTU). The differences in feminist, racial, and ethnic identities between white women and women of color were reflected in their affiliation in various social movement organizations (see Table 4.1).

Table 4.1
Membership in Various Social Movement Organizations by Race
(Female Respondents)

	White	African American	Latina	Asian
NAACP (N = 131)	17%	72%	29%	20%*
CBTU (N = 51)	2%	41%	11%	—
APRI (N = 76)	13%	33%	19%	20%
NOW (N = 423)	41%	15%	33%	20%

Source: CLUW Membership Survey. *N = 1

More African American than white, Latina, and Asian women belonged to NAACP, CBTU, and APRI, while more white (followed by Latina and Asian) than African American women belonged to NOW. However, over 50% of the respondents surveyed indicated that they had been involved in the civil rights movement. Almost 80% of the founding mothers, three quarters of the rebellious daughters, half the fighting victims, and a good third of the political animals indicated that they had been involved in the civil rights movement. 30% of all CLUW members were members of NAACP, 14% were involved in CBTU, and 19% were involved in APRI (CLUW membership survey).

To summarize, the women of color in CLUW (like the white CLUW members) rejected a notion of feminism that neglected the experiences of women of color. Ethnic identity was crucial for them. The union served as a vehicle to address the concerns of working women of color. They defined women's issues as community and family issues, and also stated that they were not "against men." Furthermore, the Chinese and Hispanic CLUW committees that will be discussed below allowed Chinese and Hispanic immigrants to develop Chinese and Hispanic feminist identity.

Experiences of Discrimination

Just as the white members had an ambivalent relationship with the labor movement because it promoted gender discrimination as well as fighting against it, women of color also had mixed experiences. Some of the interviewees emphasized the labor movement as an ally for civil rights; some described experiences of race discrimination in the labor movement.

The African American founding mothers emphasized that the labor movement was an important ally of the civil rights movement and thus a venue to fight against racial discrimination. Aleeta Walker credited the labor movement for the leadership skills she employed during the civil rights movement. She retired from the labor movement in order to become more active in the African American community by becoming a minister in her church. When she realized that faith groups did not address economic issues, Walker started to speak about the labor movement during the church service. As a bridge-leader (Robnett 1997) connecting the social movement with the community, Walker used her position in the religious community to organize more African Americans into the labor movement. She integrated the need to address economic issues into the religious services she leads. Even after retiring from the union, she pointed to the labor movement as a means to overcome racial discrimination.

Tabitha Elton, a rebellious daughter, had a very different view of racial issues in the labor movement. For example, she explained, she noticed that the white male leadership of her union local in the South were wearing baseball caps with KKK insignia. African American members in the local who protested against this form of racism were told that they "could not take a joke." Elton found out that the white leadership of this local had "squashed" a black caucus. While dismayed, Elton also recognized the labor movement also was an ally against race discrimination: "I mean, the central focus would be justice for workers, all workers and that women can lead workers—male, female, regardless of race, ethnicity."

The labor movement also has a mixed record regarding immigrants: at times it has been supportive, at other times it has been anti-immigrant. The immigrants among the fighting victims had a distinctive sense of discrimination based on nationality, ethnicity, gender, and class. They knew that they had to "stick together" and "fight back," although they realized that many immigrants were intimidated and therefore reluctant to join a union. Latina and Chinese fighting victims reported that the union helped them learn English and obtain American citizenship. They appreciated the political freedom they enjoyed in the United States, but also pointed to police brutality and anti-immigrant activities. In spite of the discrimination they experienced, their situation as women, as workers, and as citizens was often an improvement compared to the situation in their home countries.

Alison Itt, for example, a Chinese fighting victim, explained why it was necessary for her to fight for women's rights in the United States. "We fight for equality. . . . America is a free country, and women do all this hard work, we should get respect too. That's why we raise our voice, we stay together. So we get respect." Itt found that women in the United States had to engage in collective action to fight for equality.

Like the white women, the women of color also put great emphasis on equality. They were concerned not only with sexual harassment, but also with harassment based on race, age, weight, handicaps, anti-immigrant feelings, and sexual orientation. These women of color, though aware of gender and race discrimination in the labor movement, also recognized that it was an important mechanism to address race, class, and gender issues.

Integration of Women of Color in CLUW

From the beginning, CLUW's leadership as well as its membership wanted to represent the diversity of unionized women.[4] This meant that the officer slate should be diverse regionally, racially, and with respect to unions. African American women have constituted a significant part of the national leadership since CLUW's inception. Gloria Johnson, however, in 1993 was the first African American woman to become CLUW's national president. Some activists claimed that since Johnson became president more African American women have become active in the organization. Others, however, emphasized the participation of African American women in CLUW from the very start and claimed there was no increase after the change in presidency. The latter view was supported in the membership survey, which showed no significant differences between white women and women of color regarding the time they joined CLUW. The leadership of a woman of color did not lead to increasing membership of women of color. Several members, however, remarked that Johnson's inclusive leadership style encouraged greater participation in the organization by all CLUW members.

Members of CLUW were proud of the high proportion of women of color. One white interviewee, who was in an inter-racial relationship and was active in anti-racist work, explained that she was attracted to CLUW because it was an inter-racial group. She remembered the first time she went to a meeting of the national executive board. "When I walked into the general plenary session of the NEB as an observer and saw a mixed-race group, I was floored. To be honest with you, I hadn't seen a mixed-race group like that in the labor movement, in the women's movement, anywhere before, and I remember that moment very clearly [is very moved]. I felt there was hope. And it was something I had always been looking for."

Founding members emphasized that from the beginning the leadership tried to achieve a balance based on different unions and on racial and ethnic composition among the national officers. However, one of the African American respondents had the impression that when she joined the organization in the 1970s all the officers' positions were held by white women, and that African American women and women of other ethnic groups became involved in the leadership only later. Tabitha Elton also perceived "some promotion of more diversity within CLUW" since Gloria Johnson became president. Elton enjoyed the significant participation of women of color in CLUW but felt it was a recent development. She also credited Johnson for contributing to the increased participation of women of color.

These results suggest that the initial emphasis on including all racial and ethnic groups was watered down over the years and then was emphasized again under the new leadership. However, leadership and membership, white women and women of color all emphasized that CLUW sought to involve women of color and expressed pride concerning the high participation of African American women. CLUW members generally were very proud about the organization being highly racially and ethnically integrated. Moving from the national to the local level, however, one finds that the chapters were less diverse and more homogeneous than the organization as a whole. In some chapters only white or only African American women participated, in some the majority of the members belonged to one racial-ethnic group. In mixed chapters, the executive board seemed more homogeneous than the chapter.[5]

Respondents explained the racial-ethnic composition of the chapters in terms of the characteristics of the local work force, area, and labor movement. Bringing up race relations in interviews within CLUW sometimes caused defensive responses. Some white respondents were worried that African American women were less concerned in electing white women as delegates to the NEB and conventions. African American women mentioned "lily-white" chapters, or that white women did not want to join a chapter because they perceived CLUW as an organization of African American women. An African American respondent recalled a debate about the constituency of CLUW. "And we heard the talk about it, it was not the talk that CLUW had too, had, was too white, the underlying talk was, was it too black? Would we lose other people? That was my interpretation, that was never said, that is my interpretation. . . . That was just an undercurrent with the officer, it was not all officers. Let's leave it alone, because I know what officer I am talking about and I don't want to go into details."

Thus there was awareness of a racist "undercurrent" and of a reluctance to address race relations within the organization. This respondent emphasized that she offered me an interpretation, her interpretation, that some members—she did not specify if these members were white or women of color—were afraid that the organization could become "too black," while there had never been a concern that the organization might have been "too white."[6] She explained that one of the unions with many African American members supported the participation of observers as well as delegates at national meetings. Thus, while it might seem that the meeting was dominated by African American women, not all of them were delegates and participated in the decision-making process. A white respondent noticed that only one of her union delegates was white and the others were African American. She thought "it's power instead of race, more that we have the power to elect and we elect who we want." Although African American women were somewhat more likely to attend conventions, according to the survey, the differences were not significant.

Usually, the chapters were dominated by either white or African American women; women of the same race appeared to be more easily recruited. Chapter members then had to counteract the impression that the chapter was a "black" or a "white" group. When a chapter was perceived as dominated by one group, members of other groups felt uncomfortable and were less likely to join. In this way the chapter stayed or became homogeneous. Though members felt that CLUW chapters could be more diverse and do more outreach to communities of color, they also noted that the chapters were more inclusive than the regional labor movement or their unions and that CLUW had a record for building bridges between the labor movement and communities of color.

Some members noticed that CLUW had few Hispanic and Asian members relative to African American members. Some scholars argue that Hispanic families are more patriarchal than other American families, and that this is reflected in the lower unionization rate of Hispanic women. However, this notion is rejected by other scholars (Zavella 1988). Hispanic and Chinese CLUW members mentioned language barriers and felt not sufficiently included. One of the Hispanic founding mothers said: "But I don't feel that women who are in position are doing enough to reach to the sisters and bring them up. I don't think so. The Blacks have made more progress in CLUW than the Hispanics, and Blacks have been more pushing and more accepting this than the Hispanic women. And sometimes I feel that our women who are not so fluent in English cannot tolerate that because they [African American women] are rough and they are sometimes rude." This hints at differences among different racial-ethnic groups within CLUW. Some Chinese members were involved in the formation of the Asian Pacific Labor Alliance and shifted their involvement from CLUW to APALA, where they held national leadership positions.

Despite the high participation of women of color in CLUW, one could also note within the organization both segregation and competition between different racial and ethnic groups. These conflicts were not addressed openly. Nevertheless, even if full integration had not been fully achieved, the organization was committed to racial ethnic integration, and just as white women had, women of color achieved skills and found support in CLUW.

Organizational Structures for Women of Color

Some members thought not only that more Hispanic and Chinese women should be involved, but also that their needs should be addressed. One questionnaire respondent wrote: "I strongly believe that CLUW should deal with more issues concerning the Hispanic women. Many of our Hispanic members need the help, information, and support from a group like CLUW. Some of the topics which should be offered: family planning, AIDS and the Hispanic family, housing." Other Hispanic members however, credited CLUW with educating the leaders of the unions with fewer minority members about the needs of minority workers.

Although there was no open debate about racial-ethnic differences, CLUW recognized early on that women of color "had more needs," and therefore the national-level minority committee was created. Thus diversity was framed in terms of "needs" rather than contributions to the organization. Thus far the minority committee had not addressed issues of minorities or diversity *within* CLUW, but only at the workplace or in the union.

The minority committee and the affirmative action committee merged in 1995 at a NEB meeting where the overall attendance was very low. The affirmative action committee had been dominated by white women, while the minority committee had been dominated by African American women. This situation hints at the difficulties at creating an integrated organization, if even committees that deal with race issues are segregated by race.

In the 1980s a Hispanic caucus was formed in the New York City chapter to better address the needs of Hispanic women. Later, a Chinese caucus was modeled after the Hispanic caucus. These caucuses allowed immigrant women to communicate in their native language and to pursue their cultural traditions. Karmen Andes, a Hispanic founding mother, pointed out that socializing and connecting to the culture of Hispanic women was a strategy to get this group involved in the labor movement and the political process. She explained, "In [the garment workers union] we have a lot of classes. We have workshops with children. Acting, performing, singing, we have knitting, embroidery, quilting making, things that they like to do and they are very active. . . . So we do that a lot because we always, every mother, every Hispanic mother, even the American likes to have a piñata party for the kids because it is fun. And they learn about the traditions of the Latin American." At the same time they became acquainted with the labor movement and learned about current political issues and women's rights.[7] The caucuses allowed them to develop union feminisms that encompassed rather than ignored their ethnic identity.

The merger between Chinese tradition and American feminism was exemplified by the symbol of the Chinese CLUW committee, which was developed by a Chinese artist and consisted of the Chinese symbols representing power and equality. The creation of the symbol stood for continuity with respect to ethnic identity along with transformation of this identity. Thus it allowed a Chinese feminist identity, which did not have a place in their homeland.[8] As Allison Itt put it, "So this is our symbol for the Coalition of Labor Union Women. This symbol was designed from one of our members, and [Chinese activist], he is artist, he is teacher, he designed this for us. So this is a Chinese symbol. You know we are asking for equal. And this bamboo means 'stay strong.' "

In addition, Chinese CLUW activists participated in the formation of the Asian Pacific Labor Alliance, where they held national leadership positions, while they were not represented among the national leadership in CLUW. These Chinese CLUW members obviously saw better chances to pursue the interests of Asian American union women in APALA than in CLUW.

AGE, GENDER, AND MARITAL STATUS

In 1994, CLUW's membership was on average older than that of the labor movement. Only 6% of the respondents were between 25 and 34, 94% were older than 34, and two-thirds were 45 or older. In contrast, of all female union members, 16% were younger than 34, and fewer than half are 45 or older (see Table 4.2).

This age distribution reflected an aging membership, though the cause was not a failure to recruit new members. About one-fifth of the respondents joined CLUW in 1993–1994. Of this group, one-sixth were 55 or older. However, half of the respondents who joined CLUW in this period were 44 or younger, compared to about a third of the respondents who joined between 1978 and 1992. Prior to 1977, more than half those who joined CLUW were 55 or older. The age distribution raises the question of whether the organization was attractive to young(er) union members (CLUW membership survey).

As Table 4.2. shows, the small number of young members in CLUW cannot simply be explained by the fact that the unionization rate of younger workers was lower than that of other age groups. Moreover, other labor organizations were able to reach out to younger people. For example, members of APALA, the AFL–CIO support group of Asian-Pacific-American union members, which was founded in 1992, were somewhat younger than the average union member. This organization reached out to universities and cooperated with the Organizing Institute of the AFL–CIO (field notes, Las Vegas 1993; Chen and Wong 1998). Although some women, especially CLUW staff, came to CLUW from women's studies programs, the organization so far did not have formal connections to such programs.

Table 4.2
Age of Female Union Members in 1994

	Female Union Members (BLS)	CLUW Members (CLUW Survey)
16–24	5%	—
25–34	11%	6%
35–44	16%	27%
45–54	19%	39%
55–64	17%	19%
65 +	8%	8%
	N = 6,642,000	N = 447

Sources: BLS Employment and Earnings, vol. 43, no.1 (1995), p. 210;
CLUW Membership Survey.

In the early 1990s, participants in a CLUW conference were concerned when they realized that only one (staff) person was under thirty years old and only ten participants were under forty. CLUW reacted to this development by establishing a "mature women" committee. Some members, however, criticized that CLUW was unable to reach out to younger people. In 1995 a Young Workers Conference was held in connection with one of the national meetings. This conference was co-sponsored by Frontlash, the AFL–CIO support group organizing young workers. One delegate who was very disappointed by the meeting recalled: "I had visions of a lot of young people, being there, being part of the panels, kind of hearing their stories and figuring out ways to work with them. What are some of their issues, what do we need to be looking at to include them. And all it was, was listening to the same people, that we usually hear from, speak." While some members described the conference as "terrific," others were critical that young women played only a small role in the conference and CLUW officers played a much larger role.

Marital Status and Motherhood

Respondents often explained that CLUW had difficulties attracting young women because they had families and young children. One survey respondent wrote on the questionnaire: "My inactivity is due to family obligation, three- and five-year-old children and working, and not having any more time in my life. It is very difficult to work and be involved with progressive activities with children. No matter how supportive and family active the husband/father is, children need the quality time and home life which takes a good amount of time by both parents." Although single mothers especially need the union and benefit from CLUW's efforts, it was often too expensive for them to pay for a babysitter and logistically improbable to bring children to meetings. Offering child care programs was not always possible for unions or chapters because they would be liable in case of accidents and could not afford the insurance.

The gendered division of reproductive labor makes it more difficult for women both to attend union meetings and to take on leadership positions in the union. Male stewards can often count on the support of spouses to take responsibility for the children, while female stewards have the responsibility for arranging child care when they are active for the union (Roby and Uttal 1993). According to this study, female shop stewards tend to be single (27%), living only with children (27%), or living only with a partner (21%); only 25% live with children and a partner. The majority of male stewards (66%), in contrast, live with children and a partner, while only 11% live only with a partner and 5% only with children (Roby and Uttal 1993). Both single and married mothers need to arrange for child care, but compared to their shares of the population, single mothers are more likely to be active than married mothers. This suggests that spouses or partners create more work for women with children than help with household and child care.

Over half of the respondents of the CLUW survey were married, a fifth were divorced, and over 70% had children. However, male respondents were almost twice as likely as female ones to be married, while a much higher proportion of female respondents were divorced, single, or widowed (see Table 4.3).

Table 4.3
Marital Status of CLUW Members by Sex

	Women	Men
Married	44%	79%
Divorced	24%	9%
Single	18%	5%
Widowed	8%	5%
Partnered	5%	3%
Separated	1%	—
N = 513	446	67

Source: CLUW Membership Survey.

Overall, female and male respondents showed only small differences regarding attitudes toward women's participation in unions. 71% of the female and male respondents agreed that "women's responsibilities in the family and at work limit union participation," and 75% of the female respondents and 65% of the male respondents agreed that "the lack of day care makes it difficult for women to take leadership roles." There were greater differences with respect to day care: 7% of the female respondents and 41% of the male respondents found "providing more day care" very important for bringing women into leadership positions. However, about the same proportion of female (57%) and male (55%) respondents found "sharing household and child care responsibilities with family members" very important in this respect. Male (76%) and female (80%) respondents found leadership training very important (CLUW membership survey). The small gender differences in attitudes suggest that men may think sharing household chores would help, while it is unclear if they are ready to do it. At a workshop at the Biennial Convention in Las Vegas in 1993 someone suggested that husbands and children should be invited to the CLUW meetings, so that the women can get involved, rather than suggesting that the husbands should take care of the kids (field notes, Biennial Convention 1993, Las Vegas).

Men's Participation in CLUW

Men represented 13% of the membership (CLUW membership survey).[9] Male respondents were as likely as female respondents to participate in the organization, but were less likely to hold officer positions. They were however, more likely than female members to be white and to hold a union office. By including men, CLUW demonstrated that the organization was not anti-male. The National Executive Board in 1993–1995 had two male members.[10] Two types of male CLUW members could be distinguished: (white) union officials who supported CLUW with dues to demonstrate through their membership that they support union women, and rank-and-file activists, who were active at the chapter level and seriously committed to supporting women. One of the latter, stressing gender, wrote on his survey: "As a white male I have always been a feminist and have done a lot of organizing of women, so CLUW is necessary. More effort needs to be put into energizing the local organization, and less on the formalities/structure/appearances. In fact, I am not organizing now (and only working part-time) because I am raising our two children, while my wife works. Domestic engineers of the world, unite!"

In contrast, another respondent transcended gender in favor of a wider collective identity. "I joined CLUW to support my sisters because their cause is justice. I encourage all people to work for that goal. Not just for women. Or justice for blacks, or justice for gays, or justice for any one group. We need justice for all people. We are all brothers and sisters and we must learn to live together and work together in this world. An injury to one must be considered an injury to all." He thus invoked labor rhetoric ("an injury to one is an injury to all") while at the same time emphasizing diversity with respect to race, gender, and sexuality, rather than prioritizing class.

At the Biennial Convention one male unionist participated in the Minority

Issues workshop. He described himself as part of the "male power structure of his union" and spoke about the dilemma of supporting women's issues. "I am part of the male-dominated power structure in my union and I want to make those changes. And I know, if I take a real radical stand on making some of those changes, I won't be in office in the male-dominated union that we have. Somebody else will be in there who does not fight for diversity, who does not fight for the rights of women and minorities" (field notes, Biennial Convention, Minority Issues Committee). He argued that one would have to look at the constituency of the unions and make the leadership aware that women and minorities need to be addressed because their issues are the issues of every union member. This respondent made a case that he could not be too radical without losing his position and thus the chance to influence the union local with respect to gender issues.

Male membership in chapters ranged from dues-paying members to active membership and participation in the chapter leadership as active board members. Respondents who endorsed the participation of male unionists argued that they would not be able to achieve changes in the labor movement without the cooperation of men. One chapter president, however, had the impression that the male unionists involved in her chapter did not encourage women in their locals to join the chapter. "I have more men who are members of CLUW in this area. When I say that, I mean labor leaders who are members, but they have not encouraged their women to join, you see? They have joined. So [that I don't bother their women]. But if they would just encourage their women to join, their women to get involved and we could bring that unity here, we would have a dynamic group throughout the state." Obviously the participation of men in CLUW chapters could thus also prevent women from becoming more active in the labor movement and thus undermined the goals of the organization. More supportive male members invited CLUW members to participate in meetings of the labor council or contributed to publicizing CLUW.

UNION AFFILIATION AND POSITION

In order to represent unionized women workers, CLUW sought to attract and represent a broad range of unions. In 1994 CLUW members represented 100 different unions, but more than half of the surveyed members belonged to six unions: American Federation of State, County, and Municipal Employees (14%); United Autoworkers of America (13%); Union of Needletrades Industrial and Textile Employees (ca. 10%); Communication Workers of America (9%); American Federation of Teachers (8%); and Service Employees International Union (5%) (CLUW membership survey). These unions represented workers in the public and service sectors and the textile industry, and telephone operators and teachers—sectors of the labor market that with the exception of

UAW were overwhelmingly female. Again with the exception of UAW, these unions were characterized by a high proportion of women among the membership and leadership. The UAW's concern with women workers was reflected in the large number of UAW members in CLUW. AFSCME and UAW strongly supported the participation of their female members in CLUW.

One third of the white respondents belonged to the female-dominated service and retail sector unions; otherwise they were more or less equally distributed across the unions. More than a third of the African American respondents belonged to the public sector union AFSCME. The number of Hispanic women and Asian respondents was too small for generalizations. Compared to all unionized women, service sector workers and teachers were underrepresented in CLUW, while members of public sector unions and industrial unions were overrepresented (see Table 4.4). Furthermore, the organization was not representative of working women due to the small proportion of unionized women workers (10%).

Table 4.4
Women Members of Labor Organizations, Selected Industry Groups, 2001

Industry group	Women members (thousands)	Organized women in all industries	Women employed in this industry	Percent of all women workers* employed in this industry
Public administration	711	11%	26%	5%
Educational services	2,828	42%	36%	13%
Services	1,342	20%	6%	36%
Wholesale and retail trade	495	7%	4%	21%
Transportation, communication, public utilities	675	10%	25%	5%
Finance, insurance, real estate	106	2%	2%	8%
Manufacturing	538	8%	9%	10%
Mining and construction	40	1%	5%	1%
Agriculture, forestry, fishing	11	0	2%	1%
All industries	6,750	100	12%	100

Source: Hirsch and McPherson (2002); *organized and unorganized.

CLUW members represented a heterogeneous group not only with respect to union affiliation, but also with respect to the position they held in their union—union leadership and staff, rank-and-file activists, and members who were not active in the union. CLUW recruited unionized women workers primarily through labor movement organizations, as I discuss in detail in the next chapter. It thus recruited primarily those who were already active in their union and other labor organizations like the local labor council.[11] Women who were not familiar with, felt alienated by, or were critical of the labor movement were less likely to participate.

CONFLICT AND CRITICISM IN CLUW

CLUW had a membership that was familiar with and loyal to the labor movement. Although CLUW included members from different unions, racial and ethnic groups, and men and women, it was less heterogeneous in its stance toward the labor movement. Although some women from leftist groups participated from the beginning, several of the rebellious daughters reported experiences of discrimination in the 1970s, a lingering effect of McCarthyism on the labor movement (Schrecker 1998). For example, Margitta Guirard noticed that she was excluded from meetings and confronted by decisions that were being made while she was absent. She recalled: "So when I was on the Executive Board, I asked to be on the Bylaws committee, but [name] was also on the by-laws committee and I started noticing that all the meetings were, they would say, 'You missed it.' Well, I didn't know about it, they were deliberately excluding me from the meetings. And then they were writing bylaws and giving me a fait accompli. And so I was being shut out of the bylaw meetings. And I think they thought that I was a Communist sympathizer because I was always appealing to them not to exclude these people from the Left."

At the chapter level homophobia could be a problem. One chapter activist experienced a conflict about the endorsement of Pride at Work, an organization of gay and lesbian union members. "We had several very homophobic members, one of whom was a board member at a board meeting where a respected leader from CLUW brought up her participation in Pride at Work in an almost casual way without a lot of forethought. Because we had sort of assumed that people were on the same wavelength, it didn't occur to anyone that we would get backlash. This conservative board member gathered together other members in her office the next morning and called me at work from a group of people to complain about the issue of gay rights coming up at a CLUW meeting, and said some very homophobic and very troubling things, and a short time later left the organization." She thought in retrospect that CLUW should have incorporated gay rights as part of the overall CLUW program rather than as a single issue. It should have been incorporated into the political agenda. She pointed out: "There is no way that we can support affirmative action without talking about race.

There is no way that we can talk about women's rights on the job without talking about the issue of gay civil rights laws that prevent discrimination in the workplace. There are ways to talk about our issues without talking about some issues of race and gender and sexual orientation that are threatening and upsetting to some people. Not just to conservatives, but to many people."

These examples show that the role of outsiders and critics of the labor movement—and thus open debate about shortcomings and flaws of the labor movement—was limited. Rather than openly addressing and discussing controversial issues, members tended to leave the organization or exclude others from meetings.

Furthermore, accountability to different movements and movement organizations as part of achieving an integrated identity encompassing race, class, and gender could be problematic. One African American respondent recalled a conflict during the mobilization for the ERA. CLUW and the National Women's Political Caucus had called for a boycott of a NAACP convention in a southern state that had not endorsed the ERA. She listed several reasons the NAACP held many conventions in the South, including race relations and the number of large, viable NAACP chapters. In addition, she explained, the NAACP was a civil rights organization, and, although the support for the ERA was compatible with the goals of the NAACP, it was not the "mission of the organization. . . . So it would have been sending the wrong signal if this resolution were acted on by CLUW. It would have put the African Americans in a position of saying, 'Well, you're telling me I can't go or can't expect my union to support us in this organization because they're holding this convention?' No, I think we've got to look at this thing in a different light."

She argued that through such a boycott CLUW would have risked losing support for the ERA from the NAACP, as well as losing CLUW members belonging to the NAACP. The decision of CLUW's leadership to endorse the boycott of conventions in the South forced African American women to choose between supporting the women's or the civil rights movement. The respondent was critical of forcing members to make such a choice. Other African American women supported putting pressure on the NAACP.

While the CLUW newsletter *CLUW News* reported on activities in which the organization or individuals had been involved, it did not discuss controversies. Similarly, at chapter and NEB meetings I did not observe much dissent in the plenary sessions. One respondent put it this way: "Actually to be honest, at this thing [NEB meeting] there is not a whole lot of room for criticism."

In an interview with two NEB members at a conference, one developed the idea that somebody should tell CLUW to put out a questionnaire to solicit feedback. "It might be a good idea if somebody told National CLUW maybe they need to put out, after the end of the conference like this, an evaluation sheet where people could say, this is what I liked about it, this what I did not like. I felt there needed to be more of this and this is what the conference was supposed to be about. Because I think if that, something like that was done, you do get feedback on those. And this can remain anonymous."

This respondent was one of the few NEB members who was a rank-and-file union member and paid for her participation at the national level herself. I observed that she sometimes took a critical stance at national meetings. The quote indicates how reluctant even this outspoken NEB member was. First, she suggested that "somebody"—maybe the researcher—should bring this idea to the attention of the leadership. Second, it was obviously necessary to create a means to express criticism, rather than voicing it in a plenary session. Third, in order to assure participation in the survey, the evaluation sheets should be anonymous. Thus, rather than an absence of conflict, there was a great reluctance to acknowledge and deal with conflicts openly. Given the heated debates within the women's movement, the tendency to avoid conflict within CLUW can certainly not be explained by "women's nature." Rather, it expressed the organizational context of CLUW as part of the labor movement with its emphasis on "discipline."

The political animals described conflicts between male and female union members, and also conflict and competition between women in general and in the union—in CLUW in particular. They often used the phrase "women are their own worst enemies," and criticized women who did not support other women. Heather Stone noticed the following about women in the labor movement: "I think they help other women to get in positions, as long as they're not challenging their position. Yes, I think that they pretty much do that. I think CLUW as a whole definitely is supportive of women and women's issues. How supportive are they when it gets down to home turf and home network? I guess what you really need to try and discover is if there is truly a different attitude between women and women in the labor movement and men and men in the labor movement."

Obviously, women do both—they support each other and compete with each other. Some political animals also spoke about "personality" problems in CLUW chapters. Smith, a chapter officer, described how she and two other officers did not get along with each other. "The [one officer] would step in and take over, and then the [other officer] would get mad. . . . And somebody else would get mad, because of somebody else. And we never really got to put things together. . . . It was always like everybody is having hurt feelings."

The political animals did not have any suggestions how to deal with such "personality" problems. In general, rather than discussing such problems openly within CLUW, members withdrew their participation. However, in contrast to many rebellious daughters and fighting victims, who tended to leave CLUW when they were frustrated with the organization, the political animals brought up conflicts at national meetings.

The four types varied in their assessment of conflict and cooperation in CLUW and the labor movement in general. The founding mothers emphasized mentoring and mutual support among CLUW members and hardly perceived tensions between the women's and labor movements. In contrast, the rebellious daughters focused on the conflicts between women and labor. The political animals and fighting victims criticized CLUW meetings that were not run properly, and felt that there was not enough exchange between the national office and the CLUW chapters. Unlike the fighting victims, the political animals appreciated informal interaction in the context of CLUW meetings as long as it was separated from business. The fighting victims had experienced support from male unionists, as well as discrimination based on race and gender. The political animals were concerned that women did not support each other more.

In addition to a general reluctance to deal with conflict, respondents were very hesitant to talk about conflicts with me, an outsider. They were against discussing "dirty laundry" in public, discussing "family matters" with an outsider. This unwillingness to discuss controversies can also be explained in terms of the emphasis of the labor movement on union solidarity and unity. It might also be related to the still marginal position and the related insecurity of women in the labor movement.

CONCLUSION

Compared to other organizations of the women's movement, CLUW was exceptional because of to the high proportion of women of color, reflecting the higher unionization rate of African American women compared to white, Hispanic, and Asian women. In addition, from the beginning the leadership emphasized that the officers must represent women from different backgrounds. CLUW was less diverse with respect to age (the organization was aging), attitude toward the labor movement (there was little critical position), and sexual orientation (at least one chapter experienced conflicts due to homophobia). The reluctance to address conflicts was an indicator for CLUW's identification with the norms of the labor movement, the emphasis on solidarity, in contrast to the conflict culture of the women's movement.

The organization allowed the forming of new groups as long as they were consistent with union ideology (e.g., no competition between unions or between union and non-union members). This organizational setup—which allowed groups for Hispanic and Chinese members, but not for non-unionist working women—made diversity possible and at the same time suppressed conflict.

NOTES

1. The findings are consistent with the results of a survey among five chapters (New York, Los Angeles, Chicago, Pittsburgh, and Twin Cities) carried out in 1992 by CLUW. Among the 417 respondents, 60% chose the category white, 24% African American, 4%

Hispanic, 2% Asian/Pacific, 1% Native American, and 9% other or no answer.

2. The proportion of African American women was highest among the founding mothers (40%) and fighting victims (30%), while a vast majority of white women were rebellious daughters (80%) or political animals (75%). The proportion of Asian American and Hispanic women was highest among the fighting victims (10%), followed by the rebellious daughters (8%), political animals (6%), and founding mothers (2%) (CLUW membership survey).

3. White and Hispanic respondents were significantly more likely to belong to NOW than were African American and Asian American respondents (CLUW membership survey).

4. It should be kept in mind that unionized workers represent only a small proportion of all working women and thus are not representative for this group.

5. This description is based on participant observation, interviews with chapter presidents at NEB meetings, and ten chapter questionnaires. Only five of the ten questionnaires provided information about the racial-ethnic composition of the chapter. The organization did not collect data about the racial-ethnic composition of the chapters.

6. However, Olga Madar, the first national president of CLUW, a white woman, emphasized that there had been significant efforts from the inception of the organization to select an integrated National Officers Council.

7. The inclusion of social, recreational, and cultural activities has a tradition in women workers' education programs (Kornbluh and Frederickson 1984).

8. The symbol therefore exemplified the construction and re-construction of culture (Tuchman and Levine 1993), and was an example of cultural appropriation (Fantasia and Hirsch 1995; McAdam 1994).

9. Since I did not conduct biographical interviews with male CLUW members it is not possible to classify them according to the membership typology I am using.

10. I tried to set up interviews with them, but they did not attend the NEB meetings. One wrote me a letter explaining that he supported CLUW, but did not participate in the NEB meetings. It is unclear why he became a delegate, if he did not plan to participate in the meetings.

11. Comparable to the AFL–CIO, labor councils are federations of unions at the local and regional level.

5

Organizational Structure and Collective Identity: CLUW as a Labor Organization

The organizational structure of the Coalition of Labor Union Women reflected the culture of the labor movement. However, the development of this structure was contested. In its first two years of existence, CLUW experienced heated debates about its organizational setup. These conflicts were grounded in the histories of the women's and labor movements in which the founding members gained organizational experience and developed political identities and loyalties. Differences in the political socialization of CLUW's founding members resulted in different perspectives on and expectations about the organization.

Organizational strategy and structure as an expression of collective identity can be traced back to political socialization, since both strategies and identities are shaped by the membership (Klandermans 1994; Moore 1993). Whittier (1995) analyzed how different micro-cohorts shaped the women's movement in Columbus, Ohio. She emphasizes that movement endurance and movement transformation are closely related. New members or micro-cohorts construct different and lasting identities based on the movement context and mobilizing conditions at the time they enter the movement and at the same time raise new issues and question prevailing notions of feminism (Whittier 1995:253).

In addition to generational differences, political opportunity structures also need to be taken into consideration. The neo-institutionalist approach (DiMaggio and Powell 1983; Hasse and Krücken 1999; Powell and DiMaggio 1991) emphasizes the influence of the environment on organizational change. Based on a case study of the two Lesbian and Gay Film Festivals in New York (1994/1995), J. Gamson (1996) argues that organizational bodies "filter identity formulations" mediating between the constituency and the environment (rather than identities being constructed "bottom up" from the constituencies or dictated "top down" from the environment). He showed how the two festivals (Experimental Festival, New Festival) responded differently to the drying up of resources. The Experimental Festival moved away from lesbian and gay labels and experienced an organizational shift in order to attain connections to the art world. The collective identity of the New Festival shifted from political to consumer category. Both festivals became increasingly multicultural. Gamson concludes: "Collective identities emerge from groups along this continuum of loose-to-tight relationships to a community base; it seems likely that the more detached a cultural organization is from its community base, the more prone it is to emphasizing identity frames consonant with its particular cultural opportunity structure" (259). In a historical and biographical perspective, the environment of an organization encompasses the allied and opposing organizations and state structures that constitute the political field (Ray 1999) as well as members' experiences and expectations. Clemens (1993) interprets the formation of women's clubs and the emergence of lobbying as an answer to the exclusion of women from the vote. The decision for a specific organizational form "invoke[s] a culturally familiar set of scripts for collective action and thereby shape the expectations and probable reactions of others" (Clemens 1997:51). The choice of an organizational form thus reflects the political socialization of the founding members and the context in which it emerged; furthermore it demonstrates to whom a group feels accountable. Decisions about organizational structure and strategies point to some dilemmas of pragmatic political action: getting things done might mean to make compromises concerning one's ideals in order to create a functioning organization.

Collective identity is thus expressed in the organizational structure, which determines who can belong to the organization, how one can participate, and how decisions are made. Bureaucratic and collectivist organizations represent two ideal types[1] (Rothschild-Whitt 1979). CLUW was bureaucratic, but its informal structure also exhibited collectivist characteristics. For instance, social relations were often communal, holistic, personal, and expressive, typical for collectivist organizations, rather than impersonal, role-based, segmented, and instrumental, typical for bureaucratic organizations. Although there was a hierarchy of positions, network contacts played an important role in recruitment into the organization. Within CLUW, the incentives for participation were as much solidarity and value realization as power. In spite of the bureaucratic features typical of the labor movement, interaction at CLUW meetings and conventions was often shaped by the emotion culture of the women's movement (Taylor and Rupp 2002).

The structure of an organization not only represents its ideology and collective identity and defines the range of strategies and alliances open to it, it also determines the organization's relative independence and its access to the resources available. In this respect one can distinguish "insider" and "outsider" organizations (Spalter-Roth and Schreiber 1995). Insider organizations are part of and accountable to another organization—state agencies, social movements, political parties, or religious organizations. Accountability constrains the actions of an organization by defining with whom to form coalitions, what issues to address, and in what way to address them. Being part of an institution, however, also means having an "official" status, credibility, and access to the resources of the institution. Outsider organizations are independent and thus less constrained, but they also lack official status and access to resources.

In CLUW's early years, the resolution of three conflicts had a decisive impact on its development as an organization. Two of these conflicts, as in any new organization, involved the fundamental questions of membership and governance (see Figure 5.1). The third concerned support for the farmworkers union. In each case, CLUW's character as an insider organization was consolidated. The leadership wanted to avoid any risk that the organization would be seen as undermining the labor movement. In my analysis of the three conflicts, I will address questions of organizational style (bureaucratic/collectivist), emotion culture, and autonomy and accountability.

DEFINING THE MEMBERSHIP

The central conflict of the organization from its inception concerned who could be a regular member of CLUW. From the beginning, membership was restricted to union members, according to each union's definition of membership. For instance, if a union acknowledged as members workers who were currently laid off or between jobs, CLUW accepted them as regular members. This restriction to union members was disputed throughout the existence of the organization. Some members argued that the organization was unique because it was restricted to union members; and that opening the organization up to all women, as one of the national officers put it, "would change the whole nature of CLUW. Then you are like any other women's organization, you are not different than any other group." As a women's organization what made CLUW unique was its insider status in the labor movement.

Restricting the membership to union members made CLUW an organization of and for unionized women workers. In its report in the constitutional convention, the CLUW newsletter emphasized that the majority wished to restrict the membership to union women, downplaying the controversy: "In the Convention's opening hours, members decisively rejected a proposal to open up CLUW membership to all workers—not just those who are union members. That vote reaffirmed the Coalition's goal of developing action programs within the frame-

Building Movement Bridges

framework of the trade union movement" (*CLUW News*, 2. no. 1 [1976]:6).

The founding mothers emphasized that the new organization should work within the framework of the trade union movement. The rebellious daughters were interested in organizing working women more broadly and therefore argued for opening the organization to all women, organized or not. They sup-

Figure 5.1
CLUW Organizational Chart

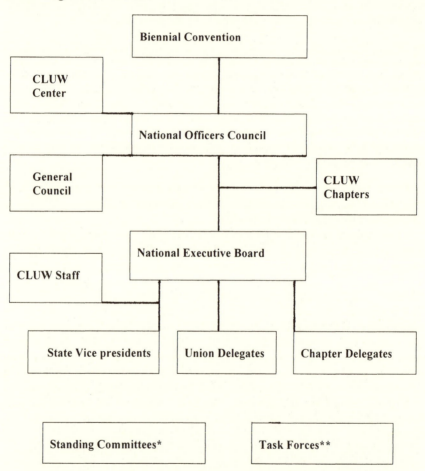

*CLUW's standing committees include: affirmative action, increasing women's participation, legislative, minority, older and retired persons, organizing the unorganized, public employees, publications and public relations, elections, finance, recruitment; **task forces include child care, substance abuse, technological change, women in non-traditional jobs.

ported unionization, but given the low unionization of women generally, they also wanted to change the meaning and practices of unionization to better include all working women. The founding mothers were convinced that it would be easier to change the labor movement from within by broadening the labor agenda as an insider organization; the rebellious daughters wanted CLUW to be a critical outsider organization. In particular, rebellious daughters who were active in the labor movement because they wanted to organize unorganized women workers criticized the exclusion of non-unionized women workers. Some left the organization because they did not agree with the decision, but others came to the conclusion that it was the right decision to restrict the membership to union members. One of the rebellious daughters recalled:

We lost on that question. And in retrospect I am not certain it was a bad decision at all. I mean, at that time I felt very strongly that we should be including all working women, but as the years have gone by, I think the fact that CLUW does just represent women in unions has given us more credibility within the labor movement than we would have had if we would have been viewed just as a women's movement or organization. It gave us an official status within the labor movement. That's important I think to help push the agenda that we are fighting for. So that issues like child care, working family issues, pay equity had to be taken more seriously by the leadership of our unions. Because we were part of the unions and pushing for it.

Like this respondent, over time some rebellious daughters adopted the strategy of the founding mothers to strive for acknowledgment of the unions in order to change the labor movement from within.

This restriction of membership to union members reflected the political climate and the position of the AFL–CIO at the time CLUW was formed. The decision excluded members of socialist groups, a legacy of McCarthyism (Schrecker 1998). Although there were some references in the interviews to involvement in "progressive movements," membership in the Communist Party and other organizations of the Old and New Left rarely surfaced. However, recent research (Horowitz 1998; Weigand 2001) suggests that the second wave of the women's movement was significantly shaped by the experiences of women who had been active in the Communist Party USA and Popular Front, who sought to address race, class, and gender. Some of them were also active in the labor movement. CLUW thus experienced the tenuous relation between labor as a formal organization and labor as "the Left." Members of socialist feminist groups participated at the national level as observers; some were involved at the chapter level.

Another reason to restrict membership was that it preempted the accusation of dual unionism, that is, competing with existing unions and undermining union solidarity. The membership rule did mean, however, that retirees and men who are union members can belong to CLUW as regular members, but working women who are not union members can become only associate members.

The category "associate member" was created in 1979 and amended in 1984 in order to allow non-unionized members to join the organization, though not as full members. But few people were interested in paying dues without having the right to participate fully in the organization. Furthermore, associate members had difficulty finding a role in CLUW and felt marginalized. Some found it upsetting to be an auxiliary or associate member, but nevertheless stayed active in their chapter and supported CLUW.

Recruitment and Membership Development

CLUW included only a small proportion of working women, even only a small proportion of female union membership. Many more women were initially interested in CLUW's formation than actually joined the organization in the first years. About 3,200 women participated in the founding convention in 1974, but only about 1,000 members took part in the constitutional convention in the following year. In 1975 CLUW had 2,500 members and 24 chapters. Glick (1983) has argued that the growth of the organization was hampered by infighting in chapters and by the fact that the leadership was not interested in quick growth. A different explanation is that the founding of CLUW coincided with the 1974–1975 recession (Foner 1980). Precise membership figures were not available because leadership was reluctant to publish concrete numbers. This is normal for organizations of the labor movement (Baden 1986), especially during times when they experience membership loss. Between 1974 and 1977, membership increased from approximately 2,500 to 5,500 (*CLUW News*). CLUW reported 15,000 members in 1985 and about 20,000 in 2000. Given that union membership declined nationally over this period, it is surprising that CLUW membership has remained the same or even increased. Among the respondents to the survey, 7% said they had participated in the founding convention, while 20% joined the organization in 1993 and 1994 (CLUW membership survey). This means that the founding members represented only a small part of the membership,[2] and that the organization has continued to recruit members. It also means that many members left the organization, because of dissatisfaction with the organization, retirement, or for other reasons.

CLUW recruited members through unions, chapters, and individual member contacts. About 75% of the new members were recruited through their own union or through personal contact (friend, colleague, union member). Others learned about CLUW accidentally at an AFL–CIO convention and thought "A feminist labor group—how cool!" Some learned about CLUW through the labor council or their union, and some were even assigned by the male leadership to "check CLUW out." Some male union members withdrew support, however, when they got the impression that involvement in CLUW enabled "union sisters to defeat their brothers." This suggests that male leadership supported CLUW as long as it was seen as an auxiliary, but did not support CLUW's goal to bring more women into union leadership positions.

The distribution of the approximately eighty chapters reflected union density: Around union cities Los Angeles and New York and in the more heavily unionized areas of the Northeast and Midwest, several chapters often existed in one state, while some non-unionized right-to-work states in the South did not have any chapters at all. Obviously, it was easier to found chapters—whose members should come from at least five different unions—in highly unionized areas.

Women who were already actively involved in the labor movement learned about CLUW. CLUW put less emphasis on reaching out to women who were not active in the labor movement. This can be explained by the fact that many active CLUW members strongly identified with the labor movement. Chapter members had to be national members (though members of the national organization do not have to join at the chapter level). President Miller argued that members cannot be forced to join a chapter:

When we established CLUW we said, you must be a member of national CLUW first. No one can belong to a chapter without being a member of the national. There are two things involved here. First, there are areas of the country where, whether we want to admit it or not, people did not want to affiliate with their local chapter, and without being offensive, let me say, with very good reason. There were chapters that were organized . . . there were chapters that fell apart, chapters that were reorganized. So it was mandated that people join national CLUW, but it was optional for them to join their local chapter. (Glick 1983:403)

This indicates that the organization was run from the top down rather than from the grassroots level up.

Conflicts and tensions between some local chapters and the national leadership were grounded in different perceptions of CLUW as insider organization (the position of the national leadership) or outsider organization (that of some members). The chapters were chartered by the national organization, which granted exceptions to the rule that at least five unions need to be represented in the chapter. The national also intervened in cases of leftist participation at the chapter level. National CLUW interfered in chapter activities in Boston and New York, reacting to the "dominance" of "leftists" in the chapters (Glick 1983; see also Troger 1975; Withorn 1976).

Recruitment into the chapters occured mostly through unions or labor councils. In a few cases the founding of a chapter was initiated by a members of a college Women's Studies Center, or through a labor history society. This means that only active union members were recruited into the chapters, while members who did not participate in their union local or local labor movement hardly had a chance to hear about CLUW.

Participation at the Chapter Level

The frequency of chapter meetings differed from monthly to less than quarterly, and the activities differed depending on the resources and organizational affiliations of the leadership and the interests of the membership. The chapter meetings offered women from different unions opportunities to exchange experience and develop joint strategies. Ironically, women who already held offices in their union locals felt that they did not have enough time and energy to participate in CLUW meetings. Some felt that CLUW chapter meetings were too long, not well structured, and did not offer new information. One respondent said she resented the fact that people spoke out of turn and did not focus on one point at a time. The meetings therefore were very long. "I kept looking at my watch and saying, 'I don't want to have to be going to meetings that's going to take two and a half hours to get through and really feel like you're coming out with something, but not as much as two and a half hours worth.' " Recruitment into CLUW chapters thus suffered from a lack of activities in which members and new recruits could be involved.

Chapters led by rank-and-file members or retirees tended to be less active and did not seem to attract staff members and local union leaders. Although retirees had time for the chapter, they often lacked connections to the labor movement and other social movements, and their position in the union tended to be marginal.

If members worked in shifts, chapter meetings had to be scheduled late at night or on weekends and were held at members' homes. Meetings of executive boards were held at the home of one of the members, sometimes along with a potluck dinner. Some members emphasized socializing aspects like car-pooling to meetings, "making it a fun night," and involving the whole family in the chapter activities. Other members found the meetings inefficient, especially if they were new in the chapter: they felt excluded from the familiarity of the long-time activists. Others criticized that the meetings and even the election process were not run properly:

We have a meeting and they'll say, "Well I think [you] will still be the treasurer." They call up and say, "You were just elected, you are going still to be the treasurer." No election. It's not run the right way. I think the chapter needs somebody from National CLUW to come in and investigate what we are doing and tell us what we are doing wrong. As far as meetings and elections and stuff like that.

This respondent felt forced to be an officer, because no one in the chapter wanted to run for the office. This account stands in contrast to the criticism of low officer turnover. In chapters with low activity levels, it was difficult to find members who were willing to take an officer's position.

Overall, respondents saw a need for a support group of labor union women. While some found that CLUW fulfilled this need, others were disappointed by chapter activities and the lack of opportunity to get involved:

> I've had stewards that I've encouraged to be involved in CLUW who have then come back to me and said they go to meetings and they talk about things. But they're not pulled in to be active resources, or given jobs to do that have an end result. It's like going to committee meetings over and over and over again and not having any real outcome. After a while you say, "Why am I devoting my time and my energy in this area, when this hasn't borne any fruit?" There's no outcome to this."

Overall there was relatively little exchange among the chapters except for workshops on "recruitment and chapter building" at national meetings. Some chapter members voiced disappointment regarding the lack of information from the national level. Others were not interested in national developments.

Some respondents who were not active expressed that they would be interested in participating in chapters but there was either no chapter in their area, or the chapter activities were unattractive or not announced. Other women who had been active in CLUW reduced their involvement after they advanced in the labor movement. Many said they did not have time to attend chapter activities, but they also criticized CLUW for not reaching out to and representing women in the local labor movement. Other women stopped going to meetings because they found the activities uninteresting. Some women who dropped out of CLUW were still interested in participating in women's groups. Respondents who were not active in CLUW said that it was not clear to them what the organization did for women workers. To them, CLUW appeared as a social club, reflecting personal agendas and a lack of political focus. These members did not consider joining CLUW.

Some members claimed that the change of the national presidency has led to change in organization activities. One respondent had the impression: "I think people are coming back to CLUW that had left CLUW because we are doing things a little bit different and we are giving the members what they want in terms of workshops. People are no longer bored to death and talked to death. They are allowed to participate and feel like they are included, and their voices can be heard." This means that, after a period of stagnation, the organization experienced some revival. In order to build membership, members not only have to be recruited, but also need to be encouraged and able to participate in the organization. Furthermore, the organization needed to be open to the interests and needs of newer and younger members.

Union Support

CLUW was a member-sustained organization, but also received direct financial support from the AFL–CIO and direct and indirect support from individual unions. Union support meant, for example, that the union local provided a meeting place and money or facilities for postage, printing, and copying. Meeting at a union local meant honoring the rule that labor-related meetings should take place at labor localities and not in private places or homes. It had the disadvantage that members from another (competing) union not necessarily felt comfortable. Labor councils[3] provided a more neutral space. Sometimes members also met at private home, although, as one respondent put it, "it is considered wrong to carry on meetings outside of the official familiar places of meeting" because it is seen as divisive and as a threat to labor unions.

Some international unions and union locals encouraged members to join CLUW and paid the dues for their members, though this supports only a small group of participants (10% of the female respondents and even fewer of the male respondents). Some members considered it a sign of support for CLUW when the union—local or international—paid dues for members. Others found the idea that their CLUW dues would be paid by the union ridiculous. In their view, individuals joined CLUW in the process of asserting themselves in the labor movement. Since the membership dues were very low, they did not constitute an obstacle to joining the organization.

I see these two sides as an expression of different perspectives on the organization and different strategies to improve the situation of women in the labor movement. Members who emphasized CLUW's character as a women's movement organization and an outsider organization found it logical to pay CLUW dues themselves. Other members saw in the support of the unions an acknowledgment of CLUW, and perceived unions paying CLUW dues for their members as support for CLUW and for women in the labor movement. Both strategies are necessary, of course; women need to assert themselves and fight for their rights, but they also need the support of unions. The structural conflict between these positions lies in the fact that outsider organizations can take a critical stance but might not be acknowledged by the institution they are criticizing, or by society in general. In contrast, insider organizations are acknowledged but are restricted by their loyalty and accountability to the parent organization.

By virtue of the recruitment practices, drawing women active in the labor movement to start with, the chance of CLUW becoming too much of a women's movement organization was limited. Due to its membership rules and recruitment practices, CLUW was an insider organization

DEMOCRACY—OPPORTUNITIES AND OBSTACLES TO PARTICIPATION

Another contested issue in the early years of CLUW concerned the endorsement of union democracy. In general, labor unions are formally democratic organizations—the leadership is elected by the membership, which votes on policy issues and meets in representative or plenary bodies. While unions have formal institutions of democracy to represent the rank-and-file, this does not necessarily mean that members participate in the union. Advocates of "union democracy" argue that union membership should include member control and involvement (Fletcher 1998). Like most non-public organizations, unions do not "normally provide for the expression of differing organized points of view, such as could be carried out by legitimized political parties or caucuses within the institutions" (Cook et al. 1992:45). Caucuses exist, however, as informal structures and are tolerated as long as they do not challenge the fundamental requirement of "militant organization, the need for 'solidarity,' for disciplined, united, unquestioned action when required" (Cook et al. 1992:44). The formation of distinct groups— such as ethnic minorities or women—has often been seen as undermining solidarity.[4] In addition, it is not unusual for international unions to control and destroy insurgent locals (Foner 1980; Feldberg 1987). Solidarity is a key concept in the organizational repertoire of labor, whereas the women's movement, while it invokes "sisterhood," is open to conflicts.[5]

Participants in CLUW's founding convention fought successfully for the inclusion of the following sentence in the constitution: "Additionally, the Coalition will encourage democratic procedures in all unions." But how was democracy practiced within CLUW? From the beginning, discipline, a union codeword that emphasized the need for unity and implied that open debates over conflictual issues would undermine the success of the organization, was emphasized. In the CLUW newsletter, President Olga Madar commented with respect to the constitutional convention in 1975 "Without a cohesive organization, we in CLUW cannot build the discipline that will enable us to act together, to concentrate our activities and to direct our efforts toward common goals" (*CLUW News*, 1, no. 3 [1975]).

Two other interrelated factors also threatened democracy within CLUW. On the one hand, CLUW leaders clung to their offices. On the other, CLUW leaders felt accountable to their union, which supported their participation. Representation was thus a continuing problem in CLUW. The organization did not live up to its participatory ideals. This seems to be especially problematic for an organization founded in the context of the second wave of the women's movement.

Bureaucratic decision-making was a means to restrict participation to delegates. On the one hand, such a procedure limits full participation and thus is undemocratic. On the other, it secures that conventions are not dominated by large or strongly represented unions. Furthermore, it prevents the domination of meetings on procedural questions. It also symbolizes the socialization of the leadership into union culture.

Margitta Guirard, a rebellious daughter, left CLUW after attending one of the early national conventions, in Washington in 1977. Guirard described herself as "convention-savvy" and explained that she expected AFL–CIO conventions to be "engineered," but that she always expected a floor fight or that someone would "throw a wrench in the works." However, that feeling [was] completely gone in Washington, there was not a desire to throw a wrench in the works. There wasn't, everything was like silk, or every speaker was positive, . . . and nobody said anything nasty, there were no fights. Everybody agreed to everything. It was like a convention of the Stepford Wives. It was like surreal, it was so weird. . . . And like after a few hours, I got, I either have to get out of there or I am gonna fall asleep. . . . And I knew then, that there was something irrelevant about CLUW. I couldn't explain it. It wasn't like anybody had sold out or anybody had like, it was not like anybody was really fucked up. It was just, it was just another inside organization.

The convention described in this quote was much smaller—only about 300 participants—than both earlier and later conventions, in which about 1,000 delegates, alternates, and guests participated. Guirard's description suggests that the convention was muffled and lifeless. The participants achieved unity by excluding conflict. She felt that at this point CLUW had lost its importance as an outsider organization of women who criticize the labor movement for its sexism.

Although the majority of CLUW's membership seemed in favor of a formal structure for the organization, some were concerned that the structure was not democratic enough. They pointed out that CLUW leaders constituted an "old girls" network that was based on the bureaucratic structure and reluctance of the labor movement to engage in open conflict. Those in favor of the organizational setup instead emphasized mentoring and sisterhood and denied differences within the membership. The term "sisterhood" paralleled the term "brotherhood," which was common in the labor movement. The term implies a relationship that goes beyond a voluntary association; it suggests family bonds.

Obstacles and Incentives to Participation at the National Level

It is common in the labor movement (as in other organizations that exercise representative democracy) to restrict full participation in conventions to the delegates. At the national level, CLUW members could participate as national officers or as chapter or union delegates to the National Executive Board or biennial convention.[6] Non-delegates and non-members could participate in the national meetings as observers, but alternates and guests were seated separately from delegates, and voting rights were restricted to delegates. This arrangement had already been practiced at the constitutional convention in 1975 (Glick 1983:332). Furthermore, union delegates were placed with other members of their union from elsewhere in the country, as were chapter delegates, a fact which was disliked by some members. There was a long-standing demand to allow all CLUW members to participate in the convention. According to the July 1977 issue of *Bread and Roses*, the newsletter of the Chicago Coalition of Labor Union Women, the "Chicago CLUW's executive board is urging as many members as possible to plan to go to the convention. We want to show interest and concern that future conventions be non-delegated, and that all CLUW members be able to vote on convention issues." Representation was thus a continuing problem in CLUW.

About one third of the members of the questionnaire respondents said they were active in the organization. A fourth participated at the chapter level, another fourth at both the chapter and national level, and about one sixth at the national level only. In general, officers and staff were more likely to participate at the national level and rank-and-file members at the chapter level (CLUW membership survey). Participation at the national level was closely related to access to resources, that is, whether the union paid for participation. This support was much more likely to be the case for union officers and staff, though some unions (such as AFSCME) also supported the participation of rank-and-file members. Some members criticized that the national meetings were too expensive. CLUW leadership claimed that they tried to keep meeting costs low in order to keep attendance affordable for rank-and-file members. A travel fund existed, but it only supported the participation of a very small number of members.

One of the respondents was concerned that sending women union members to CLUW conventions was a means to reserve participation in the union convention for male members of the union. "I thought that . . . it was pretty obvious . . . that they are saying, you go to your women's thing here in CLUW. But when the big things involving our union come up all of us guys are going to go and make those big decisions." So while the support for participation by rank-and-file members was acknowledged and applauded, it was also perceived somewhat skeptically.

At both local and national level meetings, long-time members shared friendships and memories of the early years of the organization. In spite of a special program for first-time participants at the national level, new participants sometimes felt excluded and left the organization. The tension between socializing among long-time members and a lack of activities (and leadership positions) for new members led to a high turnover of members who did not find a position in the organization.

The participants cherished the national meetings as occasions where they could get together with friends. This seemed more important than voting on resolutions, which usually were passed with little debate. Some participants criticized that speakers sometimes spoke to a half-empty floor. This pattern of participation, or rather non-participation, suggests that being part of the decision-making body was not the most important aspect of the meetings of the National Executive Board. There could be several explanations for this. First, members might have felt that those participating in the meetings represent their interests. Second, members might have thought that they could not influence board policy. Third, members might have thought it did not matter what the organization decided, because it did not have a lot of impact anyway. Because crucial decisions about the participation of women in unions were made in the unions themselves—neither by AFL–CIO nor by CLUW—it was plausible that

members used CLUW meetings for personal exchange, learning, and information.

This situation suggests that the Coalition of Labor Union Women experienced goal displacement (Michels 1962), meaning that maintaining the
organization and one's position had become more important than pursuing the
goals of the organization.[7] This might be an inherent risk for voluntary organizations that offer few activities in which members can participate. Relationships to
other members then become the main reason for participation in the organization. One of the NEB members observed, "Nothing changed in the organization
that much, nothing major. The same people who were the founding officers are
still the officers; there have not been new officers other than maybe about one or
two. There are the same people as on the day it was founded and elected." She
suggested:

I think people should stay in office for an allotted time period and then new people
should be elected. That way, your organization does not become stagnant. . . . In that
way, you don't end up with people who are totally entrenched, that don't necessarily look
at new ideas as being positive, but sometimes look at them as being criticism. And the
organization tends to grow when you bring in new people. If you have the same people,
talk about the same ideas, with the same program, there is a tendency that the organization kind of dies.

She noticed that this had happened before the change of the presidency in 1994,
she noting that "people get disenchanted with the executive board."

Leadership Turnover

In the American labor movement (and not only here), union leadership tends
to stay in office for decades. The race between Thomas Donahue and John
Sweeney for the leadership of the AFL–CIO in 1995 was a rare exception (Myerson 1998). Similarly, in CLUW the nomination and election of officers was
uncontested and ritualistic. In contrast to the high membership turnover, there
was low leadership turnover at the national level. National officers usually
stayed in office until they retired or gave up their union office—losing power
and resources in the labor movement. Many members of the officers' council
had been national officers since the founding of the organization or were involved in preparing the founding convention and became officers when the officers from their union left their union for another position, retired, or died.[8] (See
Table 5.1)

Officers who retired were usually replaced by a younger member of the same
union. Some of the younger officers were mentored by older ones and inherited
the office. Changes in the council thus were due not to turnover but to newly
created positions. Between 1977 and 1997 the number of officers increased from
seven to nineteen. Furthermore, some women who had achieved leadership in

the American labor movement—for example, Barbara Easterling and Linda Chávez-Thompson[9]—did not belong to CLUW's national leadership but participated as guest speakers at CLUW meetings. In addition to the fact that their commitments did not allow them to take on a role in CLUW, this suggests that CLUW leaders might have been more marginal in the labor movement than other women union leaders. It also indicates that women might have to avoid a feminist affiliation in order to move up in the labor movement.

Since the leadership was to represent a wide range of union women, a particular union could have only one representative in the national officers' council. All national officers held offices or staff positions in their unions at the national or regional levels. Their unions covered the expenses connected with participation in the council. This means that the council was composed not of rank-and-file union members but of union leadership who had the public support and trust of the union they represented. As Milkman (1985b) points out, union officers enjoy limited autonomy and may be concerned about jeopardizing their jobs if they criticize the labor movement openly. This means that those who were more critical of their unions were less likely to participate at CLUW's national level. Respondents mentioned that it was important for them to know that their involvement in CLUW was supported by their union. One of the officers explained:

I asked the boss, I said, "I am involved with this organization, I need to know if you are going to put the blessing on it, because I don't want there to be a conflict between my job and the organization." And he clearly told me that he was proud of the name recognition for our union with me being active, so he would support whatever the activities were. . . . And then after I became national vice president, [my union] picked up the finances for that, so it made it easier to go to all the meetings and to participate and I did not have to pay my way.

This respondent's loyalty clearly belonged first and foremost to her union. Her position in her union was also her "job." The quote also indicates how the unions benefited from supporting the participation in CLUW of their members: the officers represented their unions on the officers' council. Thus the union not only gained exposure but was also seen as a woman-friendly organization. Some of the national officers were national vice presidents and heads of women's or human rights departments in their unions. Some, but not all directors of women's and civil rights departments were national vice presidents of their unions. Others were active in their unions at the district level. One national officer expressed the following position:

I think, obviously a woman who has been able to move politically and successfully in her own union, is going to have greater support for involvement in the Coalition of Labor Union Women by the current leadership. . . . If she has not been able to rise in her own union by getting elected for whatever reasons, the barriers may be too high or she might not have developed the skills. . . . Then she can to a local chapter of the Coalition of La-

Building Movement Bridges

bor Union Women. . . . There are many entry level places to enter the labor movement. . . . Or start within a local union, which is what the majority of people did at the beginning of the Coalition of Labor Union Women

This respondent expressed a very hierarchical and "orderly career" sentiment, arguing that members should move up from the local level to the national level of CLUW. Coming up from the ranks is the most common path to union leadership (Gray 1993).[10] Those who held officer's positions argued that candidates for such positions had to be in a leadership position in their union, which means having influence and access to resources that would help CLUW pursue

Table 5.1
CLUW National Leadership (1974–1997)

Office	1974–1975	1975–1976	1977–1979	1979–1981	1982–1983	1984–1985
President	Madar UAW	Madar UAW	Miller ACTWU	Miller ACTWU	Miller ACTWU	Miller ACTWU
President Emerita	—	Madar UAW	Madar UAW	Madar UAW	Madar UAW	Madar UAW
National/Executive Vice President	Wyatt AMCBW	Wyatt AMCBW	Wyatt AMCBW	Wyatt AMCBW	Wyatt AMCBW	Wyatt AMCBW
National/Executive Vice President Emerita	—	—	—	—	—	—
Treasurer	Johnson IUE	Johnson IUE	Johnson IUE	Johnson IUE	Johnson IUE	Johnson IUE
Corresponding Secretary	Tarr–Whelan AFSCME	Miller ACWA	Komer UAW	Komer UAW	Glenn SEIU	Glenn SEIU
Recording Secretary	—	Fryman CWA	Fryman CWA	Foreman CWA	Foreman CWA	Foreman CWA
Vice President	Day IBT	(MidWest VP)	Day IBT	Day IBT	Day IBT	Day IBT
Vice President	Miller ACWA	(Eastcoast VP)	—	Halpin AFT	Halpin AFT	Stryker AFT
Vice President	Duke CWA	(Southern VP)	McGhee AFSCME	McGhee AFSCME	McGhee AFSCME	McGhee AFSCME
Vice President	Glenn SEIU	(Westcoast VP)	—	Newton OPEIU	Newton OPEIU	Newton OPEIU
Vice President	—	—	—	—	Dubrow ILGWU	Dubrow ILGWU
Vice President	—	—	—	—	Komer UAW	Komer UAW
Vice President	—	—	—	—	Thompson IAM	Padia TNG
Vice President	—	—	—	—	—	—
Vice President	—	—	—	—	—	—
Vice President	—	—	—	—	—	—
Vice President	—	—	—	—	—	—
Vice President	—	—	—	—	—	—

its goals. Women who are in leadership positions in their unions furthermore provide role-models for other union women.

However, women labor leaders could be role-models at any level of CLUW, not just as national officers. It is certainly true that the representation of full-time union officers among CLUW's officers secured CLUW respect within the labor movement. But it does not seem inevitable that top offices in CLUW should be restricted to full-time officers or that participation of full-time officers should be restricted to top offices in CLUW. This explanation rather appears as a rationalization for almost oligarchic tendencies in the organization.

Table 5.1
CLUW National Leadership (1974–1997) (continued)

Office	1985–1986	1987–1988	1989–1991	1991–1993	1993–1995	1995–1997
President	Miller ACTWU	Miller ACTWU	Miller ACTWU	Miller ACTWU	Johnson IUE	Johnson IUE
President Emerita	Madar UAW	Madar UAW	Madar UAW	Madar UAW	Madar UAW	Madar UAW
National/Executive Vice President	Wyatt AMCBW	Wyatt AMCBW	Day IBT	Day IBT	Day IBT	Day IBT
National/Executive Vice President Emerita	—	—	Wyatt AMCBW	Wyatt AMCBW	Wyatt AMCBW	Wyatt AMCBW
Treasurer	Johnson IUE	Johnson IUE	Johnson IUE	Johnson IUE	Foreman CWA	Foreman CWA
Corresponding Secretary	Glenn SEIU	Glenn SEIU	Glenn SEIU	Padia TNG	Padia TNG	Padia TNG
Recording Secretary	Foreman CWA	Foreman CWA	Foreman CWA	Foreman CWA	Scarcelli UFCW	Scarcelli UFCW
Vice President	Day IBT	Day IBT	Scarcelli UFCW	Scarcelli UFCW	Hervey ACTWU	Hervey UNITE*
Vice President	Stryker AFT	Stryker AFT	Van Blake AFT	Van Blake AFT	Van Blake AFT	Van Blake AFT
Vice President	McGhee AFSCME	Roberts AFSCME	Roberts AFSCME	Le Beau AFSCME	Le Beau AFSCME	Le Beau AFSCME
Vice President	Newton OPEIU	Newton OPEIU	Newton OPEIU	Wells OPEIU	Wells OPEIU	Wells OPEIU
Vice President	Dubrow ILGWU	Dubrow ILGWU	Dubrow ILGWU	Dubrow ILGWU	Dubrow ILGWU	Dubrow UNITE
Vice President	Komer UAW	Komer UAW	Komer UAW	Komer UAW	Forrest UAW	Forrest UAW
Vice President	Padia TNG	Padia TNG	Padia TNG	Binns IAM	Binns IAM	Binns IAM
Vice President	—	Zakowski USWA	Zakowski USWA	Zakowski USWA	Zakowski USWA	Zakowski USWA
Vice President	—	—	—	Shelleda SEIU	Shelleda SEIU	Shelleda SEIU
Vice President	—	—	—	Bailey APWU	Bailey APWU	Bailey APWU
Vice President	—	—	—	—	—	Huerta UFWA
Vice President	—	—	—	—	—	Sanford IBEW

* ACTWU and ILGWU merged in 1995 to form UNITE.

Some current national officers were never active at the chapter level or even in the National Executive Board except as dues-paying members and observers at Board meetings. They succeeded their retiring mentors. This suggests that leadership selection was based more on their position in their union than on their participation in CLUW. Furthermore, the election process was ritualistic as well as emotional. For example, after Gloria Johnson was unanimously elected president, the delegates from her union played the song "You Are the Wind beneath Our Wings," which is not a labor song, in her honor. One delegate remarked: "Gloria, your love for us makes it so easy for us to love you. Your ability and leadership are the stepping stones we use to move forward. And if we falter, we are sure that you are there to reach out and lift us up again. Your courage removes our own fears. Your very presence in our midst is why we can and will succeed" (field notes, Seventh Biennial Convention, Las Vegas, 1993).

Johnson was not introduced with an agenda or program. In addition to emphasizing Johnson's achievements in CLUW and the labor movement and her participation in the organizations of the civil rights movement, the nomination was very emotional and personal. Johnson's organizational affiliation and standing played a much bigger role than her stance. Johnson herself thanked the delegates—especially from her union—and pointed out that mutual support was an important aspect of belonging to the organization.

Our role must go far beyond legislative issues, negotiating issues, educating issues, it must go to the heart and soul of what the labor movement should be all about. We each have experienced problems, difficulties. [refers to having had cancer, the death of her son, and the letters she received from CLUW members in each case] And to me that is the most important thing in the world, to know that I can reach out any time, any place, anywhere and have someone who is going to reach out for me. [applause] And that's what CLUW is all about. [applause]

Johnson and those who nominated her presented her participation in CLUW, the labor movement, and social movement organization less as a matter of political action than as one of mutual support in personal relationships. The nomination process emphasized personal and expressive relations among members and officers. Taylor and Rupp (2002) identify an "emotion culture" as typical for women's movement organizations. In their comparison between the efforts of male-dominated labor unions and the women's peace movement of the late nineteenth and early twentieth centuries, they argue that international solidarity was achieved by the latter through drawing on emotion templates like family relationships. Barker (2001) points out with respect to the Solidarity movement in Poland that male labor organizing also is packed with "human emotionality." He observed "fear, courage, anger, laughter, nervous breakdown, pride and solidarity" (175) (see also Flam 1996). Similarly, Fantasia (1988) describes the development of "cultures of solidarity" among female and male workers in labor fights. However, the display of emotions is highly gendered and results in emotion norms (Hochschild 1983).

A candidate's union affiliation and position had significant impact on her chances to become a national CLUW officer. The assembly of CLUW delegates at national conventions had only limited influence on the selection of candidates. The influence of the unions thus reached into the decision-making process. However, in instances in which a union tried to determine who would run for an office, CLUW had made clear that the organization would not defer to the union. One respondent recalled: "I mean, we had some disputes with unions about who gets to serve. We had instances when the international union has tried to tell CLUW who is going to represent them on the board. And we have to say, you know, 'Sorry [laughs], this is our organization, you don't get to tell us.' So that the officers are elected by CLUW." She emphasized CLUW's autonomy from the labor federation. Younger or more recently elected national officers found that the other officers were very helpful in helping them up the ladder.

Some members criticized the low officer turnover and spoke of an "old girls network"; they were disappointed that women held on to power as much as men do. However, this criticism was not voiced openly. Off the record, respondents told me that they would like to see officers share the power they had in CLUW and in the labor movement, for example, through introducing term limits, in order to involve more members and prevent the stagnation of the organization. One respondent pointed out that, although involvement was constantly encouraged, it was not available, "because standing officers and active members do not wish to rotate or step down to allow diversity. Perhaps time served on committees and as officers both national and in chapters should be limited."

All this means not only that full membership was restricted to union members, but that through the recruitment practice only those already active in the union were reached. Participation at the national level was furthermore de facto restricted to those who received funding from their unions—either as staff members or officers or because the union supported participation of rank-and-file members. Thus the organization consisted of not only a small segment of working women, but also a small segment of union women. It also meant that the unions had an influence on CLUW through supporting the participation of their members. This financial support represented acknowledgment of union women and women's interests through their unions; at the same time, unions might expect that members whose expenses they paid would represent the interests of the union in CLUW. Therefore, it was less likely that members who did not have the support of their union participated in CLUW at the national level. This means that, although CLUW was formally independent, the indirect influence of the unions on the organization was significant, and CLUW felt first and foremost accountable to the unions.

Respondents reported that the new president of CLUW, Gloria Johnson, distributed tasks more than the previous president did. Except for the creation of two new vice presidential positions, the structure has not changed, but the change in the presidency seemed to have revived the organization in several regards. Interviews and observations suggest that the atmosphere had changed and more members felt that they could participate. The more inclusive leadership style gave more members the chance to practice and improve their skills and enhance their visibility, while preventing burnout. The participation of national officers in events of the women's and the labor movement not only gave the individuals more exposure, but also better represented the diversity of women and unions that were involved in the Coalition of Labor Union Women, and the labor movement in general.

NEUTRALITY IN UNION DISPUTES: COMPETITION AND COLLABORATION AMONG UNIONS

The "Teamsters and Farmworkers (UFW) issue" constituted the third major conflict at the founding convention. Like the membership question and the debate about union democracy, the third contentious issue of early years of the organization also concerned "union solidarity." Here as well, the decision was about CLUW becoming an insider organization, loyal to the labor movement. Not getting involved in the union dispute signaled to the (male) leadership of the labor movement that CLUW considered itself part of the structure rather than being "divisive" or a competing organization.

The two unions, the Teamsters and the UFW, were competing with each other in an organizing drive. As already noted, the Farmworkers union played a large role in the political socialization of the rebellious daughters. Most of the women participating in the founding convention, even rank-and-file Teamster members, supported the Farmworkers (Glick 1983). The Farmworkers stood for rank-and-file activism and had many female workers. The Teamsters represented the labor union establishment. The Teamsters union was also much richer and could provide more financial resources for CLUW than could the poorer Farmworkers union. Against the will of its rank-and-file members, CLUW leadership took a position of neutrality in the dispute. However, several CLUW chapters at the East Coast supported the farmworkers with the knowledge and approval (and financial support) of national CLUW.

Founding mothers I interviewed described solving the Farmworkers issue as an example of the solidarity among women across union boundaries. The embrace of the representatives of the two unions (Josephine Flores and Clara Day) was very meaningful to the founding mothers because it symbolized the reconciliation of their conflicting loyalties to the Teamsters and the Farmworkers:

In the most touching display of trade union unity to be seen in many decades, the two women turned suddenly toward each other and embraced. The entire audience rose and cheered, some with tears streaming down their faces. And Edith Van Horn, a United Auto Workers staff representative for many years, tried to carry on. "This is what CLUW is all about," she said, her voice choked with emotion. And then she added, "In 54 years, I've never been prouder to be a woman." (Jordan 1974)

Why all this emotion for a decision that was to "not decide"—that actually favored the Teamsters and ignored the position of a significant part of the CLUW membership? The decision was about CLUW's collective identity, an outsider organization—critical of the labor movement—or an insider organization—loyal to the labor movement. The founding mothers sought the recognition—and support—of the (male) union leadership. To take the rank-and-file members' side for the maverick Farmworkers union would have signaled to the leadership of the labor movement that CLUW's leadership was not in control of the organization. The resolution signified the loyalty and accountability of the founding mothers toward the labor movement, regardless how democratic or undemocratic the unions were.

Clara Day, who represented the Teamsters in this union conflict, had been a national officer since the founding convention; the representative of the Farmworkers did not become a national officer at the founding convention. More than twenty years later, in 1995, Dolores Huerta, one of the leaders of the Farmworkers, who had been a member of the CLUW National Executive Board and frequently addressed the conventions and national meetings, became a vice president when two new officer's positions were created. The fact that Huerta did not become an officer in 1974 suggests that it was important to seek the approval of the Teamsters union rather than emphasize the unity of women across unions. The Farmworkers union was poor and thus could not contribute to CLUW financially. Furthermore, the Farmworkers represented union democracy and rank-and-file activism. The election of Huerta in 1995 was a tribute to a famous woman labor leader, it contributed to more ethnic diversity on the national officers council, and it suggested that the organization felt secure enough in the labor movement to make place for a maverick. After all, the conflict between the Farmworkers and the Teamsters had been resolved twenty years earlier.

Not getting involved in organizational disputes and restricting membership to labor union women were both strategies to assure the (male) leadership of the labor movement that CLUW was a subordinate part of the labor movement and considered itself as part of the structure rather than being "divisive" or a competing organization.

MUTUAL SUPPORT—CLUW'S RELATIONSHIP WITH THE AFL–CIO

CLUW became a "support group" of the AFL–CIO. No such relationship was mentioned in the constitution of the organization, and the *CLUW News* did not report the event. The support was clearly hierarchical insofar as CLUW relied heavily on the funds of the AFL–CIO and its unions. But respondents—whether they represented CLUW or the AFL–CIO—described the support between the two as mutual: the AFL–CIO supported CLUW with resources and CLUW supported the AFL–CIO through disseminating its politics and getting women involved in the labor movement.

One of the respondents explained:

We call us a "support group" because mostly and fundamentally we support each other. However, we are not the AFL–CIO. We are the women's movement within the AFL–CIO. And I think we are . . . considered to be more progressive in certain areas of the labor movement and in regard to women's issues and children and family. So we are looked at with respect, and hope and admiration from . . . the members of the AFL–CIO.

Members emphasized that being a support group does not mean giving up independence or that CLUW agreed with the AFL–CIO leadership on every issue:

Now this independence meant that we don't have to agree 1000% of the time or 100% of the time. And on the issue of choice we certainly did not agree. And they took no position, saying that it's going be up to the various unions to carry out the whole question rather then the AFL–CIO. So it is an advantage, tremendous advantage to everybody that we remain in the situation that we are for those reasons.

As this respondent pointed out, in spite of the financial support CLUW received, the organization was independent from the AFL–CIO and did take dissenting positions. For example, the AFL–CIO did not take a position in the debate about reproductive rights, while CLUW supported a women's right to choose. Moreover, unions were represented in CLUW that did not belong to the AFL–CIO.[11] In the 1995 race for the AFL–CIO presidency, CLUW took a neutral position because members belonged to both sides.

But overall, CLUW tended to support the position of the AFL–CIO. At the Seventh Biennial Convention in Las Vegas, delegates adopted a resolution urging President Clinton to send labor union women to the 1995 International Women's Conference in Beijing. After the AFL–CIO called for a boycott of the conference because of human rights violations in China, some CLUW members attended the conference, but not representing the American labor movement or CLUW. Some respondents were disappointed about this development. My observations indicate that CLUW members' loyalty belonged first to their own union, followed by CLUW and then the AFL–CIO.

STRIVING FOR AUTONOMY: THE CLUW CENTER FOR EDUCATION AND RESEARCH

In 1978, CLUW founded the CLUW Center for Education and Research in order to survey the participation of women in union leadership. The Center was set up as a tax-exempt organization. This status made it feasible to apply for grants and gave its staff more leeway in collaborating with women's organizations than the officers of CLUW, who always felt accountable to their unions.

In the 1980s and 1990s the CLUW Center received grants from various foundations, in order to survey collective bargaining, for example. The Center prepared the day-long conferences prior to the NEB meetings and biennial conventions to which representatives from women's organizations were invited. In addition to traditional labor issues like labor law reform or boycotts, these conferences address the issues discussed in this chapter—child care, pay equity, reproductive rights, or sexual harassment—as well as HIV, and political education in general.

CONCLUSION: CLUW AS LABOR ORGANIZATION

The self-organization of women in the labor movement often has been seen as "divisive"; in addition, "women's work culture" has been excluded from the unions. In order for unions to be successful in organizing and maintaining loyal and active women members, they need to address "women's culture," which Feldberg (1987:300) defines as "the ways of getting things done that women value, their sense of honor, the obligations they acknowledge to coworkers, and the connections they make between their work and their womanhood." Such women's work cultures emerge in female-dominated areas. Feldberg argues that unions have to change in the following way to attract women members: "They would have to make room for 'women's culture' and for more meaningful rank-and-file participation, they would have to share leadership and skills, and they would have to learn to value the leadership, skills, issues, and solidarity that 'women's culture' contributes . . . unions would have to adapt to most women's family responsibilities" (321).

The formation of CLUW in the context of the male union culture established an institutional base for women in the labor movement. While some argue that CLUW has concentrated on gaining more power for women in the unions in the form of leadership positions without challenging the basic structure or character of the labor movement (Milkman 1985b), others note that CLUW was able to create independent space to network and organize for its own position (Needleman 1998). The leaders of CLUW emphasized accountability toward the labor movement and tried to reconcile it with accountability to feminist principles. This made CLUW credible among the officials of the labor movement. Members of feminist organizations who cooperated with organizations of the labor movement understood CLUW's position, but saw its impact on the women's movement as limited. CLUW adopted the organizational style of the labor movement and thus demonstrated its loyalty and accountability toward the unions. Using insider tactics, CLUW introduced outsider issues like child care, reproductive rights, sexual harassment, and pay equity on to the labor agenda, as

I will discuss in the next chapter.

Participation in CLUW was hampered by its bureaucratic structure and oligarchic tendencies. National officers, National Executive Board members, chapter officers, and chairs of committees and task forces tended to hold on to their positions. Little emphasis was put on recruiting new members. Those who joined the organization were disappointed at the lack of information about activities at the local level and the few chances to become active in the organization. The lack of activities at the chapter level can be partly explained by the fact that many CLUW members were either rank-and-file activists—which means that they were active in their union and in CLUW in addition to their paid work and family obligations—or retired. Staff members of unions and officers had more resources to initiate activities at the chapter level. There are two explanations for the low turnover of officers at the local and at the national level. First, CLUW officers who held staff or officer's positions in their union remained in the CLUW office as long as they held an office in their union. Just as they defended their union position against challengers, they held on to their CLUW position. Second, rank-and-file activists held on to their CLUW office because they did not have another office in their union or the local labor movement. Those who were active at the national meetings—as delegates to the National Executive Board and biennial conventions—were enthusiastic about the information and support they received.

CLUW's hierarchy and organizational structure echoed the organizational culture of the labor movement. This was intended by the founding mothers and criticized by some rebellious daughters. In the view of these rebellious daughters, unorganized working women were those who needed an organization like CLUW most, but they were denied full membership.

Being an insider organization in the labor movement had certain implications for the organizational structure, strategies, and alliances of CLUW. The officers' positions and participation at the national level were virtually reserved for officers and staff members of unions or for rank-and-file members who received financial support from their unions, while the activities that were offered at the local level were primarily targeted to rank-and-file members.

These conditions affected participation in the organization. It was important that staff members and officers participated at the chapter level because they provided the chapter with resources and connections to the labor community and organizations of the women's movement and other social movements. Furthermore, it was important for rank-and-file members to learn about the problems that women in higher leadership positions faced, and to have role-models.

National officers and NEB members tended to stay in their positions for several terms. Some have held offices and NEB positions since the organization was founded in 1974. Not surprisingly, the fact that officer turnover was quite low was criticized by those who did not hold such positions, while those who held officer's positions legitimized their long tenure and were less critical of the low turnover. In addition to the formal, bureaucratic side of CLUW, there were also informal, socializing aspects like the friendships that developed among CLUW members.

As an insider organization in the labor movement, CLUW played the role of a "watchdog" on women's issues, a role limited by the fact that CLUW was also a "support group" of the AFL–CIO. Rather than criticizing the labor organization and its affiliates, CLUW pointed to the need to integrate women and minorities and their interests more fully into the labor movement. Thus CLUW pursued a mainstreaming strategy. CLUW members who were also members of other feminist organizations provided access to the labor movement for those organizations. As an outsider organization, CLUW would have lost credibility, influence, and access to resources in the labor movement. Insider status allowed cooperation with outsider organizations. CLUW thus opened the labor movement to the women's movement.

The organizational choice thus indicates more accountability to the labor movement than to the women's movement. The newly founded organization intended to demonstrate to the labor movement that its culture and concerns were understood. The organization sought the acknowledgment of the labor movement, and it indicated toward the unions that it perceived itself as part of the labor movement and wanted to change it from within. In short, CLUW's organizational strategy was to be an insider organization, loyal to the labor movement. The leadership of the organization were convinced that this would be the best strategy to advance feminist issues in the labor movement.

NOTES

1. Max Weber (1979) introduced the notion of an ideal type as a heuristic device or method of investigation. Ideal types are constructed with reference to the real world; they inform about typical elements that fit together in a coherent way. Ideal types do not refer to the average or most common type.

2. As I will discuss in the next chapter, the founding members represented a large part of the leadership.

3. Labor councils are federations of unions at the local or regional level.

4. For a discussion of skepticism as well as support for minority caucuses, see Needleman (1998), La Luz and Finn (1998), Chen and Wong (1998).

5. In the following chapter I will discuss the diversity of feminist organizations.

6. The national officers met about monthly, the NEB three times a year.

7. The goals of the organization will be discussed in the next chapter.

8. The first president and vice president became emerita and thus remained part of the officers' council after their retirement.

9. In 1995, Barbara J. Easterling, who as first woman became secretary treasurer of the CWA in 1992, became the first woman to serve as secretary-treasurer of the AFL–CIO, as running mate with Thomas R. Donahue, who succeeded Lane Kirkland as AFL–CIO president. At the labor federation's October convention, the John Sweeney–Rich

Trumka slate prevailed and Easterling returned to her CWA post. A running mate of John Sweeney and Richard Trumka, Linda Chavez-Thompson, became the highest-ranking woman in the labor movement when she was first elected to the new position of AFL–CIO executive vice president at the federation's 1995 convention. At the time of her election, Chavez-Thompson was a vice president of AFSCME and a member of the AFL–CIO Executive Council.

10. Gray (1993:383) distinguishes three other paths to union leadership: founding a union, inheritance, and technical expertise. Technical expertise is the most readily available route to union leadership for women.

11. The International Brotherhood of Teamsters and the United Automobile Workers did not belong to the AFL–CIO at the time CLUW was founded; they affiliated later with the labor federation. Some independent unions are not affiliated with international unions and thus not part of the AFL–CIO.

6

Feminist Goals and Outcomes: CLUW
as a Feminist Organization

> It became a question of wouldn't it be smarter if women got together
> from all the unions to work out general programs. . . . It became very
> much like the needs of the Blacks or the Hispanics to get together in
> their particular organizations. Like in the NAACP or the Urban
> League or the civil rights movement generally.
>
> Aleeta Walker, founding mother

CLUW adopted the bureaucratic culture of the labor movement and was financially dependent on labor unions and the AFL–CIO. Thus CLUW was clearly a labor organization. But was CLUW also a feminist organization? While some argue that bureaucratic organizations are by definition anti-feminist (e.g., Ferguson 1984), others suggest disentangling organizational form and outcomes and acknowledge a wide variety of different feminist organizations (Martin 1990; Ferree and Martin 1995). As Martin puts it, "No other social movement of the 1960s or later has produced the rich variety of organizations that the women's movement has" (183).

According to their degree of independence from institutions and organizations that are not part of the women's movement, three types of feminist organizations can be distinguished. First, autonomous feminist organizations represent all branches of the feminist movement, from liberal to radical feminism. Autonomous feminist organizations vary in their organizational structure: some are collectivist, others bureaucratic; they can be mass-membership organizations as well as small groups. NOW and the Center for Women's Policy Research represent such autonomous feminist groups. Other examples are the YWCA and the League of Women Voters. Second, feminist caucuses are associated with, but independent from, another organization. They have feminist goals and leadership, but they are related to another organization or movement. Although they are formally independent, they feel to a greater or lesser extent accountable to another movement or organization. Third, and least independent, femocratic organizations are part of another organization. Examples of femocratic organizations are the Women's Bureau of the Department of Labor and women's departments of organizations like labor unions and agencies.

Thus feminist organizations can be insider (femocratic) or outsider (autonomous) organizations. Both types of organizations might use insider tactics like lobbying, testifying, writing legislation, providing training and education, mobilizing constituencies, and supporting women candidates (Spalter-Roth and Schreiber 1995; Schlozman 1991; Judis 1992). Autonomous feminist organizations might be limited in their influence on policy outcomes, but contribute to the emergence and persistence of feminist consciousness and feminist culture and help sustain the women's movement (Taylor 1989; Whittier 1995). Thus, for different types of feminist organizations, there are different criteria of success (Katzenstein 1995; Staggenborg 1995).

The difference between insider and outsider organizations thus lies in accountability, not necessarily in the use of tactics. Among the three types of feminist organizations, autonomous feminist organizations are most accountable to feminist principles, while femocratic organizations are held accountable by the organization of which they are a part (Eisenstein 1995; Reinelt 1995). Feminist caucuses—feminist organizations that are not part of another organization but represent a certain constituency within a larger organization—have to negotiate whether they feel more accountable to the women's movement or to the organizational background (labor movement, peace movement, environmental movement, political party, voluntary association) from which they emerged.

Thus, according to Martin (1990), distinct from organizational form, degree of independence, or self-identification, an organization is feminist if it meets the following criteria: it "a) has feminist ideology, b) has feminist guiding values, c) has feminist goals, d) produces feminist outcomes, e) was founded during the women's movement as part of the women's movement" (185). All these criteria apply to CLUW. The organization saw women as disadvantaged and sought to empower women, improve their status, and address their needs. It was founded during the height of the second wave of the women's movement. CLUW constituted a feminist caucus in the labor movement and resembled the AFL–CIO. It was one of the AFL–CIO's support or constituent groups. In contrast to autonomous organizations like Nine-to-Five,[1] an organization of clerical workers, or Union WAGE (Balser 1987), CLUW set out to work within the unions rather than criticizing the labor movement from the position of an outsider.

I will show in this chapter how this accountability to the labor movement constrained CLUW with respect to the four main goals that were adopted at the founding convention—organizing the unorganized, bringing women into union leadership, affirmative action, and getting women involved in the political process. Although CLUW contributed to empowerment through organizing women into unions and supporting women in union leadership, these feminist outcomes were limited to a small number of women.

EMPOWERMENT VERSUS UNION LOYALTY: ORGANIZING THE UNORGANIZED

The long-standing explanation for women's underrepresentation in unions— that women are not interested in union membership—has been clearly rejected. Moreover, recent studies show that women are even more interested in union membership than men (Clawson and Clawson 1999; Cornfield 2001). Since women on average still earn less than men, unionization is especially attractive for them, representing higher wages, better fringe benefits and working conditions, and greater job security (Spalter-Roth et al. 1994). CLUW was especially interested in supporting unionization of sectors with a high proportion of non-unionized women workers and minorities.

Empowerment

Unionization not only provides better benefits and workplace representation for working women, it also empowers them. Empowerment is an important feminist goal. Morgen and Bookman (1988:4) define it as a "process aimed at consolidating, maintaining or changing the nature and distribution of power in a particular social context." This process takes place in interaction. At union meetings, new members learn to assert themselves and stand up for their rights and interests in the workplace. By encouraging women to join unions and become active in their union locals, CLUW contributed to such empowerment processes. CLUW explicitly used the discourse of the feminist movement in calling one of its brochures "Empowerment: A Handbook for Union Women" (CLUW 1982).

Alison Itt, a Chinese immigrant who encouraged Chinese garment workers to participate in a strike, provides a good example of empowerment processes in the context of a labor struggle. She overcame anxiety, developed the courage to fight against an employer, and felt empowered by being able to convince others and have an impact on them. As an organizer she was able to persuade other workers that they had to "stick together," although it is especially difficult to organize workers who as recent immigrants are very vulnerable and afraid to lose their jobs if they participate in a strike. Itt was successful in convincing them that if they went back to work they would not get respect. She focused on "strong" people and encouraged them: "the strong one brings the weak one." She convinced other workers to participate in the strike by telling them:

"Believe that you just try hard, nobody can step on you. Stay strong." That's what I tell my fellow sisters. I am always very nice to people, but people go wild, I go wild [laughs]. I tell everyone you don't have to be scared. When there is some strike and sometimes that we have, we have strikes we organize the job and some big guys want to pull out the jobs, they think they can work with that. No, you are not going to shut us out because we are on strike, you cannot. The people go, "Oh, this lady is very strong." You have to go like this, otherwise people step on you. We always are reasonable, but if you don't, nobody cares.

She described that, although she was a "nice" person, she needed to protest in order to get respect. This case of the conflict between the Chinese garment workers and their employers illustrates very nicely the emergence of what Fantasia (1988) has labeled "cultures of solidarity," which emerge in workers' struggles.

Empowerment is closely connected to involvement in collective action. In this respect the distinction between mobilizing, which can be defined as bringing a large number of women to a protest event, and organizing, getting people involved in contentious politics, is helpful (Payne 1989). Organizing has long-term consequences for activists, not only in the workplace and the union, but also in other areas of their lives. Several of the interviewees described how they became empowered through joining the union. Samantha Torrell became active in the union because she felt that she was underpaid. She did not want the (male) union leadership to be active on her behalf. "And the guy who was running [the union] . . . was a little tight Italian and I knew that he was one of these guys who would put his arm around you and say, 'We'll take care of you girls,' and I said, 'Uh-uh.' I've had enough of people taking care of me. I'll take care of me.' " While the union offered her support, Torrell did not want to be taken care of by union officials, but became active in the order to fight for her rights. She "fell madly in love with the union" and attended training programs for union women. She became involved in a pilot study for objective job evaluation, participated in organizing drives, and eventually became president of a large union local.

Getting involved in the labor movement has far-reaching effects, as Kora Scott described:

As a matter of fact it is because of CLUW that I got involved with all those things. Before I was a union member, but I just kind of went to my own individual union. But since I got involved in CLUW I became Executive Board member of the labor council. And I work with the AFL–CIO. I have started doing lobbying at the General Assembly at [state]. . . .. Kind of broadened me as an individual getting involved in CLUW and I owe a lot to CLUW. . . . Since I got involved in CLUW I've got really involved [in political and union action].

Empowerment refers not only to the recruitment and involvement in the union, but also to the involvement in the development of bargaining contracts. As one member pointed out, it is important that the contracts are developed by union members and business agents rather than labor lawyers so that the contracts are understood by the membership.

It's better that contracts are developed by people like myself included with the bargaining unit members because the contract serves you in the workplace. It should be readable to you, as a dues-paying member, and it shouldn't have all this legalese that is not understandable. . . . Why would I give you a document that you clearly can't understand? Then that would bind you to me constantly to be there to interpret it.

Some union locals encourage members to take courses at local colleges to train worker advocates. Then arbitration can be taken on by the workers themselves instead of being put in the hands of lawyers (Adams 1998). Here the notion of "union democracy" is emphasized. Members should not be serviced by the union but get involved in the local and be able to participate and take matters in their own hand rather than feeling alienated.

Organizing Women into Unions

Although CLUW restricted membership to unionized women, it urged women to join unions—and thus become eligible for membership. Of course, organizing women into unions also means strengthening the labor movement. In this respect, CLUW was clearly a support group—supporting unions, but at the same time supporting working women. This is a feminist strategy insofar as it improves women's working conditions and contributes to a gender-mainstreaming of the labor movement through increasing women's union membership, demanding women's representation among the leadership, and addressing women's needs.

Organizing the unorganized was clearly a central goal for the labor movement, although it was neglected after World War II until the mid-1990s (Foerster 2001; Bronfenbrenner et al. 1998). However, since unionization is an important means to improve women's working conditions, salaries and fringe benefits are also feminist issues. Furthermore, although unions should be interested in an increasing membership, women workers have often been neglected or overlooked. Thus it was important to urge unions to become more active in organizing women workers and to develop new strategies for decentralized workplaces. In addition, for many women participation resulted in experiences not only of discrimination but also of empowerment.

CLUW did not itself organize women into unions; instead, it educated and encouraged its membership to organize women workers through their unions. The emphasis of CLUW was training at conferences and education through material CLUW provided. CLUW supported organizing drives and labor fights through picketing. During national CLUW conventions, members joined picket lines to show solidarity. Individual chapters supported local labor struggles. CLUW became involved in organizing campaigns after a union called on the organization, under the condition that there were not two competing unions. Members pointed out to me that the organization had won respect from the labor movement for supporting organizing drives and strikes. "So we've won the respect of unions. Especially when we join with their picket lines, we help organizing when it is appropriate and it is desired. And we play a very positive role."

According to CLUW's premises—staying neutral in labor disputes and working within the framework of the labor movement—CLUW as an organization was restricted to supporting organizing drives and strikes and calling for more emphasis on organizing women workers. For example, CLUW leaders addressed conventions of labor unions and the AFL–CIO and emphasized that more effort to organize women workers was needed. In addition, CLUW encouraged members to initiate organizing drives within their unions, which did not violate CLUW's principle of neutrality.

Education. In the early 1980s, the CLUW Center for Education and Research developed materials addressing organizing issues. Through these materials as well as conferences, CLUW educated its members to organize women workers through unions. Through that decade, CLUW held several national conferences on "Organizing the Unorganized." Some of these conferences were held together with the Baltimore/Washington Women's Organization and the Industrial Union Department of the AFL–CIO.

In 1989, the Organizing Institute (OI) of the AFL–CIO was founded in order to reverse the decline in union leadership through more pro-active organizing.[2] The organization trained union organizers, who organize workers and offer organizing workshops. At the local level, CLUW cooperated with the OI in 1992, for example, when the Union of Needletrades, Industrial, and Textile Employees (UNITE) established a "worker's center" in Brooklyn. CLUW together with APALA, the OI, and the Trade Union Women's Summer School trained women rank-and-file immigrant workers (Chen and Wong 1998). However, the OI was not represented at the "Young Workers" Conference in 1995, and in 2002 there was no direct link to the OI on CLUW's homepage. This may be explained by the fact that it always takes time for organizations to establish cooperation.[3]

CLUW encouraged its membership to unionize women workers or urge their unions to become active, and honored the federation structure of the labor movement. Within the labor federation, the affiliated unions and their locals are independent. Decisions about organizing are made at the local or regional level. The OI, in contrast, initially represented an independent structure that sought to influence the federation. It was thus perceived—and by some rejected—as a centralizing element. It was seen as threatening by union leadership as well as by those supporting grassroots democracy (Foerster 2001).

Achievements. The success of CLUW's strategy—not organizing directly but providing organizing training and support for unions that are on strike—was limited. Overall, members found that the organization should put more effort into organizing the unorganized at the national and chapter level. Especially for the members who were interested in organizing the unorganized, it was disappointing that CLUW excluded non-unionized women from regular membership. Some of these members were therefore no longer active in CLUW, but have become active in other women's organizations that deal with working women's issues. Furthermore, some of the members understood organizing women as not only recruiting new union members but contributing to empowerment processes that are linked to getting involved in the union (Fletcher 1998).

However, if CLUW would have been serious about organizing women into unions, the organization could have been more pro-active in addition to offering organizing workshops at the biennial conventions. This could have included cooperation with other AFL–CIO support groups representing minorities as well as with the AFL–CIOs Department of Organizing (La Luz and Finn 1998). Representatives of the other AFL–CIO support groups regularly participated in CLUW's national meetings. Furthermore, CLUW could have approached unions with a high proportion of union members or which target female-dominated sectors of the labor market, and aim at non-unionized workplaces and worksites with a high proportion of women workers. CLUW could also have surveyed unions and evaluated them with respect to their efforts to organize women workers. However, this would mean that CLUW members—and officers—who belonged to unions that were not yet active in organizing women workers would have had to face and share this criticism. This might have jeopardized the union's support for CLUW and the participation of members and officers. Cooperation with the OI might have posed a similar problem, since not all AFL–CIO unions were equally involved in the Institute.

Becoming a union member and becoming active in one's union can be a very empowering experience and is thus an important feminist outcome. In this respect "organizing the unorganized" contributed to the empowerment of working women. However, as long as CLUW deferred to the unions with respect to organizing women workers—not even criticizing them for not doing so—this empowerment was limited. Owing to the massive membership loss due to structural change, many unions have understood by now that they have to organize women and immigrants in the service and public sector as well as professionals to make up for the membership loss in the industrial sector, and have started hiring female organizers (Needleman 1998).

Rather than criticizing the labor movement for neglecting to organize women workers, CLUW tried to change the unions from within by promoting unionism and encouraging women to join unions. CLUW saw its role as restricted to creating greater awareness among women workers and unions, rather than initiating organizing drives, which would have been interpreted as being divisive and fostering competition between unions.

ACHIEVING AND HOLDING ON TO POWER: BRINGING WOMEN INTO UNION LEADERSHIP

CLUW sought not only to organize women into unions but also to bring women into leadership positions and thus to gain more power and influence within the unions. The organization saw an increase of women in union leadership as a means to change the labor movement from within. CLUW's leadership did not openly criticize the unions for excluding women from leadership positions; rather, it sought to educate and encourage women in order to ensure their participation and movement into policymaking roles. CLUW supported the formation of women's committees and women's caucuses within labor unions at all levels. I will now first address the reasons for women's underrepresentation in union leadership: then I will discuss the strategies that were employed by CLUW, which include education, mentoring, and support networks.

Barriers to Women's Leadership in Unions

The obstacles to women's union leadership are manifold. They include the centralization of union functions, the small number of leadership openings, the fact that women are outsiders in the male union culture, and the persistence of gender (and race) stereotypes (Needleman 1998). CLUW members believed that collective action and strategies targeting individuals were needed in order to improve the status of women in unions. One of the founding members identified individual and structural barriers that women faced in the labor movement. She explained that CLUW addressed both individual and structural barriers, but that the organization could affect individuals more immediately and effectively than structures. "The one thing that we know for sure, that is that we can affect as a coalition and more immediately, is the development of individuals. And also have the individuals realize that they have a responsibility to develop their own skills, so that they can effect structural changes. They become a part of that structure." She emphasized that individual members can change the labor movement through their participation by becoming part of it. According to this CLUW member, changes at the individual level—making women labor leaders—lead to structural changes.

In order to come up with strategies to increase the number of women in leadership positions, it is important to understand the reasons for their underrepresentation. CLUW members overall agreed that women did not lack leadership skills, though many thought women lacked self-confidence. As already discussed, a vast majority of the members emphasized that family obligations constituted an obstacle to achieving union leadership positions. Members who did not participate in church and community found that these represent obstacles to women's union leadership, while those participating in church and community rejected this notion (CLUW membership survey). These differences were due to different participation patterns of the members described in Chapter 5.

Male and female members differed with respect to the assessment of the male union leadership. Although more than half of the male members (58%) were of the opinion that men deny women leadership positions, many more women (84%) were of this opinion (CLUW membership survey). Overall, CLUW members observed some changes in union leadership. For example, fewer male union leaders did not want to share leadership positions and men who were not in favor of women's union participation would no longer dare to say this publicly. While some members described the unions as "male-dominated power structures," others pointed out that unions "always knew that women were very good loyal members of the union and they always knew that they make good organizers, and good managers of locals, but the establishment of CLUW gave the impetus to really make it clear." The founding mothers in particular emphasized that women are a resource for the labor movement. For example, Eliza Dombrowski said, "And I think as union presidents of basically male unions have met CLUW members, . . . they began to see that we can be valuable allies." However, the women in the labor movement had to prove to the male leadership that they were valuable allies.

Overall, female respondents found that male union leadership and the division of labor between the sexes, rather than deficits in women, was responsible for the underrepresentation of women in union leadership. However, despite the fact that organizational factors were mentioned as obstacles to women's participation in union leadership, the strategies CLUW employed did not focus on the labor movement but on individual women. CLUW offered members leadership training, mentoring, and a support network.

Training for Women in Union Leadership

CLUW provided training materials and organized conferences on bringing women into union leadership. The training materials were developed by the CLUW Center for Education and Research. The Center's first project was an assessment of women in unions in 1979 (Glassberg et al. 1980). The report identified institutional and personal barriers to women trying to achieve leadership positions in their unions. Based on these findings, the Center designed leadership training programs and materials (*Color Me Union* 1983; *Empowerment: A Handbook for Union Women* 1982) and conducted workshops for state AFL–CIOs, international women labor leaders, and women's conferences of unions. The material was also useful for women who headed women's and civil rights departments in unions with a small or virtually no budget. Furthermore, CLUW members participated as speakers in each other's conventions.

CLUW held one-day conferences prior to the meetings of the National Executive Board or of the National Convention. The topics of these conferences were related to the four goals of CLUW—organizing the unorganized, affirmative action in the workplace, bringing women into union leadership, and political action—and other issues of concern to labor union women (for example, health care reform, sexual harassment, pay equity). These conferences were organized by CLUW committees and task forces, national officers, and staff of the National Office, CLUW Center, and local chapters, and were open to members and non-members. However, the target group were CLUW members, who also represented the vast majority of the participants. Although the CLUW chapters in the area used the NEB meetings to showcase their city, the meetings were not generally used for outreach and recruitment of new members, according to my observations.

CLUW provided crucial resources for heads of women's departments, especially those without a budget, because CLUW officers could be invited to speak at conferences and CLUW material could be distributed in the union. It was also useful for those working in labor education programs. In addition to organizing conferences, CLUW participated in conferences of other organizations. Furthermore, CLUW participated in the UCLEA Summer School for Union Women, which provided leadership training. Respondents were enthusiastic about the experience of participating in CLUW conventions and National Executive Board meetings. Rather than decision-making and learning about issues like pay equity and sexual harassment prevention, meeting women who had achieved leadership positions in their unions seemed to be more important to the conference participants.

Mentoring

Mentoring might be even more important than leadership training. A study of union stewards showed that 40% of the women of color and 34% of the white women had received the most important encouragement in their leadership by a union officer or member (Roby 1995). Elkiss (1995) points out that mentoring provides "critical on the job leadership training." A great majority of respondents found encouragement and mentorship most important for bringing women into leadership positions (CLUW membership survey). They found mentors who encouraged them to become more active in the labor movement and who showed them the ropes. Some CLUW members found mentors in CLUW who helped them in their way up to union leadership; often these mentors insisted that their mentees (protégés) join the organization in order to benefit from training and networking possibilities. In some cases the mentee succeeded the mentor in the CLUW position.

However, mentoring within CLUW was only one aspect of achieving leadership positions in the union. As long as men hold the majority of union leadership positions, they play an important role in bringing women into leadership positions. If male union leaders recognize the importance of mentoring, they acknowledge their responsibility to bring women into leadership positions. For example, Jacqueline Lanois credited both male and female mentors for her union career:

It was union officials that thought I would be good to work for the union. I hadn't even dreamt of doing that. They thought I would be good. So they kind of convinced me. And at each level that I moved into, somebody saw that I had capabilities that I hadn't yet realized that I had. Once I got into the positions I just went ahead and did hopefully a good job because otherwise I wouldn't have ended up as director of the council.

Lanois said that she did not have self-esteem when she joined the union as a switchboard operator. At the time of the interview, she was in a management position in her union because her mentors "recognized the potential."

Support Network

Especially the long-time members who have participated in CLUW since the beginning experience CLUW as a support network. CLUW provided them with a "safe environment" or independent space (Needleman 1998) in which they could seek advice and share problems. Networking with women from their own and other unions, along with meeting union women from other countries, expanded their knowledge about union and women's issues. In CLUW meetings they could exchange experiences and find allies. Meeting members of other chapters at national meetings was beneficial for the union, the chapter, and the individual. Ella Turner referred to CLUW as the "women's AFL–CIO" and the CLUW leaders as "sheroes." She emphasized the camaraderie among CLUW members:

CLUW has been good for working women, for union women in this country, because it gives them a place where people can understand each other. Women have a different kind of what I call camaraderie than men do. And we tend to be much more understanding and much more caring about what happens to the person. And that's what CLUW has been for a lot of women. Whenever women run into problems within their respective unions or within their local unions or whatever, they can always call CLUW and ask, "What is it that I should be doing?"

For example, Lanois stated: "What I really, really have been impressed with, is the fact that there's so many women who have joined together for a common cause. They're working together and working together in harmony and working together with the expertise and whatever is needed to really move forward, and the leadership, the genuine leadership they have there, and the willingness to be available to you."

Especially for women in male-dominated unions who had little or no day-to-day contact with other women in union leadership positions, CLUW offered an opportunity to come together with other such women. Members of unions that represented a predominantly female work force felt isolated in their union posi-

tion, in which they mediate among workers, union, and management. Jody
Hunter recalled that she thought "it would be really good to know women who
are involved in the unions." She emphasized that it is important for women to
have "their" network. "Because traditionally I think the men's networks have
been cut off from the women. And I think that . . . the informal network of
CLUW is just as important as the formal things they do such as workshops. . . . I
think the informal network of friendships is just being able to call somebody. . . .
I just think that's worth a lot."

Friendships were informal resources that developed in chapters. Samantha
Torrell used to go to CLUW meetings to "bounce a lot of things off." When her
mentors left the CLUW chapter and she took on a leadership position, the chapter was no longer a support group for her.

I mean, you could go to the meeting and say 'Shit, I'm pissed at these people!' Now I
can't do that because now I'm the big guy and they used to be the big guys, the other
people that there were there and I was the little guy. Now, I have to do it. . . . CLUW is
really what I consider a support group because you go and you're with people who feel, a
lot of times, who feel the same way about things as you do, and that's a really necessary
thing. . . . I find that I'm now the support group for other people, but I still need support
myself. So I have to go other places to find my support, that's all.

CLUW members who belonged to chapters in which retirees and rank-and-file
members predominated also reduced their participation in CLUW, although they
felt a need for a support group.

Aside from education, formal training, mentoring, and information sharing,
emotional support through informal bonds was perceived as very valuable. Respondents emphasized that mutual support was an important reason for them to
participate in the national meeting. "That's what the conferences are really
about—to give you that extra energy. It's like a vitamin shot, you know. So that
you can come back and feel that you are going to do this and you accomplish
this for many women who need the help." The "vitamin" consisted of sharing
information and support and meeting union officers. The mutual support experienced at these meetings was very important to some NEB members: "We created what for me has been the most outstanding thing in my life, and that is sisterhood. . . . We say, 'I need something to carry me until the next NEB meeting.'
So you see we reach out and so many of us come here."

This means that in addition to bringing women into leadership positions, the
support they found in CLUW helped women union leaders to stay in these positions and continue their work in the unions. As Cynthia Delgado, one of the
founding members, put it:

We come here so drained and so frustrated that we need that sort of a stimulation, listening to our sisters, or maybe just to hug, or a pat on the back. Or knowing that we all care
about it, that we are working for the same thing. That it has given the greatest sisterhood

to me that I have known. The church . . . brings folks together from different walks of life, but the Coalition of Labor Union Women has brought women together for a common concern greater than anything in the history of the trade union movement.

Another CLUW member described friendships and networking within CLUW:

I think the experiences of the working together, I guess the friendships established, the, just the ability to share problems with others. The cooperativeness, I guess, the willingness of women to help each other. And we travel to conferences together, we march on picket lines of each other. It's just a nice feeling to know that we are part of a group and belong to a group, a support group, I guess. Knowing that you can turn to others for help if you are having any problems.

Many personal and emotional aspects of the support CLUW provided were expressed, sometimes in terms comparable to those during the nomination of national president Gloria Johnson. Emotional support was especially important for union staff and officers who had been active in the labor movement for a long time, raising women's issues over and over again in their union. Thus through training, the attendance of unions offers possibilities for developing networks, mentoring relationships, and friendships. This means that CLUW constituted a support group and was perceived as a valuable resource. The independent space it provided was important for creating a women-friendly organizational culture, and thus had feminist outcomes. However, CLUW offered little for women who did not participate in national meetings and whose chapters included mostly retired or rank-and-file members.

Structured Opportunities

In addition to independent spaces, "structured opportunities" (Needleman 1998) like the establishment of women's and civil rights departments, the development of special training programs, and the conscious inclusion of women and people of color in visible and critical leadership positions are important strategies to bring women and minorities into union leadership (Needleman 1998). CLUW's explicit goal of getting women into leadership positions required that the organization acknowledge structural factors as well as strategies to overcome them. More than half the respondents found the establishment of affirmative action programs and sharing household and child care most important for bringing women into leadership positions. Thus members thought that a combination of policies as well as a rearranging of the division of labor at home were needed. The stance toward affirmative action was controversial and changed after 1995.

Since CLUW was founded in 1974, the number of women in union leadership positions has increased at all levels. However, the participation of women in leadership positions in 1994 lagged behind the participation of women among the membership (see Table 6.1).

In 1994, the proportion of women in union leadership positions was highest in unions of professionals like the American Federation of Teachers, industrial unions, and public and private sector unions with a high proportion of women members. In some cases the number of women in union leadership increased, in others it remained stable or even decreased slightly. Various factors contributed

Table 6.1
Female Membership and Leadership in Selected Labor Organizations (1979, 1985, 1990, 1994)

Labor Organization	Year	Women Members (thousands)	Women Members (%)	Women Officers and Board Members	Women Officers and Board Members (%)
ACTWU[1]	1979	331	65%	6	15%
	1985	228	66%	3	(%
	1990	160	61%	5	10%
	1990	n/a	n/a	4 (2)[2]	19% (50%)[3]
AFGE	1979	130	49%	0	0%
	1985	61	31%	2	10%
	1990	n/a	n/a	n/a	n/a
	1990	n/a	65%	3 (0)	17%
AFSCME	1979	408	40%	1	3%
	1985	450	45%	4	14%
	1990	600	50%	5	17%
	1990	689	52%	5 (4)	16%
AFT	1979	300	60%	8	25%
	1985	366	60%	11	14%
	1990	455	65%	11	17%
	1990	(ca.) 560	70%	13	16%
CWA	1979	259	51%	0	0%
	1985	338	52%	1	6%
	1990	338	52%	1	6%
	1990	338	51%	3 (0)	21% (0)
HERE	1979	181	42%	1	4%
	1985	200	50%	2	8%
	1990	143	48%	1	4%
	1990	n/a	n/a	n/a	n/a

to the increased number of women in union leadership positions: the proportion of women among the membership and the formal and informal support of the (male) leadership, as well as a decline of officer's positions.

The increase of women in leadership positions was in several cases a mathematical development: the number of women among all officers did not increase, but the Women staff members of the AFL–CIO acknowledged CLUW's contribution in terms of leadership development, but emphasized that the increase of women in union leadership and the creation of the positions of women's coordinator in the civil rights department were a result of the diffusion of feminist consciousness in the labor movement and society in general, and not just due to CLUW. The women who made these claims were AFL–CIO staff members. Since they represent the labor federation, they were restricted in praising

Table 6.1 (continued)
Female Membership and Leadership in Selected Labor Organizations (1979, 1985, 1990, 1994)

Labor Organization	Year	Women Members (thousands)	Women Members (%)	Women Officers and Board Members	Women Officers and Board Members (%)
IAMAW	1979	119	13%	0	0%
	1985	114	15%	0	0%
	1990	n/a	n/a	n/a	n/a
	1990	n/a	17%	0	0%
IBEW	1979	304	30%	0	0%
	1985	330	30%	0	0%
	1990	240	30%	0	0%
	1990	n/a	n/a	n/a	n/a
IBT	1979	481	25%	0	0%
	1985	485	26%	0	0%
	1990	400	25%	0	0%
	1994	n/a	20-30%	1 (0)	4% (0)
ILGWU	1979	279	80%	2	7%
	1985	219	85%	3	13%
	1990	145	83%	4	22%
	1990	125	85%	4 (0)	21% (0)
IUE	1979	102	40%	1	4%
	1985	80	40%	2	8%
	1990	n/a	n/a	n/a	n/a
	1990	n/a	40%	3 (2)	14% (66%)
SEIU	1979	312	50%	7	15%
	1985	435	50%	9	18%
	1990	420	45%	13	34%
	1990	n/a	50%	13 (0)	24% (46%)

1. ACTWU and ILGWU merged in 1995 and formed UNITE.
2. Women of color. The number of women of color among union leaders was compiled for the first time in 1994. Five of the eleven unions and the NEA have women of color among their national officers (ACTWU, AFSCME, AFT, IUE, SEIU). Women of color represent between 25% (NEA) and 80% (AFSCME) of the women officers in these unions.
3. Percentage women of color.

Sources: 1979 data from Glassberg et al. 1980; 1985 from Baden 1986; 1990 from Cobble 1993, and 1994 CLUW Survey.

organization and might have been reluctant to credit CLUW with these changes, which might be perceived as criticism of the AFL–CIO. However, the increase was still limited, and the extent to which CLUW was responsible for it is debatable. One informant who has been an AFL–CIO staff member since the early 1970s had the impression that the effect had been tremendous. "CLUW was formed about then and as CLUW grew and became more active it certainly had an impact on the unions. And during that period from which I first came on until now there has been a tremendous change in women being officers, being active in their unions, being top officers, being international vice presidents, etc. And there is of course an increase in activity in EEO, affirmative action, all that."

Achievements

Some of the rebellious daughters agreed that there are still not enough women in union leadership positions, but that the labor movement had changed because there were more women in the movement, as members and in leadership positions, and that women's issues were more acknowledged. Other rebellious daughters pointed out that the labor movement was in such a desperate condition that it had to open up to women, regardless of CLUW's existence, but that CLUW certainly contributed to the increase of women in union leadership and the inclusion of women's issues on the labor agenda. Moreover, not all members were interested in achieving leadership positions; some were more concerned with empowering and changing the lives of working women. For example, Marguitta Guirard described in the interview that she became very depressed when she realized that she had a bigger impact on women as an organizer than as a business agent. Instead of being proud of her career and reputation in the labor movement, she felt ambivalent and disappointed that she had not significantly improved the situation of working women. On becoming a noted labor leader, she recalled that she felt:

I should be happy, because I sort of got a lot of fame. But I am not helping anybody. I am not changing anybody's life. . . . When I was organizing daycare centers, peoples lives were dramatically changing, . . . people were becoming radical feminists. They were getting divorced or having an abortion. And they were . . . going to law school and getting degrees. These were high-school dropouts who were suddenly becoming powerful women. And I thought, "What happened?" I am not changing people's lives. Now, it's just about "Can I get a gas card?" and "Can I get my salary up?"

Guirard was disappointed by a labor movement that was restricted to servicing members rather than empowering them. She did not perceive raising someone's salary as social change. The fact that she lost arbitrations, grievance proceedings, and campaigns contributed to her feeling of powerlessness. Later she realized that her lack of impact could be explained by the anti-union climate that began in the late 1970s and continued through the beginning of the 1990s. Guirard criticized labor leaders for being more interested in advancing their own careers than in standing up for workers' rights. She pondered that the expectations of the rebellious daughters might have been too high, and that rather than empowering the powerless they were only able to bring about changes in the leadership. "Our expectations were that we were going to empower people on the bottom. . . . And really it really was just [have] leadership turnover [laughs] . . . Because this is what happened in my union. We were supposed to throw out the reactionary labor leaders and put in this militant pro-Black, pro-woman, pro-rank-and-file. And you know, all we really did was change bureaucrats."

However, even the members who stated that the labor movement was still a "bastion of male chauvinism" found that it had changed a lot since CLUW was formed and brought more women into leadership positions, who pushed the unions on women's issues and did legislative work at the state and congressional levels.[4]

Overall, the members agreed on the causes for women's under representation in union leadership, but disagreed somewhat with respect to the best solution. Nevertheless, despite the fact that they saw the reasons for women's under representation as structural, they focused on educating and empowering individual union women. This means that, although female respondents understood the structural causes for the under representation of women in union leadership, they found improving women's skills and networking to be the most important way to achieve these positions. They argued that women needed to become active in their unions in order to be respected. In CLUW, women unionists could obtain the necessary skills to run for office in their unions and other labor organizations.

CLUW members who were active at the national level benefited most from leadership training, mentoring, and support networks. This means that CLUW provided collective self-help and mutual support for those who had already achieved union offices and were active in CLUW. Access for women who were not yet active in their union or CLUW was more limited. The great majority of CLUW members agreed that CLUW should put more effort into bringing women into union leadership positions.

Instead of giving members the opportunity to develop leadership skills within CLUW, for instance through a high turnover of officers' positions, the organization offered leadership training in which women union leaders shared their experiences with each other. Leadership in one's own union was a precondition for becoming a leader in CLUW. This strategy was useful for women who were already in leadership positions and who used CLUW as a support group. It also meant that women who did not move up in their union held on to their position in CLUW to compensate for their limited influence in their union.

OVERCOMING DISCRIMINATION: AFFIRMATIVE ACTION AND
SENIORITY RIGHTS

The labor movement and the women's movement have been at odds regarding affirmative action[5] and seniority rights. In the perspective of the labor movement, seniority rights represent job security for employees covered by a bargaining contract. However, for newly hired women and minorities, seniority rights represent institutionalized racism and sexism because these regulations do not credit time spent working in segregated jobs, lines, or departments toward opportunities available in areas that had previously been reserved for white males. At the time CLUW was founded, during the 1974–1975 recession in the labor movement, the focus shifted from transfer and promotion via seniority systems to layoff and recall, and produced great conflict between anti-discrimination agreements and collective bargaining agreements (Wallace and Driscoll 1981).

Feminists criticize seniority rights as discriminatory practices. Seniority rights privilege those who hold a position for a significant time period. The seniority of women and minorities is often lower than that of white men in the same workplace. Furthermore, affirmative action policies turned out to be disadvantageous for women and minorities, who lost seniority in moving into a new position. As "last hired," they were the "first fired"—consistent with seniority rights. Furthermore, women who entered sex-atypical trades experienced harassment (Fonow 1993; O'Farrell and Moore 1993).

Since CLUW was fighting against discrimination within the framework of the labor movement, it had to reconcile these two different, controversial, and seemingly irreconcilable perspectives on seniority rights in order to remain loyal to both feminist principles and the labor movement. CLUW, in its loyalty to the labor movement, pointed to the employers who profited by dividing workers on sexual, racial, and age lines. In its statement of purpose, CLUW argued that affirmative action could be accomplished through the process of collective bargaining, and thus through the union. CLUW set its agenda to "encourage women to learn what their rights are under the law and become more knowledgeable of the specifics of collective bargaining and of the contract clauses and work place practices which discriminate against them. . . . [and] . . . to encourage women, through their unions, to recognize and take positive action against job discrimination in hiring, promotion, classification, and other aspects of work."

CLUW framed its support for affirmative action in language that was compatible with union practices. In addition, CLUW planned to "educate and inspire our union brothers" to help achieve affirmative action in the workplace. Rather than address structures and policies directly, CLUW thus focused on individuals—men and women in the labor movement who should change the structures from within. The organization thus sought to overcome institutionalized racism and sexism through consciousness raising and education of union members. At the meeting of the National Coordinating Committee of CLUW in Houston in the spring of 1975, CLUW adopted a resolution on affirmative action and seniority in the work force. "CLUW's NCC will urge the organization's members to seek to improve the seniority system in their union contracts to eliminate aspects that have not served women and minority groups fairly" (*CLUW News*, 1, no. 2 [1975]: 1). This resolution constituted a plea rather than a protest.

CLUW targeted individuals rather than labor unions and the AFL–CIO, where it would have had little leverage. By affirming seniority rights while acknowledging that they put women and minorities at a disadvantage, CLUW demonstrated its accountability to both the labor movement and the women's and civil rights movements. Rather than criticizing the unions openly, CLUW called on its members to improve the seniority system from within through monitoring recall and rehiring actions and improving union contracts. However, seniority rights were not explicitly addressed in the CLUW publication "Effective Contract Language for Union Women" (1979).

CLUW President Olga Madar aggressively defended seniority rights against feminist attacks in a *CLUW News* editorial entitled "Safeguarding What We Have." She argued that

"more women, young and old, are released from their jobs out of line with seniority than are laid off in line with seniority. . . . Despite some of the inequities that continue to exist between men and women at the organized workplace, union women are better off than unorganized working women. They make more money, they have the security of a seniority agreement, and they have the recourse to their union." (*CLUW News*, 1, no. 2 [1975])

According to Madar, employers, not unions, were to blame for gender discrimination. She suggested three remedies for improving women's working conditions: diligent monitoring and enforcement of contract clauses and legislation; renewed political and legislative activity; and accelerated efforts to organize unorganized women. In addition, in a letter to Karen De Crow, then president of the National Organization for Women, she criticized NOW for implying that seniority rights were responsible for layoffs of women and pointed out that more women were losing jobs in unorganized workplaces than in organized workplaces. She suggested to NOW "that you monitor those unorganized work places and insist that they lay off in line with company-wide seniority. I promise that you will help save more women's jobs than by attacking the seniority system" (*CLUW News*, 1, no. 2 [1975]:3).

In 1976, a member of the Chicago CLUW chapter invited CLUW representation at a November conference on affirmative action. Among those invited were leaders and staff of working women's groups such as Women Employed, Nine-to-Five, Women Organized for Employment, New York Women Office Workers, Cleveland Working Women, the NOW Sears Task Force, Women's Action Alliance, and Wisconsin Feminist Project. CLUW President Olga Madar declined the invitation, arguing, "We should focus on the training of union women to find meaningful ways to use the grievance and bargaining structures of our unions for more effective implementation of title VII, equal pay, and the government Affirmative Action programs" (Glick 1983:336). Thus, CLUW rejected the invitation to build a coalition with outsider groups like Nine-to-Five and the growing network of autonomous (non-union) working women's groups.

This early decision affirmed CLUW's loyalty to the labor movement and thus set parameters in which the organization would develop. Accountability to the labor movement took precedence over feminist principles. By defending seniority rights, CLUW put itself squarely in the framework of the labor movement. However, the issue was debated within CLUW and reported in *CLUW News*:

"Spirited debate on the language of a resolution dealing with the issue of seniority and affirmative action came after a wide-ranging panel discussion. . . . Although each panelist presented a different point of view, each cited the obvious solution to the thorny issue of seniority; improving the economy and providing jobs for those who seek them—thus making the issue an academic one." (*CLUW News*, 1, no. 2 [1975]:3)

The panelists avoided taking a stance on this contested issue, trying to abstain from being disloyal to either feminism or unionism.

Clearly, seniority and affirmative action were contested issues within the organization. President Madar summarized the controversy pointing out that the committee had resolved that only a union contract would be a safeguard against selective layoffs, blaming instead the government. "The seniority system itself is not the culprit—rather the government's economic policies are the cause of the nation's highest unemployment rate since the Depression" (*CLUW News*, vol. 1, no. 3 [1975]:1). Madar thus rejected the notion that the seniority system was to blame for discrimination against women in the workplace. Four years later, at the 1979 Biennial Convention, the officers' council reported to the participants in the convention: "CLUW stands at the crossroads of the labor movement, the civil rights movement, and the women's movement. We can further the program for compliance with anti-discrimination laws and develop innovative approaches for the integration of women into society. Affirmative action in the workplace is the starting point for a renewed commitment by unions, employers, and civil rights organizations."

On affirmative action, CLUW contributed to building a bridge between the women's movement and the labor movement. However, although a majority of the members found CLUW very successful with respect to this goal, more than 80% of all four types felt that CLUW should pursue affirmative action more energetically (CLUW membership survey).

At the time CLUW was founded, some feminists argued that seniority rights would harm women workers and get in the way of affirmative action programs. CLUW leaders replied that women who were covered by seniority rights were better off than unorganized women workers. CLUW's strategy was to educate women and help them achieve leadership positions in their union, in which they could influence bargaining contracts and resolutions. Rather than criticizing the labor movement, the organization sought to change the unions from within as legitimate members. In addition, CLUW was part of coalitions on affirmative action that consisted of unions, civil rights, organizations, and women's organizations.[6]

ENCOURAGING WOMEN TO PARTICIPATE IN THE LEGISLATIVE AND POLITICAL PROCESS

The statement of purpose further called for the active participation of women in the political and legislative process with special emphasis on areas that particularly affect women. These issues included full employment and job opportunities, shorter work weeks without loss of pay, child care legislation, a livable minimum wage for all workers, improved maternity and pension benefits, improved health and safety coverage, expanded educational opportunities, mass action on state and federal legislation for equal rights for women, and guaranteed collective bargaining rights for all workers. CLUW urged union women to run for political office at local, county, state, and national levels. In addition, the Equal Rights Amendment (ERA) was a key concern: "Until final ratification of the Equal Rights Amendment is won, the Coalition will make the fight for the ERA a priority through a mass action and educational campaign" (CLUW constitution).

Prior to CLUW's founding, the Equal Rights Amendment was contested among union women and between the labor movement and the women's movement. While some pointed out that the ERA would abolish much needed protective legislation, others welcomed the ERA for setting an end to discriminatory side effects of the same protective legislation. Furthermore, it led to tensions with respect to race, since many of the states that had not ratified the ERA were in the South. As already discussed in Chapter 4, a boycott of such states was problematic for NAACP members (the majority of them African American), sinde the organization often met in the South. From the beginning, CLUW has fought for the ratification of the ERA and an extension of "truly protective legislation for all workers" (*CLUW News* vol. 1, no. 1[1975]:7). In the *CLUW News* the discriminatory side effects of protective legislation were regularly discussed in the context of health and safety at the workplace.

CLUW members were involved in lobbying and political campaigning. Many members of the National Executive Board were on the political action committees of their union local and active in the Democratic Party. At one NEB meeting, virtually all participants indicated that they had been involved in political campaigning although only very few ran for office themselves (field notes).

Over 80% of the respondents were involved in the Democratic Party, with no significant differences between racial and ethnic groups (CLUW membership survey). In addition, a large majority of members were involved in lobbying and campaigning as part of the classical repertoire of political action.

Involvement in political campaigns has aimed to support candidates who support a labor and feminist agenda. This was sometimes an ambivalent experience when a labor candidate was pro-life and pro-gun, or when a feminist candidate was not a supporter of a labor concern like the North American Free Trade Agreement. One informant recalled how she switched her vote to a pro-choice, anti-labor candidate, although as a delegate she was expected to vote for the anti-choice, pro-labor candidate running for the Democratic endorsement for the U.S. Senate.

And I sat there and I held my vote with this, and I was in tears, I was sitting there and I was absolutely in tears, because I kept being pressured by both sides, you know, and I stayed there. I hung with, and, she was gaining votes, he was gradually losing votes. So finally when I came around, I was told, it got to 14 ballots. I was switching my vote, which I did. But it was one of the hardest things I think I have ever gone through, this all-night-session balloting.

Thus CLUW members, who felt accountable to the labor movement in general, to their union in particular, and also to the women's movement, in particular CLUW, were torn between their loyalty for these movements. As union members—and especially as union delegates—they were expected to choose the labor position over the feminist position. Conversely, as feminists they were expected to support feminist positions. Strauss (1959) points out that loyalty is an expression of identity and that building loyalty always means to loosen allegiance to an older loyalty. Strauss' observations refer to conversion. However, CLUW members did not seek conversion. Rather, they felt loyal to both movements and therefore felt torn when they had to choose one over the other. If they were forced to make a choice, they most often opted for the labor position.[7] Otherwise, as the example shows, they went through hell.

While participation in electoral campaigns aims to bring supportive candidates into office, lobbying aims to persuade legislators to support feminist and labor issues. CLUW offered conferences and education not only on political campaigning, but also on lobbying at the local, state, and national level. CLUW members received information about feminist issues through the newsletter and CLUW meetings. At conferences CLUW invited speakers from the labor, women's, and civil rights movement in order to address how issues like the North American Free Trade Agreement, labor law reform, or health care reform relate to working women and what union women could do to support these issues.

CONCLUSION

As a feminist inside organization, CLUW tried to change the labor movement from within by bringing women into unions and women's issues on to the labor agenda. Accountability to the labor movement constrained CLUW in its pursuit of these goals. Rather than criticizing the labor movement or protesting against its practices, CLUW encouraged women to get involved, achieve leadership positions, and make unions more women-friendly. CLUW was more successful in affirmative action and getting women involved in the political process than in organizing the unorganized and bringing women into leadership positions. In both respects, CLUW presented itself as an ally of the labor movement.

The emphasis of the new AFL–CIO leadership on organizing, which resulted in the creation of a separate Organizing Department, may bring new impulses for CLUW's goal to organize the unorganized. The labor movement has realized that its survival depends on organizing women and minorities. CLUW thus represented an important ally, and it could in turn expect to find allies in the Organizing Department and the other support or constituent groups. The new leadership of the AFL–CIO also provided a positive opportunity structure for bringing more women into leadership positions. While the AFL–CIO and some of its affiliated unions provided structured opportunities for bringing more women and people of color into union leadership, CLUW represented an independent space in which union women found leadership training, mentorship, and support networks. Emotional bonds were very important for those active in the organization.

CLUW endorsed a feminist ideology, pursued feminist goals, achieved feminist outcomes, and was founded during the fight for the Equal Rights Amendment. Thus, even if the organization did not label itself feminist, it meets several criteria for a feminist organization (Martin 1990). In addition, CLUW constituted a feminist caucus in the labor movement. In contrast to autonomous organizations like Nine-to-Five (Milkman 1985b), an organization of clerical workers, or Union WAGE (Balser 1987), CLUW set out to work within the unions rather than criticizing the labor movement from the position of an outsider. As an insider organization, CLUW bridged the women's and labor movement gap by framing women's issues as labor issues and labor issues as women's issues in four areas: reproductive rights, pay equity, sexual harassment, and child care. Furthermore, the organization formed coalitions with women's, labor, and civil rights organizations around these issues.

NOTES

1. Nine-to-Five, an organization of women office workers, began in Boston in 1973, founded by Karen Nussbaum (see endnote 4 below; see also Chapter 2). Initially, Nine-to-Five was an outside organization, organizing non-unionized office workers (Milkman

1985b). Later it affiliated with the Service Employees International Union and formed District 925, which organizes clerical workers. In addition to SEIU District 925, Nine-to-Five still exists as an autonomous organization.

2. In the beginning, the Organizing Institute constituted an independent entity within the AFL–CIO. After Sweeney became president of the labor federation in 1995 and the Department of Organizing and Field Services was split into two departments, the Organizing Institute became part of the Department of Organizing (Foerster 2001)

3. The AFL–CIO Organizing Institute cooperated with one of the other support-groups—the Asian Pacific Labor Alliance (APALA). APALA and the AFL–CIO Organizing Institute were both founded in the beginning of the 1990s and had their offices in the same building. This, as well as the constituency of these organizations might contribute to close contact and cooperation.

4. The director of the Working Women's Department, Karen Nussbaum, was the founder of Nine-to-Five. Nussbaum was the director of the U.S. Labor Bureau under then president Clinton. In 1996 she became director of the Working Women's Department. The case of Nine-to-Five and its founder shows how outsider organizations and strategies can be followed by insider organizations and policies sticking to one's political agenda. How far such gender-mainstreaming processes result in broadening the base or if they must be seen as a watering down of principles needs to be determined.

5. This will be addressed in the next chapter.

6. Affirmative action here is discussed only with respect to the workplace, not with respect to union positions.

7. Coalition building will be discussed in the next chapter.

8. The striving to reconcile women's issues and labor issues will be discussed in the next chapter.

7

"Together We Will Make Unionists Feminists and Feminists Unionists": CLUW as a Bridging Organization

CLUW was not only a labor organization and a feminist organization. Through pursuing women's issues using the style and the structures of the labor movement it also served as a bridging organization and contributed to bringing women's issues onto the labor agenda. Through organizing women into unions and bringing women into leadership positions, CLUW sought to transform the unions from within and presented "unobtrusive mobilization," an important strategy to achieve feminist goals (Katzenstein 1998). The representation of women and minorities among union membership and leadership has significant impact on the issues unions address, since women union leaders are more supportive than men union leaders of organizational benefits and policies to help employees with their family responsibilities (Martin et al. 1988). Women's workplace problems—for example sexual harassment—are different from men's and less likely to be covered by the provisions of union contracts (Gwartney-Gibbs and Lach 1993).

CLUW contributed to the development of a feminist labor agenda in different ways. First, CLUW supported issues like child care or dependent care that had been previously neglected by both the women's movement and the labor movement.[1] Second, CLUW supported issues new to both labor and feminism, like pay equity. Third, CLUW framed feminist issues like sexual harassment and reproductive rights as labor issues and thus made them part of the union agenda. CLUW employed frame alignment processes in which individual and social movement organization (SMO) interpretative orientations were linked, "such that some set of individual interests, values, and beliefs, and SMO activities, goals, and ideology are congruent and complementary" (Snow et al. 1986:464). Four such processes—which serve to broaden the constituency of a movement or movement organization—can be distinguished: frame bridging, frame amplification, frame extension, and frame transformation. CLUW employed frame bridging and frame extension in particular, as I will show with respect to reproductive rights and sexual harassment. Fourth, CLUW highlighted the gender dimensions of labor issues (for example, occupational health and safety, NAFTA, labor law reform, health care reform) as women's concerns.

CLUW was more successful in some areas than in others. In general, it was more successful if an issue could be used as an organizing tool and less if it threatened union solidarity. Some issues, like child care, became safer, while others, like sexual harassment, remained delicate. In each of these cases, by highlighting women's concerns CLUW contributed to the gender-mainstreaming—that is, making gender issues a part of regular politics—of the labor movement and thus to agenda-broadening and coalition-building between the women's movement and the labor movement.

Naming is an organizing activity since the direction of an activity depends on the particular ways in which objects are classified (Strauss 1959). For example, as long as reproductive rights are framed as a women's issue, the labor movement has no reason to become active on behalf of it. If, however, the issue is perceived as a labor issue, labor unions have good reason to take it on. Unions engage in coalitions and expect support for labor issues from progressive groups like NOW and the NAACP. One can then expect the labor movement to join progressive groups to support women's and civil rights issues. Indeed, labor unions have supported the civil rights movement, for example, the 1963 March on Washington. In addition, union women were active in the President's Commission of the Status of Women and in the formation of NOW (Rupp and Taylor 1987). After initial conflicts, the labor movement supported the Equal Rights Amendment and thus the women's movement.

CLUW can therefore be seen as a bridging organization since it contributed to coalition-building between the women's movement and the labor movement and to broadening the agenda of both movements. Such bridging work included reconciling contrasting positions in cases where the labor and feminist movement had opposing views, for example with respect to protective legislation, support for the Equal Rights Amendment or affirmative action, and seniority rights. While the labor movement endorsed seniority rights and protective legislation as hard-won rights for workers, the women's movement criticized these policies and practices as discriminating against women.

As a bridging organization, CLUW contributed to coalitions and alliances between the women's movement and the labor movement. Framing issues as a common concern is crucial for political success. For example, when day care workers in West Berlin went on strike in 1989, their struggle was framed as a workers' concern rather than a women's concern (Ferree and Roth 1998). Thus the labor movement—and not the feminist movement or women politicians—felt responsible for the strike and neglected the gender dimension. Although the strike of the day care workers was truly a women's concern, the day care workers made it possible for mothers to go to work and earn the low wages typical for women's work. The failure of the strike was partly due to the fact that effective coalition-building and institutionalized communication between the women's movement and the labor movement was lacking. Such institutionalized communication as can be provided by bridging organizations like CLUW did not take place. Even in cases where success in bringing a women's issue onto the labor agenda is limited, bridging work is important because it lays the ground work for future collaborations. It challenges "exclusive" solidarity—prioritizing one issue, like class—and contributes to "inclusive" solidarity, addressing the interrelatedness of class and gender (Ferree and Roth 1998).

Mesomobilization (Gerhards and Rucht 1992), which involves the participation of movement organizations that belong to a number of different movements, requires, however, not only cultural integration through framing processes but also a structural basis for mobilization by coordinating political actors. CLUW formed coalitions with women's, labor, civil rights and other social movement organizations. Members affiliated with various social and political organizations contribute to these coalitions as bridge builders and bridge leaders. Bridge builders are familiar with different movement cultures and thus can translate between different movements and movement organizations (Rose 2000). Bridge leaders serve an important function to anchor social movement activities in the community (Robnett 1997). CLUW contributed to coalition-building between labor, women's, civil rights, religious, and other groups at the national, state, and local level.

FROM CHILD CARE TO FAMILY BENEFITS

From the beginning, CLUW was active with respect to child care, which was presented by the organization as a key concern for working women. In this case, CLUW employed *frame extension*—identifying the values and interests of the labor movement and portraying feminist objectives and activities as congruent with them—to make the case that reproductive work should be addressed by workers' organizations.[2] Affordable, high-quality day care is an issue for working women that has long been neglected by both the women's movement and the labor movement. On the one hand, as long as women are primarily responsible for child care, the availability of high-quality, affordable day care is a precondition for mothers of young children to work. On the other hand, a great majority of these low-paid day care workers are women, many of them women of color.

In the United States, child care is mainly subsidized through tax breaks that mostly benefit well-to-do families, while public day care is restricted to poor families and is thus stigmatized. The unionization rate and wages of day care workers are both low. Public regulation of day care could improve both the quality of care and the wages of the day care workers. However, it would also increase costs, which hit low-income families especially hard. Since private day care meets many of the needs of working families, there is little public mobilization for public day care (Morgan 2001).[3]

CLUW supported legislation for a national child care bill (like the Mondale-Brademas proposal of the early 1970s) that would expand access to public services. CLUW members were mobilized to urge their unions and the entire labor movement to make comprehensive child care legislation a high-priority issue. In 1977, CLUW formed a child care task force and demanded from the federal government a major role in "directing and providing comprehensive, voluntary, flexible hours, bias-free, non-sexist, quality child care and development programs, including child care facilities for Federal Employees" (*CLUW News*, vol. 3, no. 2 [1977]). Federally funded child care and development programs should have "low-cost, ability to pay fee schedules that make these services accessible to all who need them, regardless of income and should provide for parent participation in their operation" (ibid).

Lobbying

In 1979, a CLUW delegation—all national officers and the chair of the child care task force—visited Sweden, France, and Israel to study public child care. The resulting study, "A Commitment to Children," pointed out that, while families "bear the most difficult burden, the entire community pays the cost of illness, failure and defeat in lost productivity, low talent and lost revenue." At the same time, the community would benefit from a child's success. Therefore, it would be only sensible that the national community assume responsibility for the child's success—as in France, Israel, and Sweden (*Commitment to Children* 1977, 1). CLUW made clear that in these countries' unions played a major role in the effort to expand facilities and improve the quality of care and called for the support of U.S. unions for such policies. Furthermore, concerning President Ford's veto of a bill to help day care centers meet federal safety and staffing standards, CLUW argued that these savings might be "wiped out by swollen welfare rolls, as working mothers are forced to give up jobs to stay home caring for children dislodged from closed day care centers and some present welfare recipients lose jobs in the centers, critics say" (*CLUW News* vol. 2 [1976]). CLUW thus argued that the lack of the public day care that was crucial for working mothers might lead to an increase in the number of welfare recipients. In 1979, *CLUW News* reported that the child care bill introduced by U.S. Representative Cardiss Collins was a direct result of the national CLUW petition of

1979. The bill called for a "national, comprehensive program of high-quality, affordable child care, including parent education, health services, and special attention to bilingual migrant and handicapped youngsters" (*CLUW News*, vol. 5 [1979]). CLUW continuously lobbied for child care bills, and testified in hearings on the Family and Medical Leave Act of 1993. As for other issues, CLUW frequently either sent telegrams to governors, senators, and representatives protesting cuts of child care services and programs or encouraged members to do so. At almost every convention, a resolution was passed calling for "good quality, affordable child care," naming the lack of a national policy on day care for working parents a "disgrace." Furthermore, CLUW warned that employer-sponsored day care could undermine the unionization of day care workers.

However, efforts to promote the cause of public child care faced a hostile political climate. The proposals for public day care in the 1970s and 1980s came in a time of "growing backlash against the welfare state, the political resurgence of neo-liberalism, and the politicization of the family and mother's employment by the New Right" (Morgan 2001:8).

Bargaining

In addition to lobbying for child care legislation, CLUW encouraged labor and management to negotiate child care programs in their collective bargaining agreements. Consequently, child care was covered in the booklet *Effective Contract Language for Union Women* (1979). This teaching and discussion guide for CLUW chapters described how a contract was written and won and made suggestions for contract language regarding child care and other issues.[4] Ten thousand copies of the booklet were distributed and in the later 1980s more bargaining contracts contained family-focused language. However, CLUW members who were not (any longer) active in the organization did not necessarily know about the bargaining language CLUW provided. One respondent stated: "I would love to have language submitted to me on bargaining—what issues do I need to cover in actual language to bargain a day care privilege, in some way in a contract."

CLUW argued that public day care became an increasingly important issue with the rise of female labor force participation and the changing family, but from the beginning, day care was framed as a concern not only for women, but for the entire family. CLUW stated its commitment to "strengthen family life by providing parents and children with the security of excellent care which they can afford while they work, study or even take a break from the rigors of housework and child rearing" (*CLUW News*, vol. 3, no. 1 [1977]). CLUW rejected the notion that (a) all women are mothers, and (b) only women are responsible for child care.

In 1990 CLUW issued a new guide that significantly broadened the issue of child care to dependent care: *Bargaining for Family Benefits: A Union Mem-*

ber's Guide (1990). This time the authors could draw on contract clauses that had been put into actual practice. It addressed flexible work policies including paid leave, providing child care, elder care, additional new parent benefits, and the working conditions and unionization of child care workers. The guide presented CLUW as the "only national organization for union women" (p. vi), and addressed itself to "the millions of working women and men of the 1990's who want their union's contracts to help them balance the demands of work with their family responsibilities." CLUW did not single out day care workers as a specific group that needed to be organized. Some members, in particular the rebellious daughters, however, were especially interested in organizing day care workers. Due to the small work sites, day care workers are more difficult to organize than worksites with many workers.

Framing Child Care as a Labor Issue

CLUW members used the example of day care to illustrate that issues can be framed as a union issue or as a women's issue. As one of the respondents stated: "Right, [child care] becomes a union issue, even though within a larger scheme it would be considered a women's issue." Day care became an accepted issue in the labor movement. Another respondent recalled:

Day care. We used to have fights over day care. We once had a conference sponsored by the AFL–CIO about day care where the men on the planning committee disagreed with the women because the women wanted to have day care provided at the day care-conference and the men didn't want it. [laughs] We had a fight over day care at a day care-conference! Now they never fight with us over it, because they understand that they have to [support it].[5]

Through frame extension, CLUW argued that child care is an issue of concern to workers, CLUW introduced this issue onto the labor agenda and provided union members—men and women—with bargaining language for dependent care. The organization of day care and the gendered labor division is at the core of gender relations. Through supporting public and paid day care, CLUW opened up work that for a long time has been private and unpaid at home for women. CLUW pointed to European welfare states as models for high-quality, affordable day care that is federally regulated and subsidized. The organization furthermore stressed that Western European unions support public day care and thus recognize it as a labor issue. Furthermore, as long as public day care does not find public support, negotiating for day care in bargaining contracts is even more important.

PAY EQUITY

With respect to pay equity or comparable worth, CLUW engaged in *frame bridging*. The organization contributed to the diffusion of information. Pay equity or comparable worth is of broad significance for both the women's movement and the labor movement and is of crucial importance for low-paid women workers, in particular in the public sector (Blum 1991). Because pay equity addresses the way gender is incorporated into the class structure (Acker 1989), it helped to broaden both movements and mobilize women workers who previously have been neglected by both movements.

Information Dissemination

While pay equity was from the beginning a labor as well as a women's and civil rights issue, CLUW helped disseminate information about pay equity within the labor movement. In 1976, CLUW was among several women's organizations, civil rights organizations, and labor unions that co-founded the National Committee on Pay Equity (NCPE). CLUW's president Gloria Johnson chaired NCPE in 1994, and several CLUW vice-presidents represented their unions on the committee. Through the newsletter, at chapter meetings, at conferences, and at national meetings of the organization, CLUW members were informed about pay equity and asked to disseminate this information further in their unions as well as women's and civil rights organizations.

CLUW chapters and national meetings offered a space where union women could meet members from other locals or unions and exchange information and experiences. For example, members of a pay equity negotiation team in Connecticut had all been active CLUW members at some point and knew other team members through CLUW. One member of the master evaluation committee recalls:

It just was a long, long struggle and again we get back to CLUW and its value because it puts the bug in people's ear. And it gives you the incentive to continue. Because this was done in steps. It was not all done at once. We would do the first part of it. And then we would forget it for a year or two. And then you would go to a CLUW conference where they were talking, "Oh, gosh, my goodness, we did do something about that. So let's go back and look at it again."

CLUW thus kept the members of the negotiating team informed about pay equity and sustained its involvement. Some members participated in the committee from 1977 (in a hearing on pay equity at the state capitol) until the pay equity negotiations were completed in 1994.

Another respondent, a long-time staff member of the AFL–CIO, believed that CLUW contributed to making pay equity a labor issue. She observed that the labor movement at the national level was in the beginning, very wary of the pay equity issue. They did not understand, they thought they would be liable, and if you read the resolutions of the AFL–CIO on pay equity you would see that each year each convention got a little bit stronger, it started not very strong and it got stronger, stronger, stronger. So in terms of broadening the issue and making it a trade union issue, I think CLUW played a critical role.

The reluctance of the unions was understandable because (as the respondent mentioned) they would be liable for signing discriminating contracts.

Organizing Tool

Comparable worth became an organizing tool for some unions, for example, the American Federation of State, County, and Municipal Employees (AFSCME) (Blum 1991; Flammang 1987). Through its educational conferences, fact sheets and other information material, and participation in labor, legal, and political action, CLUW contributed to the dissemination of pay equity information beyond the unions that were already active in this respect. Moreover, in labor unions that supported pay equity this information was not always available in all parts of the organization, since support for concerns of women and minorities within AFSCME depends on the constituency of locals (Riccucci 1990) and various levels of the union. Thus participation in CLUW benefited even members of a union like AFSCME, which is nationally in the forefront for pay equity.

While pay equity campaigns served as an organizing tool for AFSCME, CLUW helped draw attention to this issue throughout the labor movement and contributed to spreading the experiences AFSCME created among women who belonged to different unions.

Legal and Political Action

In terms of legal and political action, CLUW did more on pay equity than on child care. In 1978, CLUW's counsel Winn Newman[6] testified during hearings of the House Subcommittee on Employment Opportunities, criticizing the failure of the Equal Employment Opportunity Commission to file comparable worth lawsuits. Newman represented the industrial union IUE (vs. Westinghouse) and the public sector union AFSCME (vs. the state of Washington) in early pay equity suits that were settled out of court. In another case, after several months of negotiations between AFSCME Local 101 and the city government of San Jose, 1,700 of the 2,000 workers of the local went on strike (cf. Blum 1991). After nine days a settlement was reached in which the workers won $1.45 million compensation for pay equity over two years, the upgrade of 62 job categories, and other demands. In contrast to the comparable worth effort in the state of Washington, the negotiated pay equity policies were actually implemented in San Jose (Flammang 1987).

CLUW's long-standing support for pay equity also had limits. At the Seventh Biennial Convention (1993) there was considerable debate on a resolution that asked CLUW members to pledge not to vote or campaign for a candidate who did not support pay equity and to ask their unions and labor councils as well as women's and other organizations not to endorse such candidates. Some delegates rejected the suggestion to make pay equity a litmus test for the endorsements of candidates for political elections, who might "be supporting 95% of our issues" (meaning "labor issues"). It was therefore suggested that the resolution be softened to asking labor councils "to make the support of pay equity an important criterion for the endorsement of candidates." This suggestion was rejected by others who saw the amendment not as a single issue, but as an umbrella issue that affects all aspects of women's lives. They argued that unless CLUW was serious about pay equity and got the support from the unions, union women would never have equity or equality. One delegate spoke against the amendment, because "it violates everything that CLUW was founded on. It's like being a little bit pregnant. If you don't go the whole . . . forget it, let's go for pay equity."

After an extensive discussion the resolution was amended and passed, so the stronger version lost. Although the resolution supported pay equity and urged labor organizations to support this issue, pay equity did not become a litmus test for the endorsement of candidates. This situation is, however, not unusual for union politics: As one of the delegates who spoke in support of the amendment pointed out, other labor issues like the striker replacement bill or the North American Free Trade Agreement also did not serve as litmus tests. Such litmus tests would harm the fight for these issues more than help them. Rather than threatening candidates, the delegate suggested lobbying legislators. With the decision to adopt the amended resolution, the delegates again affirmed CLUW's position as an insider organization in the labor movement. In order not to alienate the unions, CLUW did not prioritize its strong stance. Even though pay equity was acknowledged as a labor issue, CLUW avoided taking a critical stance of a candidate endorsed by the unions. According to the membership survey, a great majority of the membership felt that CLUW should pursue pay equity more energetically.

FRAME EXTENSION: SEXUAL HARASSMENT IN THE WORKPLACE

CLUW's approach toward sexual harassment was ambivalent due to its position as a bridging organization that aimed to be accountable to both the women's movement and the labor movement. CLUW employed frame extension processes in order to include sexual harassment as one grievance among others covered by the union contract.

Sexual harassment is defined as "unwanted sexual behavior that interferes with a person's ability to conduct her[7] work or acquire an education, regardless of whether the person was the intended target" (Rundblad 2001: 353). This means that from a legal point of view it is context- and situation-specific. It is estimated that 50% of women can expect to encounter sexual harassment in education or the workplace. Two main kinds of sexual harassment can be distinguished. One is a "quid pro quo"—direct give or take when a person in power uses that power as a threat to a subordinate. The other is a "hostile environment" when the workplace or educational setting is permeated with sexual behaviors that are intimidating. Despite its prevalence, sexual harassment has only recently found public attention and is generally underreported. The term "sexual harassment" was coined in the 1970s (Brownmiller and Alexander 1999). The Thomas-Hill case in 1991 contributed to the wide publicization of the issue (Rundblad 2001). Since it is so widespread and affects a large proportion of working women, it provides an excellent organizing tool, one that was used, for example, by the working women's organization Nine-to-Five (Zippel 2000).

Bargaining, Information Dissemination, Political Action

CLUW took the feminist issue of sexual harassment and used labor strategies to solve this workplace problem of women workers. When sexual harassment is framed as a conflict between employers and employees, it becomes a union issue, union language can be developed, and the issue can be covered in bargaining contracts and grievances. The bargaining guide "Effective Contract Language for Union Women" (1979) did not cover sexual harassment, but in the year of its release it was resolved that CLUW should develop educational materials and model contract language addressing sexual harassment (*CLUW News*, vol. 5, no. 1 [1979]). In 1986, the CLUW Center for Education and Research published the report "Sexual Harassment: An Ongoing Barrier to Equal Opportunity."[8]

Sexual harassment was regularly addressed during Working Women's Awareness Week, first held in 1986. Respondents also found the workshops on national meetings very helpful. One AFSCME member stated:

I think we really get our money's worth out of the workshops that they hold. . . . It helps a lot for those of us who go back. . . . When I say we bring the people who are active, they are mostly stewards who are working with the grievance procedure, or who are responsible for making sure that everything in the work site is fine. And so it is good for us to know that sex harassment does not have to be the serious kind of sexual harassment but that it can be anything that would be offensive to another person.

Aside from organizing conferences and putting out information material, CLUW testified and submitted *amicus curiae* briefs to the U.S. Supreme Court. Furthermore, it launched a Sexual Harassment Hotline in 1986. However, more than 80% of the members felt that CLUW should pursue sexual harassment action more energetically (CLUW membership survey).

Sexual Harassment within Unions

While addressing sexual harassment in the workplace represents an organizing tool for unions and fosters union solidarity, addressing sexual harassment in the unions would undermine union solidarity.[9] CLUW therefore addressed sexual harassment in the unions informally, not openly. For example, one of the members pointed out that CLUW was not prepared to support her and respond appropriately when she experienced sexual harassment in her union. She recalled that

they couldn't help me. . . . I don't know if it was official policy or what. But they were not equipped to deal with discrimination within the unions. . . . I expected there to be a system set up within CLUW to pressure unions that were discriminating against women. I expected them to be an advocate for women within unions. Not necessarily an enemy, and not necessarily something that was destructive, but at a minimum I expected CLUW to be an advocate for women who were being discriminated against.

If CLUW had openly addressed sexual harassment in the unions, it would have been perceived as an attack on union solidarity and unity. Unions represent both the harasser and the victim. It can also happen that a female shop steward has to defend a male harasser. Sexual harassment in the labor movement was informally addressed at meetings of the National Officers' Council, the National Executive Board, or chapter meetings, which offered members opportunities to exchange experiences and seek support and advice. Chapter members informed each other about cases of sexual harassment or wrote individual letters to the editor of local newspapers. Because CLUW chapters represented a number of unions and because CLUW saw itself as part of the labor movement, the organization did not single out and criticize a union for condoning sexual harassment since such criticism would have been understood as divisive within the labor movement. Instead CLUW members addressed such issues not as representatives of CLUW, but as individual labor union women who expressed their concern for instance through writing letters to local newspapers (field notes).

In 1989 Joyce Miller protested against sexism at the AFL–CIO Executive Council meeting, "during which a number of women clad in (literally) postage-stamp bikinis posed for pictures with participants" (*CLUW News*, vol. 15, no. 2 [1989]). Miller's protest characterizing the situation as "outrageous" was ridiculed and led to the classic sexist, "feminists have no sense of humor" response. The incident was discussed at a meeting of the NEB. One delegate, who supported CLUW's president's action, argued that if she had not done so she "'would have made a mockery of what we stand for and what we believe in. We stand and support you and are proud of you!', she told Miller, as the delegates surged to their feet with applause and cheers. 'You spoke on behalf of all of us.'" This episode indicates that fifteen years after the founding of CLUW the consciousness of the AFL–CIO Executive Board had not been raised enough to abstain from sexist behavior or to be embarrassed when called on it. Furthermore, the reaction of the NEB delegates indicates that criticizing the labor federation required legitimization and approval from the members of the NEB. CLUW was torn between its loyalty to the labor federation and its accountability to feminist principles. CLUW would have lost credibility as a "women's movement" in the labor movement if it had not protested. However, by criticizing the labor movement from a feminist perspective, CLUW risked being seen as "divisive" or being ridiculed by the AFL–CIO.

Risks of Addressing Sexual Harassment in the Labor Movement

There is a key distinction between supporting sexual harassment action against employers and against unions. Criticizing employers and mobilizing sexual harassment prevention at the workplace fosters union solidarity by emphasizing the conflict between workers and employers. In contrast, addressing sexual harassment within the labor movement brings out a gender conflict within the organization and thus threatens to undermine its unity. Criticism of the AFL–CIO leadership was possible because the action was highly symbolic, visible, and involved the leadership.

The example of sexual harassment shows the dilemmas of bridging organizations very neatly. On the one hand, sexual harassment serves as an organizing tool and signals to women that labor unions take on their issues. On the other hand, addressing sexism in the labor movement can be seen as undermining union solidarity. CLUW thus constantly had to fight with an "exclusive" solidarity that asked to put labor issues first, while the organization was striving for "inclusive" solidarity, addressing labor, gender, and other issues simultaneously without prioritizing one.

The fact that CLUW did not address sexual harassment in unions openly—with the exception of the AFL–CIO incident—emphasized CLUW's role as insider organization. However, despite these shortcomings, CLUW contributed to the dissemination of information regarding sexual harassment. Here CLUW was strongly supported by the public sector union AFSCME. Furthermore, CLUW invited the working women's organization Nine-to-Five, which was very active with respect to sexual harassment, to conferences, thus building coalitions with other working women's organizations.

REPRODUCTIVE RIGHTS

Reproductive rights had been on CLUW's agenda since the late 1970s. Employing frame extension, CLUW interpreted reproductive rights very broadly, arguing that reproductive rights are a health issue that concerns men as well as women. Furthermore, CLUW addressed the violation of bargaining rights and class issues with respect to the access to abortion. In the United States, the struggle for birth control reaches back to the nineteenth century and has not always had an easy relationship with feminism. Although early feminists recognized the importance of birth control for women's freedom, not all birth control activists were feminists and not all feminists were birth control activists. It was especially problematic that birth control activism was closely related to racism and classism, seeking to produce "better" babies (Rushing 2001:450). In 1973 *Roe v. Wade* made abortion legal, but it was soon challenged by the right-to-life movement. While abortion was initially framed not as a feminist issue but as an issue of individual rights, it became more and more a feminist issue (Ferree et al. 2002).

Reproductive Rights: Occupational Health and Safety, and Sex Discrimination

Reproductive hazards were first addressed in the context of occupational health and safety and sex discrimination. CLUW's Occupational Health and Safety Task Force argued that exclusionary employment placement policies discriminated against women, and that lead exposure was detrimental to both male and female reproductive systems. Therefore, health standards on the job should be extended to male workers and "women must lead the fight to defeat this new attempt to force women out of industrial jobs" (*CLUW News*, vol. 5, no. 1 [1979]). In this way, reproductive rights were framed as a health and workers' issue. At the same time, CLUW took up established labor issues like occupational health and safety and highlighted the gender dimension linking it to reproductive rights.

CLUW suggests sensitizing and educating men about reproductive health hazards and frames the problems of reproductive freedom, job segregation, and protective legislation as "worker's issues," rather than "women's issues." CLUW argued that reproductive rights issues had so far not received enough attention and were relevant for both male and female workers and thus had to be taken on by the labor movement. "Reproductive risks are a real problem, demanding real solutions, not the diversionary ones personified by discriminatory job practices" (*CLUW News*, vol. 5, no. 1 [1979]:4).

In 1989 CLUW filed an *amicus curiae* brief in *UAW v. Johnson Controls*, supporting the UAW, which argued that the denial of battery production jobs to all fertile women under the fetal protection policy constituted sex discrimination. CLUW argued that lead exposure is dangerous not only for fertile women, but for workers, fertile or not, and suggested that the "only fair and scientifically sound solution is to eliminate the hazard—not women—from the work place" (*CLUW News*, vol. 16, no. 2 [1990]).

Discrimination through exclusionary workplace policies was identified as a conflict between management and workers rather than between men and women. CLUW "will serve to unite all workers and progressive groups behind the struggle to reduce occupational exposures to toxic substances to levels that are safe for all workers, regardless of reproductive capacity" (*CLUW News*, vol. 5, no. 1 [1979]: 4). CLUW thus framed reproductive freedom and workplace equality as an issue of the labor movement and all workers, rather than one specific group—women. Drawing on an equality frame is typical for the U.S. abortion discourse (Ferree et al. 2002).

Attack on Bargaining Rights

The Hyde Amendment (1981) prohibiting all federal health plans covering abortions not only restricted reproductive rights but also constituted an interference with collective bargaining, against which CLUW protested. Working together with public sector unions, CLUW wanted to make sure that "this is a labor issue" (*CLUW News*, vol. 7, no. 3 [1981]). In contrast to reproductive health hazards, CLUW did not have to raise the consciousness of the unions that the violation of bargaining rights is a "union issue" (*CLUW News*, vol. 7, no. 4 [1981]), and thus mobilize union solidarity on behalf of women. An attack on collective bargaining is a core concern of the labor movement. In a statement responding to the announcement that cuts would be imposed in the government employees' health program to eliminate benefits including abortion coverage and some dental and mental health payments, President Miller declared: "But it is a clear statement by the messengers of a self-interested, elitist and male-dominated administration that if sacrifices are to be made, they want them to be made by the working women of this nation—and that is both shocking and outrageous" (*CLUW News*, vol. 7, no. 5 [1981]). Abortion was thus presented as a workers' union issue with special concern to women. The *CLUW News* reported that the protests of unions representing federal employees "and groups like CLUW" were successful in leading to the restoration of existing abortion coverage (*CLUW News*, vol. 7, no. 6 [1981]).

In testimony in 1982 before the Senate Subcommittee on the Constitution in hearings on a proposed Constitutional amendment that would allow states to ban all abortions, CLUW framed abortion as an economic and moral issue. "Tens of thousands of working women—wives and mothers and single heads of families—believe pregnancy and 'choice' can make the difference between economic survival or disaster for their families" (*CLUW News*, vol. 8, no. 1 [1982]). Restricting women's reproductive rights was framed as part of a strategy to maintain women as a marginal workforce. Rather than legislating on a moral basis, the Senate should commit itself to protecting the lives and welfare of America's working women and their children. Furthermore, excluding abortion as a medical option in private, bargained-for health coverage was rejected as "intrusion into the area of collective bargaining." Again, the economic rights of women workers were framed as "workers' issues," "union issues," and "women's issues"—reproductive rights are of special concern to women workers, which had to be defended by unions.

Furthermore, CLUW president Joyce Miller linked the "right to life" rhetoric to the labor-hostile "right to work" legislation.[10] "We all know that 'right to work' is an incomplete expression that really means the right to work for less— less pay, less benefits, less dignity. It is a terribly one-sided and unfair concept. So is 'right to life,' because it totally ignores the rights of one partner in the equation: the prospective mother" (*CLUW News*, vol. 15, no. 5 [1989]: 2). Miller argued that when "freedom is unjustly taken from one member of our society, a little freedom is taken from everyone," making the case that pro-choice "affects all of us." Choice is thus not a private trouble of an individual woman, but a public problem that concerns the entire society and in this case the entire labor movement. In linking the "right to life" to the "right to work"—a central concern of the labor movement, and reminding listeners that "an injury to one is an injury to all"—the theme of the militant Industrial Workers of the World (Wobblies)—Miller drew on labor phrases and symbolism to convey that reproductive rights were a labor issue. Miller urged CLUW chapters and individual CLUW members to support the pro-choice position, arguing that they were supporting a union issue. "We must continue to get the message out, that a woman's right to make decisions affecting her own body should not be interfered with by the government. This position is absolutely consistent with the union movement's defense of the constitutional right to privacy. Reproductive rights and access to family planning by all is a union issue" (*CLUW News*, vol. 15, no. 6 [1989]).

CLUW also condemned the "Gag Rule"—the U.S. Supreme Court decision of May 1991 upholding government regulations that prohibit family planning clinics that receive federal funds from telling patients about the option of abortion. CLUW criticized this rule as creating unequal opportunities for those who cannot afford a private physician and sets a dangerous precedent in subjecting medical advice to political pressure (*CLUW News*, vol. 17, no. 4 [1991]: 4).

Labor Support for Abortion Rights

A survey the Reproductive Rights Project conducted among members of five CLUW chapters[11] revealed that a large majority of CLUW believed that abortion should be legal (90%) and supported the use of public funds for abortion (82%). Parental (71%) and spousal (83%) consent was rejected, and the availability of the abortion pill RU 486 was supported (89%) (*CLUW News*, vol. 19, no. 2 [1993]). These findings were supported through the membership survey, where 86% of the respondents agreed with the statement: "Abortion should be available to any woman who wants one." However, some members found that the pro-choice position CLUW took at the national level was in some states an obstacle to chapter level recruitment. One of the respondents wrote, "Abortion is too hot an issue for CLUW, it's too divisive. And all the emphasis on it—hurts CLUW." Here, race differences have to be taken into account—about a quarter of the white members of CLUW but a smaller percentage of the women of color were involved in NARAL (CLUW membership survey).

Although several international unions affiliated with the labor federation support a pro-choice position, CLUW had not been successful in convincing the AFL–CIO to endorse a pro-choice resolution. CLUW members regretted that the AFL–CIO did not support reproductive rights and maintained a neutral position. However, CLUW members used the example of the divergent positions of CLUW and the AFL–CIO on reproductive rights to illustrate their independence from the labor federation. Thus CLUW presented the failure to convince the AFL–CIO to endorse a pro-choice position as a proof of autonomy of the organization from the AFL–CIO.

Lobbying and Coalition-Building with the Pro-Choice Movement

In 1990, CLUW formed the Reproductive Rights Project to support lobbying against the U.S. Supreme Court's decision in *Webster v. Reproductive Health Services*, in order to fight government intervention in women's reproductive freedom. A representative from NARAL stated that CLUW's support for reproductive rights was important for the pro-choice movement. She appreciated CLUW's participation in the State Strategy Task Force:

I think it is a very positive organizational step and a very positive organizational commitment to reproductive rights and then to disseminate that information to their members and have them actually lobby. You know, not just be supportive and know that x number of members of CLUW are pro-choice, but these members are willing to stand up and speak out. So that when they go into a state or a federal legislators office, they are identified a) as labor, but b) as pro-choice labor and that's a powerful organizational message to begin to send.

CLUW provided members with organizing and lobbying skills for the pro-choice movement. Even more important is the fact that, rather than being a "white-middle-class" organization, CLUW represented working-class women and women of color. CLUW addressed reproductive rights as a health care issue that was relevant for both men and women. The organization also pointed out that the decision of Congress to forbid abortion coverage in the health care plans of federal employees was a violation of bargaining rights. CLUW was not successful in convincing the AFL–CIO to endorse a pro-choice position. Furthermore, although the majority of the membership supported a pro-choice position, some members thought that the issue was divisive and that CLUW put too much emphasis on it. As a national organization of working women, CLUW presented an important ally for pro-choice organization.

BRIDGING WORK AND COALITION-BUILDING

As a bridging organization, CLUW broadened the agenda of the women's movement and the labor movement in several respects. First, CLUW introduced child care, which had been previously neglected by both the women's movement and the labor movement. Second, CLUW helped disseminate information about pay equity, which was new to both movements. Third, CLUW framed sexual harassment and reproductive rights, an issue of special concern to women workers, as a labor issue by focusing on social rights and collective bargaining. Fourth, CLUW took union issues like occupational health and safety and applied them to issues like reproductive rights.

CLUW's framing work is an excellent example of gender mainstreaming, that is, highlighting the gender dimension of issues and transforming "women's issues" from a special concern to an issue that is of relevance to all members of the labor movement. In general, CLUW was successful in pursuing these issues if they could be used as organizing tools (child care, pay equity, sexual harassment). The achievement of these issues was limited if they supposedly threatened union solidarity (sexual harassment in unions) or if other issues were considered more important (endorsement of pay equity only if a candidate supports other labor issues). But even if CLUW did not win the support of the AFL–CIO for specific issues (like reproductive rights), CLUW members and chapters provided a large network that disseminated feminist issues among working-class women. As a bridging organization, CLUW brought labor issues onto the agenda of the women's movement and women's issues onto the labor agenda. Changes in these movements thus came about through interaction between movements and movement organizations through multiple memberships and coalitions.

Coalition between Social Movement Organizations

CLUW was part of coalitions with unions, civil rights organizations, and women's organizations. It was part of the National Committee on Pay Equity (a coalition of labor, women's, and civil rights organizations) and the Council of Presidents (a coalition of feminist organizations) as well as the NARAL State Task Force. In addition, CLUW participated in events of the women's movement and the labor movement, for example, conferences like "Workplace 2000" in 1995, which was co-sponsored by CLUW in collaboration with the Institute for Women of Work at Cornell University and the Institute for Women's Policy Research.

CLUW also invited representatives of this coalition to its meetings. CLUW's national conferences were addressed by presidents of labor unions, politicians, and representatives of women's and civil rights organizations. Although the presidents of NOW addressed CLUW conventions and meetings, so far, male union leaders have dominated, and the majority of the speakers were older white men. International guests at CLUW's Seventh Biennial Convention found it peculiar that the convention of a women's organization would be addressed by so many men (field notes). While the national leadership did not want to reject the (male) leadership of the labor movement, it also wanted to strengthen CLUW's relationship to women's organizations and to increase the number of women guest speakers. At one conference under the presidency of Gloria Johnson, union presidents were invited to participate in a panel rather than giving individual addresses. At the same time more women's organizations than before were invited.

Some of the biggest women's groups are not really active participants, like NOW for example. . . . I think CLUW did not seek out women from the women's movement, to address our meetings, although we might co-sponsor all kinds of things together. But at this next convention that's not the case. They are asking women, we are asking women from all of the big women's organizations to come and address the convention rather than a bunch of old union presidents [laughs]. If we have the labor union presidents, then it will be one panel [laughs], together, and we will get it all over with at once.

CLUW thus actively sought to strengthen relationships with women's organizations while maintaining relationships with the unions. Moreover, since John Sweeney became president of the AFL–CIO, some women assumed top leadership positions in the labor federation. Consequently, the AFL–CIO was now represented by female union leaders at CLUW conventions. Speakers at CLUW conventions thus include AFL–CIO officers and representatives of AFL–CIO support groups (A. Philip Randolph Institute, Asian Pacific Labor Alliance, Frontlash, and Labor Council for Latin American Advancement) and the Coalition of Black Trade Unionists, and also women's organizations (National Committee on Pay Equity, Mexican American Women's National Association, Wider Opportunities for Women, and the National Council of Negro Women).

At the national level, CLUW participated in nationwide conferences and events. In 1986, CLUW co-sponsored the event "National March for Women's Lives," which was organized by the National Organization for Women. In her address to the over 100,000 participants of the march, CLUW president Joyce Miller emphasized that losing the right to control their bodies "pulls women back to the lowest-paying, dead-end jobs," thus framing reproductive rights as an economic issue of particular concern to women workers. In the same speech, she addressed pay equity, criticized amendments to the Civil Rights Restoration Act, and stated, "We must denounce these amendments for what they are, the efforts of white males who refuse to give up the privilege of gender and skin color" (*CLUW News*, vol. 12, no. 2 [1986]: 1). Miller thus used this event—organized by a women's movement organization—to address economic and civil rights issues.

Two years later, in Seattle in 1988, Molly Yard, President of the National Organization for Women, addressed CLUW's Fifth Biennial Convention, attacking the Reagan-Bush administration for its attempts to persuade the Supreme Court to overturn *Roe v. Wade* (*CLUW News*, vol. 14, no. 6 [1988]:2). In the same year CLUW initiated the American Family Celebration—an event sponsored by a coalition of women's, labor, religious, civil rights, and children's rights organizations— which called for a comprehensive national family policy including family and medical leave, quality child care, services for the elderly, comprehensive health care, and equity in quality education. Among the 162 organizations participating in the event were the AFL–CIO, the NAACP, NOW, the National Women's Political Caucus, the National Council of Churches, and unions. Fifty thousand participants rallied in Washington, D.C. (*CLUW News*, vol. 14, no.3 [1988]).

CLUW joined various coalitions like the Coalition for Reproductive Freedom 1979, supported the Mobilization for Women's Lives across America, organized by the National Pro-Choice Coalition, and is represented in NARAL's State Task Force through the CLUW Center for Education and Research. CLUW collaborated with feminist organizations like the National Women's Political Caucus, the Institute for Women's Policy Research, and the Institute for Women and Work. CLUW received financial support not only from the unions and the AFL–CIO but also from feminist organizations like the Ms. Foundation.

Since Johnson became president, the CLUW national office has moved from New York City to Washington, D.C.[12] This made it easier for CLUW officers to meet and network with other organizations, given that the majority of national unions, women's movement organizations, and other agencies are located in Washington. But CLUW engaged not only at the national level in coalition-building with labor, women, and other social movement organizations but also at the state and chapter level. The involvement of chapters in coalitions depended not only on the network connections of the chapter officers and active members, but also on the environment of the chapter—a city or rural area, a region with strong labor presence, or a right-to-work state.[13] In larger cities, such as New York ("union city USA"), it was not difficult for the chapter to engage in a wide variety of activities and coalitions. Some state AFL–CIOs had a women's committee or a women's and civil rights committee with which CLUW chapters could cooperate (or compete). Chapters cooperated with unions, the AFL–CIO, civil rights groups, women's groups, and political groups, as well as community service organizations.

Some of the chapter members had connections with organizations of the women's movement, the civil rights movement, and other social movements.

Through these connections chapter presidents were informed about current developments in the community and were able to invite activists of other movement organizations to participate in chapter activities. As discussed in Chapter 6, chapters led by rank-and-file members or retirees tended to be less active than chapters led by officers and staff members. Retirees had time for the chapter but sometimes lacked connections to the labor movement and other social movements. Their positions in the union were marginal. Conversely, staff members and officers sometimes lacked the time needed for the chapter because they were overcommitted.

Depending on the interests of the leadership and membership of the chapter, chapters participated in a variety of activities. Chapters were more likely to participate in labor-oriented activities, such as supporting of union strikes or events of the labor council or state federation of labor, than in activities sponsored by women's and civil rights organizations. But it was not unusual for CLUW chapters to be involved in coalitions and events, such as the International Women's Year, the League of Women Voters, the National Women's Political Caucus, and umbrella groups of women's and civil rights organizations.

Some members were involved in a variety of social movements and social movement organizations and therefore were able to recruit speakers to CLUW event and initiate coalitions between CLUW and other groups. Such coalition-building was not without conflicts. One respondent described how, in order to create solidarity among a diverse group of women, she would first address uncontroversial issues to which they could all relate, and then turn to more contested issues in order to achieve mutual understanding.

Shaping the Labor Movement and the Women's Movement

Although respondents from the labor movement downplayed major differences between the women's movement and the labor movement, they pointed out that, except for the lack of the AFL–CIO taking a pro-choice position, CLUW has contributed to bringing the two movements closer together. A staff member of the AFL–CIO recalled that when she became active in the labor movement there was a wide gap.

When I first came on, the labor movement and the women's movement were like this [indicates a wide gap with her arms]. I mean I did not go to a NOW meeting or anything. And that has changed tremendously. And I feel that CLUW was the one that was the real bridge that brought them together. So of course that kind of activity increased, because before I wouldn't have gone to it. I would not say I would not have been allowed to, but it was not our policy to coalesce much with NOW and women's organizations. And all that has changed completely.

These changes came about via interaction between these movements and movement organizations through multiple memberships, coalitions, and the work of bridging organizations. CLUW was credited with bringing the AFL–CIO to support women's issues, such as the equal rights amendment, and the women's movement to support labor issues, like labor law reform. Several representatives of the women's movement credited CLUW with educating women who were not active in the labor movement about labor law and labor law reform. One respondent who belonged to a feminist organization explained:

And we felt that a lot of the women's movement—defined very broadly—did not know anything about labor law. Did not know much about labor law, much less labor law reform. So that part of what we saw ourselves as doing was trying to develop some educational material. The CLUW women knew it backwards and forwards, but [were] trying to get that shared and trying to get the women's organizations supportive so that we could get testified before that Dunlop Commission[14] independently of the labor movement.

As a consequence of this sharing of information and knowledge, women from the women's movement and union women testified together on labor law reform. Few women in the women's movement knew about labor law, labor law reform, and its impact on women workers. It is quite likely that due to the limited exchange between the women's and labor movement, and the weakness and bad image of the labor movement, few—men or women, feminist or not—were interested in labor law reform. However, unionized workers, especially women and minorities, gained significantly through unionization (Spalter-Roth et al. 1994). The union women brought this knowledge to the coalition. CLUW was the only organization that represented women union members across unions.

Representatives of the women's movement perceived CLUW as an "important voice" because it represented the rare case of an organization representing union women.

I think we have a history of where a lot of the women's groups saw the unions as part of the problem. And in terms of women's fight for equality in the work force, the unions were part of the problem and unions could do more and second they weren't, they did not see reaching out to unions as a very high-priority, even if though they were women in the unions. And I think historically there has always been a division with union women being very much concerned about working women's issues and union women's issues and a broader array of women's issues like the ERA or reproductive choice. (field notes)

This perspective expressed the feminist view that unions were part of the problem. The expert made a distinction between "working women's issues" or "union women's issues", on the one hand, and "women's issues", on the other. CLUW activists rejected such a division between "union women's issues" or "labor issues" and "women's issues" since they framed women's issues as labor issues—and vice versa.

However, while some feminists valued CLUW as an organization as important as the women's movement, they recognized that some women in the feminist movement perceived CLUW as conservative with respect to feminism and not critical enough of their unions. Another expert representing the women's movement emphasized the gains that were connected with CLUW's choice to be an insider organization.

I think that the glory of the women's movement is that we have feminists operating inside a whole bunch of other patriarchal structures. And the labor movement is like everything else, a patriarchal structure. So I would feel that they were being stupid if they behaved like I behave. If CLUW did. Do you know what I mean? Because after all, they are very clear that they are going to transform the labor movement and thank God! I think that is the most important part of their mission. It's the same with organizations of corporate women. You know, I don't expect them to even use the F-word feminist. But I expect them to operate as feminists inside that structure, that institution, for the purpose of changing it. So I think CLUW has been remarkably successful because they are of the labor movement, they are union women. They are loyal to the union movement. And they are loyal to advancing women. It is very powerful.

This feminist expert perceived CLUW as a femocratic organization that was part of the labor movement, and not as a caucus that was formally independent. Operating as feminists inside the structure means bringing women's issues on the agenda and—by making them part of the labor agenda—transforming this agenda. This expert pointed to CLUW's successful "unobtrusive mobilization" (Katzenstein 1990) by striving for leadership positions and contributing to the advancement of women in the labor movement. CLUW as an organization and individual CLUW members were loyal to the labor movement and to feminist principles without seeing the allegiance to either one of those movements as a betrayal to the other.

CONCLUSION

CLUW influenced the women's movement and the labor movement in multiple ways. The organization provided an independent space in which members from different unions and movement organizations could meet, inform, and support each other, frame issues in a way that allowed broad coalitions, and participate in training, education, and lobbying. As an inside organization, however CLUW was more constrained by accountability to the labor movement than by accountability to feminist issues.

CLUW was a bridging organization that framed the concerns of working women as labor union as well as women's issues. CLUW argued that women's issues were workers' issues and thus engaged in gender mainstreaming. The organization provided a meeting place for representatives of the women's and labor movements as well as civil rights organization at national, state, and chapter events. CLUW officers and members also participated in labor movement events—representing a gender perspective, and women's movement events—

representing a labor perspective.

CLUW was a bridging organization that sought to connect the labor movement and the women's movement by offering chances for cooperation from which the movements and the women they organized could benefit. Since CLUW was founded, both the women's and the labor movement have changed. On the one hand, the women's movement experienced a proliferation of feminist organizations in the 1970s and 1980s that differ widely in their organizational structures (Martin 1990; Ferree and Martin 1995; Ferree and Hess 2000). On the other hand, public and private sector unions such as AFSCME and SEIU started to organize women and minorities aggressively. In addition, many unions created women's and civil rights departments.

The case study of CLUW thus suggests that social movement interaction contributes to broadening the agenda of social movements and that CLUW influenced the women's movement and the labor movement in multiple ways. The relevance of the organization then lay in providing a respectable and legitimate meeting place for women in the labor movement. Through inviting guest speakers representing the women's movement, the civil rights movement, and the political arena, members were exposed to a variety of organizations and could make contacts with their representatives. In this independent space, members from different unions and movement organizations could meet, inform and support each other, frame issues in a way that allows broad coalitions, and participate in training, education, and lobbying. Thus a bridging organization like CLUW strengthened civil society and enabled people to mobilize and improve their lives and the living conditions of their community.

NOTES

1. Some unions, like the UE, as well as the Communist Party and the Popular Front, have supported day care policies since the 1940s (Horowitz 1998; Weigand 2001).

2. Snow et. al. (1986) describe frame extension as "attempting to enlarge [the movements] adherent pool by portraying its objectives to or being congruent with the values or interests of potential adherents. The micromobilization task in such cases is the identification of the individual or aggregate level values and interests and the alignment of them with participation in movement activities" (p. 472).

3. Morgan (personal communication) has the impression that people often support the idea of more public day care when asked, but they are already meeting their own needs in the private sector. Therefore it is hard to build a campaign for more public services.

4. It covered Non-Discrimination, Comparable Pay for Work of Equal Value, Maternity Leave, Pregnancy Disability, Child Care, Fringe Benefits, and Non-sexist Language.

5. The interview took place in 1991; the respondent did not indicate when the conference took place and in what time frame the labor movement changed in her state.

6. Winn Newman was CLUW's counsel until his death in 1994. CLUW and other organizations, for instance, the National Committee on Pay Equity and Women on the Job, a non-profit agency in Long Island, New York (National Committee on Pay Equity, vol.

15, no. 2: 13) established awards and scholarships in his honor. His widow asked to donate money to CLUW in his honor.

7. Men as well as women can be victims or perpetrators of sexual harassment. However, the majority of victims are female and the majority of harassers are male.

8. The report was written by Debbie Katz, Revson Fellow under the Georgetown University Women's Law and Public Policy Fellowship Program and founder of the Wisconsin Women's Law Journal.

9. Even if one employee harasses another employee, this is not entirely unproblematic for the union, since the union represents both. Furthermore, female shop stewards might have to represent male harassers.

10. Section 14 (b) of the Labor Act allows individual states to pass laws prohibiting union security clauses, which means that they require the "open shop." In an open shop, a union represents a bargaining unit, but no worker is required to join the union or pay dues. These laws are called "right-to-work" laws (Gold 1989:14).

11. Chicago, Los Angeles, Minneapolis, New York, and Pittsburgh.

12. CLUW's national office was hosted by the union to which the CLUW's national president belonged. Joyce Miller was an officer of the Amalgamated Clothing and Textile Workers in the New York Office. Gloria Johnson worked for the IUE, which had its headquarters in Washington, D.C.

13. Right-to-work laws that prevent union organizing are mostly found in the South.

14. This commission dealt with labor law reform under the Clinton administration.

8

Conclusion

When the Coalition of Labor Union Women was founded in 1974, there was not one woman on the AFL–CIO council. In 2003, not only was CLUW's president Gloria Johnson a member of the AFL–CIO council, but the labor federation had a woman vice president and secretary-treasurer as well as a Working Women's Department—something that was deemed unthinkable and unnecessary in the 1970s. The times and the labor movement have both changed. How has CLUW contributed to changing the labor movement, the AFL–CIO, and the women's movement? What can other organizations learn from CLUW? What are the implications of these findings for social movement research? And is there something CLUW could learn?

IMPLICATIONS FOR SOCIAL MOVEMENT THEORY

CLUW as a bridging organization draws attention to social movement interaction, diffusion processes, and the integration of heterogeneous constituencies. Bridging organizations emerge through the diffusion of feminist (as well as other forms of political) consciousness and contribute to the gender (as well as other forms of) mainstreaming of institutions and policies. They build communication channels between movements and movement organizations and provide a "free" (Evans and Boyte 1986) or "independent" (Needleman 1998) space in which members find support and information. Bridging organizations are founded by those who feel accountable to multiple social and political causes and reject "exclusive" solidarity, instead striving to create inclusive solidarity (Ferree and Roth 1998). As "submerged networks" (Melucci 1989), bridging organizations engage in discursive politics (Katzenstein 1998). Rather than openly criticizing an institution, they seek to transform it from within by reframing issues and broadening agendas of movements and movement organizations that previously had little or tense contact.

Like other social movement organizations, bridging organizations are shaped by the political context in which they emerge. Their organizational form expresses their collective identity and accountability to a movement. Depending on the homogeneity or heterogeneity of organizational forms in a movement, the bridging organization may have more or less leeway in determining its structure, which is a signal to a movement about the goals it pursues. For example, the bureaucratic structure of the labor movement and the "tyranny of structurelessness" (Freeman 1984) of women's groups in the autonomous women's movement stand for different ideals. A bridging organization has to position itself not only with respect to its goals but also with respect to its structure. But the choice of an organizational form is not just pragmatic, it is also related to the "taste in tactics" (Jasper 1997) that activists form over the course of activism. Therefore, biographies of founding members of bridging organizations help to explain how a specific organizational form was chosen or negotiated.

The case of bridging organizations brings attention to the fact that movements are neither monolithic nor isolated from each other. Within movement communities and industries there is constant social movement interaction, even when movements try to ignore each other. Movements and movement organizations share and compete for resources and build coalitions. However, coalition-building requires channels of communication. Successful mobilization requires that issues are framed in a way that they are relevant for various movements or movement organizations. On the other hand, the actual contacts have to be carried out by bridge-builders, bridge-leaders, and bridging organizations. Coalitions are always important for movement success. However, globalization and immigration make successful bridging even more important.

The community organizations and social movements of immigrants show that they share the goals of social movements like the women's movement or the labor movement, but at the same time feel that their needs, interests, and culture are neglected. Immigrant movements and movement organizations thus broaden the agenda of social movements. Social movements, furthermore, have long-standing international traditions. The peace movement provides an excellent example for international organizing. Human rights organizations like Amnesty International and environmental organizations like Greenpeace as well as the protests at Seattle and Genoa provide further examples for international organizations and mobilization efforts. Like the solidarity movements with Nicaragua and South Africa, and the principled issue networks that proliferated in the past decades, they are "activists beyond borders" (Keck and Sikkink 1998). Such cross-cultural communication and collaboration requires translation or "cross-talk" (Mische 2003). Bridging organizations seek to enable the coalition and collaboration between movements. The case study of CLUW provides important insights for the integration of a diverse constituency and collaboration among different movements and movement organizations.

THE NEED FOR CLUW

The formation of CLUW was a result of the diffusion of feminist conscious-ness and an attempt to reconcile feminist and class consciousness. Labor union women who were long-time supporters of working women and the labor move-ment, but who received little acknowledgment in the labor movement, were en-couraged by the women's movement to create a women's movement in the labor movement. Activists in the women's movement who felt that the needs of work-ing-class women and women of color were not addressed by a "white-middle-class movement" turned to CLUW to merge feminism and class action and to meet the needs of working-class women that had been overlooked by both the labor movement and the women's movement.

The formation and development of CLUW must be seen in the context of the development of the American labor movement and the AFL–CIO. When CLUW was founded in 1974, George Meany (a representative of craft unionism) was the president of the AFL–CIO, and the labor federation did not have a represen-tative responsible for "women's issues." Such a representative, regardless of the amount of budget and power devoted to the position, draws attention to the fact that in a gendered social structure, women's issues need special attention. In response to CLUW's formation, the AFL–CIO appointed a "coordinator for women's affairs" who belonged to the civil rights department. In 1980, when Lane Kirkland became president of the labor federation, the Executive Board appointed CLUW national president Joyce Miller as the first woman on the Board. This election is an example of affirmative action—and of tokenism, since Miller was the only woman on the council. In 1996, after John Sweeney was elected president, the AFL–CIO formed a Working Women's Department and a Committee of Working Women. The president of CLUW became chair of this committee and thus part of these structures. Compared to the election of Joyce Miller to the Executive Board of the AFL–CIO, the formation of women's struc-tures in the AFL–CIO in 1996 gave women's issues more weight and more re-sources in the labor movement. The inclusion of women and people of color among the AFL–CIO leadership reflected the fact that the labor federation had at last realized that women and minorities in the public and service sectors have to be organized in order to compensate for the loss of workplaces and union mem-bers in the industrial sector.

CLUW has worked with the Working Women's Department since its inception. Many of the activities the Committee of Working Women took on, like assessing the number of women in union leadership and establishing a clearing-house for women's issues in the labor movement, have been long-standing items on CLUW's agenda. CLUW and the Working Women's Department support each other. The creation of the department allows CLUW to take on a more critical outsider perspective of the AFL–CIO while at the same time supporting the department in forming such departments on the state level, using the net-works of the state vice presidents, chapters, and NEB members (union and chap-ter delegates). Women's departments (sometimes in connection with civil rights departments) exist in many state AFL–CIOs. Most of them were formed many years before the Working Women's Department. They work with CLUW chap-ters and CLUW state vice presidents.

If the Working Women's Department had been in existence in the 1970s, CLUW probably would have never been founded. The lack of women in union leadership and the lack of attention to women's issues by the AFL–CIO leader-ship made the formation of CLUW necessary. Although CLUW did not have the power to change the structure of the labor federation, it contributed to the diffu-sion of feminist consciousness in the labor movement. It provides a meeting place for women in the labor movement and a training ground for labor union women and women in community organizations who had just been introduced to the labor movement.

The founding of CLUW fell in a period of diversification and expansion of feminist organizing. Between 1973 and 1982 the feminist movement broadened. Educational and political feminist organizations aimed at changing mainstream institutions. CLUW represents "unobtrusive mobilization" (Katzenstein 1990) of women in the labor movement. In addition, CLUW contributes to the diversity of the women's movement by addressing working-class women, a large number of them women of color. This organization thus challenges the notion that the women's movement is a white-middle-class movement and contributes to the diversity of the new women's movement.

CLUW is an organization with a high proportion of women of color, which reflects the higher unionization rate of African American women. Women of color have from the beginning participated in the national leadership of the or-ganization. At the chapter level, the organization seems to be more homogene-ous than at the national level. Due to the high participation of women of color, CLUW provides an excellent opportunity to study the relationship between race, class, and feminist consciousness. Confronted with multiple systems of oppres-sion—racism, sexism, and economic stratification, to name a few—activists participate in multiple movements at the same time or consecutively. This leads to the notion of social movement interaction. I suggest two concepts as building blocks for theorizing social movement interaction: political socialization proc-esses and bridging organizations.

Political Socialization

Individual political socialization is a lifelong process in private relationships and in the public sphere, which is translated into forms of political consciousness and political participation. Because their political socialization histories differed, members of CLUW brought different expectations to the organization and participated in different ways. Life-history research and biographical methods provide an important tool for studying these processes.

CLUW membership was diverse not only with respect to race, class, and gender but also with respect to processes of political socialization and thus their accountability to feminism and the labor movement. Four types of membership and union feminism can be distinguished. The union feminism of the *founding mothers* emphasized their trade union identity, while the union feminism of the *rebellious daughters* was anchored in a feminist critique of the labor movement and a critique of the racial and class biases of the women's movement. The union feminism of the *political animals* was issue-oriented and valued the labor movement and the women's movement as equally important and mutually supportive. The union feminism of the *fighting victims* evolved from discrimination experiences and the fight against discrimination in the context of the labor movement and CLUW.

For the founding mothers, accountability to the labor movement was most important, while the rebellious daughters emphasized the sexism and racism in that movement. For the political animals and fighting victims, who joined the organization later, when the labor movement had already changed and women's issues had become labor issues—in part due to the reframing of CLUW—the organization represented the first contact with the women's movement. They did not perceive tensions between the women's movement and the labor movement as did the first two types.

Although the four types were socialized in different contexts, they had the same agenda: representing women workers. All four emphasized equality and justice regardless of race, class, and gender and saw these as dimensions that needed to be addressed equally. Whether "women issues" or "worker's issues" were emphasized did not matter as long as an improvement in the working conditions that took the concerns of women of color into consideration could be achieved. An emphasis on pragmatism rather than ideology integrated this heterogeneous group.

CLUW represented the organizational identity of a heterogeneous group of women (and men) who sought to improve the conditions of working women and women in the labor movement. Since the organization did not address the needs of members equally, some left the organization. Those who stayed changed as a result of their participation, but in different ways. As a consequence of the heterogeneity of the organization, those who came from the labor movement learned about the women's movement, and those who came from the social movements of the 1960s and 1970s learned about the labor movement. Such learning processes often took place in mentor-mentee relationships.

Bridging Organizations

CLUW chose a bureaucratic and hierarchical form, modeled after the trade union federation AFL–CIO, in order to bridge the women's movement and the labor movement. This organizational setup was perceived as most successful for transforming the labor movement from within and bringing women's issues onto the labor agenda. However, the accountability to the labor movement that was expressed through this organizational structure also constrained CLUW in pursuing its goals. The organization became one of the support groups of the AFL–CIO, and full membership was restricted to union members. Members could participate at the chapter and national level in meetings of the National Executive Board and the biennial conventions, but participation was hampered by CLUW's bureaucratic structure and oligarchic tendencies. National officers, National Executive Board members, chapter officers, and committee and task force chairwomen tended to hold on to their positions. Access to resources played a big role in participation in the organization and in the activities CLUW offered. Participation at the national level was de facto limited to members who were supported by their union. The majority of unions tended to support participation by staff and officers, but by not rank-and-file activists.

The collective identity of CLUW was a result of negotiations among the founding members of the organization. The conflicts concerned membership, union democracy, and support for the farmworkers union. In each case the founding mothers prevailed, and consequently the organization became an insider organization, restricted to union members and supporting union solidarity. This had an impact on the pursuit of the four goals of the organization— organizing the unorganized, bringing women into union leadership, affirmative action, and getting women involved in the political process. CLUW did not organize women workers directly; instead CLUW supported organizing drives when called upon by a union, and only if the union was not competing with another union, in order to avoid the impression that it would engage in dual unionism. Members who found this way of organizing inefficient, left the organization and became (more) active in their own unions or other women's organizations. CLUW members felt empowered through participation in the organization; however, not all found leadership positions or access to training and support at the national level and therefore left the organization. Founding mothers and political animals were most satisfied with the organization and had a large share of leadership positions, while rebellious daughters and fighting victims were more inclined to leave the organization after a while.

The goals and strategies of the Coalition of Labor Union Women thus were developed within the constraints of the loyalty to the labor movement and accountability to feminist principles. CLUW chose to become an insider organization, choosing accountability to the labor movement over accountability to the women's movement. As an insider organization CLUW had credibility in the labor movement, sought to raise consciousness, educated female and male unionists, and thus unobtrusively mobilized for feminist principles within the labor movement.

Although members came from a range of movements and participated in a wide variety of organizations, the culture of the labor movement prevailed and constituted the (unquestioned and unquestionable) norm. Some members left the organization early on, because they felt that the project to create a feminist group in the labor movement had failed. The organization recruited through unions and thus mostly reached women who were already participating union members. Working women who were not unionized or who were union members but felt uncomfortable in the labor movement were not reached by the organization. Furthermore, within the organization, conflicts were marginalized.

THE IMPACT OF CLUW

Although CLUW had only a small staff and few resources, the organization represented a network of tens of thousands of union women across the United States. The 350 members of the National Executive Board held positions in the women's movement, the civil rights movement, and the labor movement at the local, regional, and national levels (*CLUW Leadership Directory* 1995). They were well-organized and skilled political activists. CLUW was proud of the achievements of its members and documented them in the newsletter, leadership directory, and brochures. CLUW members held many positions and were involved in many organizations and activities. However, when they participated in an event as delegate or representative of their union or another organization, for example, the Democratic Party, CLUW members did not necessarily represent CLUW. Thus these activists were not always identified in the labor movement or in the women's movement as CLUW members. But in the labor movement they were known for taking the "women's position," and in the women's movement they were recognized as "union women."

CLUW contributed to bridging the women's and labor movements through bringing women's issues to the labor agenda and providing union leadership. Reproductive rights, sexual harassment, child care, and pay equity were framed as labor issues. Through the reframing of women's issues into "worker's issues," "family issues," or "labor issues," CLUW simultaneously broadened the agenda of the women's movement and made it more attractive to working-class women and women of color, who might not identify with a presumably white-middle-class women's movement. Coalition work depends on the possibility of framing issues in a way that is compatible with the agendas of the various groups and individuals involved.

The great majority of CLUW members supported the Democratic Party. CLUW regularly participated in "get out the vote" initiatives and in general backed the position of the AFL–CIO and its unions. While not disagreeing with the labor federation, CLUW emphasized how issues of concern to working people—for example, NAFTA or health care reform—affected women in general and women of color in particular. Rather than criticizing the labor movement, CLUW broadened the notion of workers' interest to address the needs of women of color. In this respect, CLUW engaged in gender-mainstreaming of the labor movement. Aside from affirmative action and pay equity, CLUW added child care and dependent care, sexual harassment, reproductive rights, and recently HIV prevention to the labor agenda.

Through framing the interests of women—emphasizing women of color—as labor issues, CLUW opened the labor movement to this group of workers. Furthermore, it contributed to coalition building between organizations of the labor movement, the women's movement, and organizations concerned with social justice. At the local level, CLUW chapters cooperated with and supported community groups. While the membership was restricted to union members, the issues concerned the family and the community as well as the workplace.

Not surprisingly, CLUW did not achieve all its goals. CLUW was reluctant to criticize the labor movement or to voice demands. It might have had a bigger impact on the individual than on the institutional level. That is, CLUW seems to have been most important as a support group for women involved in the labor movement, women who were already unionized, active in their union locals or at the district or national level. In CLUW these women found a network, where they could share their grievances and learn about union issues of concern for working women. Acting as a support group—for labor union women as well as for the unions and the labor union federation—CLUW changed the unions from within. By providing leadership training, networking, consciousness raising, and mentoring for union women, CLUW kept women—who felt otherwise isolated and alienated—in the labor movement and provided them, for example, with language for bargaining contracts.

The founding and ongoing existence of CLUW thus expressed the need of women active in the labor movement of a support group. This was reflected in the number of women who continued to join the organization. However, the activities of the organization were limited, and officers at the chapter and national level held on to their positions. This fact was resented by those who were interested in these positions but were not able to achieve them. Obviously, to them participation at the chapter level was not as attractive as participating at the national level, which offered workshops and other activities.

The union culture undermined electoral races in two ways. On one hand, running against another candidate from the same union would undermine union solidarity. On the other, running against a candidate from another union might mean that that union lost its representation among the officers. The influence of the unions that financed participation at the national level was significant, so it was important that they continued to be represented. Thus there were no races for offices. Since the leadership tended to be reelected until they resigned, one must assume that the membership were satisfied with them.

The reluctance to give up positions could be interpreted as an attempt to compensate for the relative powerlessness in their unions with a position in CLUW. This hypothesis would be supported by the fact that since the late 1990s there were some prominent women labor leaders (Linda Chávez-Thompson, Barbara Easterling, Karen Nussbaum) who did not have officers positions in CLUW. However, these labor union leaders supported CLUW, for example, through being keynote speakers in CLUW events.

Rather than being a training ground, CLUW thus seems to have become a meeting place for women labor leaders with limited influence in the labor movement. However, it needs to be emphasized that CLUW's founding members were pioneers and well respected in the labor movement (see Chapters 3 and 4). Furthermore, CLUW was respected by representatives of women's movement organizations for representing feminist concerns within the labor movement and seeking outreach to the women's movement. As a bridging organization, CLUW contributed to the cooperation between two movements from which both movements and their women members benefited. Moreover, CLUW put a lot of emphasis on the participation and concerns of women of color.

THE FUTURE OF CLUW

CLUW's influence on the individual level would be even bigger if the organization would give more women the chance to assume leadership positions and thus achieve leadership skills. This could be achieved by limiting the terms.[1] Furthermore, the membership criteria could be changed to give non-unionized women a better chance to participate and form caucuses. Although the constitution of CLUW does not prevent the recruitment of non-union women as associate members or the formation of caucuses for staff members and union officers at the chapter level, the collective identity of the organization so far does not allow it. The formation of such groups might contribute to keeping staff members and union officers involved and organizing unorganized women workers. Thus CLUW would be better able to achieve its goals. Furthermore, CLUW could become more financially independent from the unions if it would adopt a sliding dues structure—members with higher incomes could pay higher dues, while members with lower incomes could pay lower dues and could be eligible for travel funding to attend meetings.

Since CLUW was founded the proportion of women in union leadership has increased. However, women are still under-represented in union leadership compared to union membership. Furthermore, the increase in women's union participation is relative since it is related to structural change and the decrease of workplaces in the traditionally unionized industrial sector. CLUW provides women with a training ground for achieving leadership skills and exchanging experiences. However, new members have few chances to achieve leadership positions within CLUW—except if they found a chapter. In this way, CLUW is more attractive for women who have leadership positions in CLUW—and keep them. Given the aging membership of CLUW, attracting and keeping new members is crucial for the survival of the organization. Otherwise, CLUW would become a self-help group that would disappear when its members no longer need it.

CLUW provides a model for a development of an international labor and women's movement. CLUW invites women labor leaders from other parts of the world to its biennial conventions. CLUW members participated as election observers in the first post-apartheid elections in South Africa in 1994 and in the UN women's conference in Beijing in 1995.[2] Thus the organization shows the importance of building bridges among the women's movement and the labor movement not only in the U.S., but worldwide.

NOTES

1. However, CLUW chose the opposite: at the 2001 biennial the officers' terms were extended (*CLUW News*, vol. 28, 2002).

2. Though, they did not represent CLUW at the UN conference since the AFL–CIO boycotted China in solidarity with U.S. President Clinton's sanctions against China. Once again, accountability to the labor movement proved more important than accountability to feminism.

Appendix: Data and Methodology

This study is based on qualitative and quantitative methods: participant observation of meetings of the Coalition of Labor Union Women at the national and local levels; expert interviews and in-depth interviews with members at different levels of the organization and in different areas of the United States; and a survey of the National membership (N = 524, response rate 30%) I conducted during the summer of 1994.

PARTICIPANT OBSERVATION: ACCESS TO AND ROLES IN THE FIELD

For most of the time during my fieldwork I adopted the role of a peripheral member whose role is characterized by research exchange, membership relationships, role demands, and role changes and shifts (Adler and Adler 1987). I participated in meetings at the local, regional, and national levels, and in events of other labor organizations. From 1993 through 1995, I attended meetings of several CLUW chapters in New England. Furthermore, I participated in state-wide conferences and events of CLUW at the annual conventions of the state AFL–CIO. I also participated in a summer school of union women—a week-long training program for union women co-sponsored by the UCLEA (University and College Labor Education Association), the Education Department of the AFL–CIO, and the Coalition of Labor Union Women. At the national level I attended the Seventh Biennial Convention of CLUW in Las Vegas (November 1993), the Gala celebrating the 20th anniversary of CLUW in Washington, D.C. (May 1994) as well as several meetings of the National Executive Board and of the National Officers Council (Washington, D.C., New York).

Attending meetings and conventions allowed me to meet CLUW members, learn about their activities, pick up informational material, and observe the interactions of CLUW members. I also scheduled and conducted interviews during meetings and conventions. In exchange for being invited to participate in chapter meetings, I passed on

information concerning the activities of other chapters and at the national CLUW level. I
volunteered to speak about the position of women in German and American unions. My
role as a researcher was always very clear, and became even more visible after I started
conducting interviews with members at the chapter level.

After I had participated as a peripheral member for about a year, I became an intern at
the CLUW Center for Education and Research in Washington, DC, and thus an active
member (Adler and Adler 1987). The internship, which lasted from June through August
1994, was paid for by the Hans Böckler-Stiftung, a foundation related to the German
trade union federation. During this internship I conducted a national membership survey.
Although I offered to cover the costs (printing, postage) of the membership survey using
a doctoral dissertation fellowship, these costs were paid by CLUW. I revised the
questionnaire that I had pre-tested in New England prior to the internship. Wording and
design of the questionnaire were discussed with the director of the CLUW Center for
Education and Research, the national president of the organization, and several other
CLUW members. The questionnaire was accompanied by a letter signed by the National
President, the director of the CLUW Center, and myself. The letter emphasized that the
survey was confidential, conducted by me in the context of my doctoral dissertation and
supervised by my academic advisors, and endorsed by CLUW. In order to increase
participation, a raffle was held. Three prizes were given away. Those who returned the
questionnaire within 14 days could win $150. Those who returned the questionnaire
within 30 days could win $100. Those who returned it within 45 days could win $50. In a
letter of agreement between CLUW and me, I was granted use of the survey. I promised
to make papers based on the evaluation of the survey available to the organization.

During the internship I also mailed a short questionnaire to chapter presidents of the
Coalition. This questionnaire addressed the activities of the chapter, how these activities
were announced, and the demographic characteristics of the active members and the
officers. Questions also targeted the problems that chapters encountered and asked
chapter presidents to share experiences and advice. This questionnaire was returned by
14 (20%) of the chapter presidents.

I also participated in data collection on women in union leadership, which updated
previous surveys of women in union leadership that CLUW had conducted. These
previous surveys were published in the reports *Absent from the Agenda* (Glassberg et al.
1980) and *Developing an Agenda* (Baden 1986). Furthermore, I contributed to the
compilation of a leadership directory consisting of the 355 members of the National
Executive Board of the Coalition of Labor Union Women. It provides information about
the union office, CLUW office, other offices and affiliations, profession, and fields of
expertise of the NEB members. This NEB directory is available to unions, women's
organizations, and other social-political organizations and represents a unique body of
data.

The fact that my research was funded by the Hans Böckler-Stiftung German trade
union federation was crucial not only for financial reasons. Receiving a stipend from a
union foundation legitimated me. But in this contested field, where unions compete with
each other for union membership and disagree about political issues, it was an advantage
not to belong to any union and thus not to have to side with any of them. As an outsider I
had the chance to talk to people representing different positions within CLUW as well as
with representatives of other organizations. However, the outsider perspective also had

disadvantages. I did not have extensive knowledge of the labor movement before I began this research, and I had to acquire this information in order to put the research into context. In addition, I knew about union membership only through the interviews, not through personal experience.

INTERVIEWING LABOR UNION WOMEN

Between 1991 and 1995 I interviewed 68 formerly and presently active CLUW members as well as 14 experts on the women's movement and on the labor movement. Some interviews were as short as 15 minutes, while others lasted for several hours. On average the interviews lasted one-and-a-half hours. In some cases it took me months to set up the interview, in other cases I conducted the interview immediately after being introduced to someone at a convention. The interviews fall into two categories: life-history interviews and expert interviews.

Life-History Interviews

I conducted interviews with current and former members of the Coalition of Labor Union Women who were active at different levels of the organization, belonged to different racial and ethnic groups, were members of a variety of different unions, and represented union participation from voluntary local rank-and-file activism to national leadership. I conducted sixteen life-history interviews in which I employed an interview guide. I asked interviewees to start with their childhood and tell me how their life developed, how they got involved in the labor movement and in the Coalition of Labor Union Women. These interviews lasted between two and four hours and were conducted with members who were active at the chapter level. I also interviewed national officers and other activists at the national level to capture differences in union membership, race and ethnicity, and regional differences. These 29 additional in-depth interviews were conducted during conventions and lunch breaks and varied in length from thirty minutes to two hours.

Expert Interviews

In addition to the life-history interviews, I conducted expert interviews with national officers and other former and current members of the Coalition of Labor Union Women in New England, Washington, D.C., Chicago, and New York City. At the meetings of the national executive board in Washington, D.C. and Providence, Rhode Island, I conducted interviews with chapter presidents and CLUW members from other regions of the United States (West Coast, South, Midwest). I also conducted telephone interviews with chapter presidents who were unable to attend the national meetings. In addition, I conducted expert interviews with staff members of the AFL–CIO, representatives of other AFL–CIO support groups, and with representatives of women's movement organizations and at the national and local levels.

Changing the Interview Strategy

Originally I had planned to conduct semi-structured life-history interviews with former and current activists of the organization at the local level. In the beginning of the interview I asked the interviewee to begin by telling me about her childhood and to talk about how her life developed. After the initial narrative I asked about inconsistencies, gaps and areas that had not been included, especially regarding the participation in the Coalition of Labor Union Women. Finally, I presented a set of questions dealing with the experiences in and perspectives on the Coalition of Labor Union Women.

These interviews lasted two hours or longer. Given that the women I interviewed were working full-time, active union members, active in the Coalition of Labor Union Women and in other organizations, mothers, grandmothers, spouses, and sometimes part-time students, it was difficult to schedule interviews that would last this long.

After extending the participant observation from the local level, where I attended chapter meetings and meetings of the labor organizations (unions, AFL–CIO, labor councils), to the national level of CLUW, where I attended National Executive Board meetings and conventions, I realized that participants at the local and national levels share few common experiences. In order to understand differences between the participation at the local and at the national level, I realized I would also have to interview national leaders of the organization.

The national leadership of CLUW is composed of high-ranking staff members and officers of the unions. Although I wished to conduct extensive biographical narrative interviews with women labor leaders, I realized that due to the time constraints of national union officers this would not be feasible. I therefore changed the interview strategy and simply asked: "How did you get involved in the union and in the Coalition of Labor Union Women?"

Some women labor leaders responded to this probe with extensive narratives in which they referred to their childhood. In other cases it was not possible to elicit biographical information. Because these women were well known within CLUW, their union, or in the labor movement, they knew that they were important figures and were not surprised that I was interested in them. In addition, I felt that, rather than speaking for themselves as individuals, officers presented themselves to me as representatives of CLUW and their unions. The interviews with officers and other well-known CLUW members differed from my other interviews in that I was not able to strictly separate their private persona from their union persona or their CLUW persona.

The framing of the interview during the opening question could partly account for some of these differences. When I asked a CLUW member to tell me how her life developed, it was more likely that the private persona would dominate the interview than when I asked how she got involved in the labor movement and in CLUW. However, all the women I interviewed knew that I was studying CLUW and that learning about their lives would help me to understand "what CLUW was all about." So, despite the different ways I framed the interview, CLUW members interpreted the initial question differently. They chose how much they wanted to disclose about their private life, how much they wanted to disclose about the organization, and to what extent they presented themselves as a union member or as a CLUW member. I categorized the interview as a life-history interview if it contained biographical information about the CLUW member and the private persona emerged. I categorized interviews as expert interviews if the union or CLUW persona dominated and no biographical information was given.

Returning Summaries and Transcripts

The more interviews I conducted, the more frustrated I became with the results. I found the Coalition of Labor Union Women so interesting because it combined such a diverse membership: one third of the membership were women of color, members represented all sectors of the labor market and the labor movement. I indicated that I wanted to learn how such an organization dealt with diversity. I was interested in learning how CLUW was able to form a bridge between the women's movement and the labor movement. The relationship between these two movements was characterized by tensions as well as by cooperation. Could interviewees give examples of conflicts, and how they were dealt with? Activists hardly addressed their relationship with the women's movement, conflicts within the labor movement, and other divisive issues such as involvement in the Communist Party. Overall, most interviewees were reluctant to give me examples of conflicts. Activists at the national level tended to be more reluctant to addressed divisive issues than activists at the chapter level. Informants who mentioned divisive issues indicated that this information was "off the record."

Some interviewees did not want me to tape the interview, so I took notes and sent summaries of my notes to these interviewees in order to make sure I had understood them correctly. In cases where I received permission to record the interview, I promised to give the transcript to the interviewee, hoping that this would enhance my trustworthiness. In the cover letter that accompanied the transcript or notes, I wrote that I wanted to give the interviewee the opportunity to check if I understood her correctly (after all, English is my second language), and to offer her a chance to add something to the interview.

Reactions to Returning the Interview Transcript or Summary

I had various reasons for sending back the summaries or transcripts. To the activists at the chapter level with whom I had conducted life-histories, I sent a summary to give them an idea of what I was doing with the interview. This made our encounters less awkward when we met at chapter meetings or conferences after the interview. In the case of the high ranking national officers, the promise to return the transcript allowed me continued access to the field. I sent back notes or transcripts from 43 of the 82 interviews with CLUW members and experts from the women's and the labor movements. Twenty-one of the interviewees to whom I sent a summary or the transcript of the interview did not respond and eight approved the summary or interview transcript. Eleven edited the interview's style since I had transcribed the interviews literally and incomplete sentences, slips, and colloquialisms remained.

Only three women were concerned with the content of their interviews. One asked me not to use the interview at all. Another interviewee asked me to clear the use of the interview with her. And a third interviewee asked me to leave out certain parts of the interview. In two of these three cases, due to technical problems the interview had not been entirely recorded and parts of the interview were not audible.

The reactions to receiving the summaries and transcripts differed somewhat due to the level of involvement in CLUW (see Table A.1). Members who were active in the organization at the national level were more likely to edit the interview and be concerned about the use of the interview than were members at the local level. CLUW members who were active at the local level tended not to react at all or to tell me that my summary of the interview was "okay" when we got together at a meeting.

Table A.1
Interview Type by Reaction to Transcript or Summary Returned

Interview Type	Total Number	Returned	No Reaction	OK	Edited	X
Local Level Life-History	25	11	8	2	—	1
National Level Life-History	15	14	6	4	2	2
Local Level Expert	16	7	4	—	3	—
National Level Expert	12	6	3	1	2	—
Labor Movement Expert	6	1	—	1	—	—
Women's Movement Expert	8	4	—	—	4	—
Total Interviews	82	43	21	8	11	3

Total Interviews: number of interviews conducted
Returned: number of summaries or transcripts returned to interviewees
No Reaction: interviewee did not react at all
OK: interviewee approved summary or transcript
Edited: interviewee edited summary or transcript stylistically
X: interviewee asked me not to use interview, parts of the interview, or to clear the use of the interview with her

One explanation for the different reactions might be that I sent more summaries to activists at the local level, while I sent more transcripts to activists at the national level.

Interpretation of the Reaction of the Interviewees

I realized while conducting the interviews that the women labor leaders often spoke as representatives of their unions rather than for themselves as women in the labor movement. The boundaries between the local and national levels of CLUW and between the union and CLUW often blurred. These women emphasized how their union supported their participation and how they represented this union within CLUW.

Women who were active at the local level in CLUW or those who were no longer active in the organization were more frank about gender or racial discrimination in the labor movement, the involvement of some CLUW members in communist or socialist groups, conflicts or problems within CLUW, and their relationship to the women's movement. Overall, women who were strongly involved in CLUW, especially at the national level, and strongly identified with their union, were less likely to bring up sensitive issues such as conflicts and racial or sexual discrimination.

When I presented my preliminary findings to a number of interviewees and pointed out their reluctance to voice anything critical about the labor movement or the Coalition of Labor Union Women I heard that "one does not talk about family business in public" (field notes). Their reluctance to debate critical issues of the labor movement and of an organization of labor union women raised issues of loyalty and accountability. The interviews indicated that—at the national level more so than at the local level—accountability and loyalty towards the labor movement was stronger than to the women's movement.

DEVELOPMENT OF THE MEMBERSHIP TYPOLOGY

All interviews were transcribed. I first summarized the content of the interview and the life-history of the interviewee. Starting with childhood, I paraphrased how her life developed (school, work, family, political involvement), and the circumstances of her involvement in the labor movement and the Coalition of Labor Union Women. After this descriptive summary of the interview, I evaluated 45 interviews along six overlapping dimensions of political socialization: biographical continuity, agency, identity, injustice, interaction, and resources.

These dimensions addressed objective *and* subjective aspects of political socialization through participation in a movement organization. From an "objective" perspective, the interviewees were ethnographic informants and contributed to the understanding of recruitment processes and the organizational structure of the Coalition of Labor Union Women. From a "subjective" perspective, the dimensions highlighted what participation meant to activists. The dimension *biographical continuity* situated social movement participation in activists' lives. On one hand, this dimension focused on the objective account of developments in work and family life (for example unemployment, divorce), political involvement prior to becoming a union member, the circumstances of recruitment into the labor movement and the Coalition of Labor Union Women, and the development of participation in CLUW. On the other hand, this dimension focused on the subjective perspective on becoming an activist, what it meant to be an activist, and what effect it had on activists' lives.

Under the dimension *biographical continuity* I coded accounts of recruitment into and development of the participation in the union, CLUW, and other social movement activities and voluntary associations. Some interviewees traced their political involvement to their childhood, when they joined parents or grandparents in demonstrations or on picket lines. Other interviewees related their involvement to turning points such as divorce, death of a spouse or a child. Interviewees also described how their lives changed after they became active union members and joined the Coalition of Labor Union Women.

The second dimension, *agency*, dealt with the process of empowerment due to social movement participation. The objective aspect of agency referred to positions of power activists achieved through participation in the Coalition of Labor Union Women. The subjective aspect of agency referred to experiences of empowerment through participation in CLUW. The analysis of agency focused on powerlessness and how this could be overcome through collective action, and how activists were able to change their own lives and the larger society through their involvement in collective action.

Under the dimension *agency* I coded descriptions of experiences of power, powerlessness, efficacy and empowerment at the workplace, in the family, in the union, and in CLUW. This included accounts of assertiveness that led to union involvement. Some union members said they spoke up at the first union meeting they attended and were recruited because they were outspoken. Other interviewees described their feelings of powerlessness and how the union helped them to become assertive. Interviewees described CLUW as not only a setting in which they could learn leadership skills, but also a setting in which they could exercise those skills.

The dimension *identity* referred to the subjective construction of collective identity. I distinguish here between the collective identities of the activists and the collective identity activists imputed to the Coalition of Labor Union Women. These collective identities might be more or less congruent. The analysis focused on what collective identity activists brought to CLUW and how their political (feminist, race, class) consciousness was transformed through interaction with different occupational, racial, political, and age groups. Here I collected self-definitions as "feminists" and "union people" as well as references to their religious upbringing and their accountability to these traditions. The objective aspect of identity was holding a membership card or holding an officer's position.

The dimension *interaction* highlights mentoring, support, cooperation, and conflict that were experienced in the context of social movement participation. This dimension was also composed of subjective and objective elements. Objective aspects referred to the opportunities for interaction and exchange within CLUW and with other organizations. Interviewees were ethnographic informants who described the activities and interactions at the chapter level and at the regional level of the Coalition of Labor Union Women. The subjective component refers to how these structures are experienced by the activists. Both subjective and objective aspects address the way members interacted with each other not only in the Coalition of Labor Union Women, but in other fields (for example, in unions, women's organizations, or the Democratic Party) in which participants were involved due to their participation in CLUW.

The dimension *interaction* addresses conflict and cooperation, participation and democracy within the context of CLUW and the union. Further issues included under this dimension were loyalty, distrust, competition, solidarity, mentorship, and inclusion. How did the organization deal with diversity and how important was that to interviewees?

The dimension *injustice* also entails subjective and objective aspects. The objective aspect refers to cases of discrimination and other forms of injustice. The subjective aspect focuses on how discrimination was experienced and how it figured into activists' political consciousness and activity. A sense of injustice could stem from a variety of sources: experiences of personal discrimination or a religious and moral upbringing that emphasized the responsibility to end injustice. Thus, while an activist might have had experienced discrimination, she might not have seen this experience as the trigger of her political participation.

Under the dimension *injustice* I coded descriptions of discrimination experiences. For instance, some interviewees reported discrimination in the form of low wages or sexual harassment. Others did not speak about such personal experiences but described how they observed how others were discriminated against. For example, white women and women of color spoke about racial discrimination, but some had personally experienced it, while others spoke about others being discriminated against. In the dimension *identity* the focus was on the self-definition of the interviewee, while the dimension *injustice* emphasized experiences of interviewees.

Finally, the dimension *resources* addresses skills, knowledge, and connections that activists brought to social movement activism and those they acquired through activism. This dimension has objective and subjective aspects. Objective aspects refers to the structural opportunities available to activists, while subjective aspects refers to how the activists perceived and used these opportunities. Not only were activists a resource for movements, but participation also was a resource for activists. Members developed leadership skills and an understanding of the political process, furthermore they gained access to networks, mentors, and emotional support. These resources potentially helped members to achieve leadership positions in their communities, to move up in their union or voluntary association, and to challenge problems at the workplace and in the family.

Based on the life-history and in-depth interviews I developed the membership typology that I presented in Chapter 3 in which I described the four types—*founding mothers, rebellious daughters, political animals, fighting victims.* The typology emerged through comparing and contrasting the interviews across the six dimensions and comparing and contrasting white women and "women of color" (described in Chapter 4). The typology thus acknowledges the similarities and differences of white women and women of color.

NATIONAL MEMBERSHIP SURVEY

The national survey of the membership of CLUW addressed demographic characteristics (such as race, ethnicity, gender, age, marital status, education, etc.), recruitment into and participation in the Coalition of Labor Union Women, affiliation with other organizations (unions, social movement organizations, political parties), group consciousness, and attitudes concerning CLUW's goals and success.

Prior to the survey, I conducted a pre-test among the entire CLUW membership in one New England state. I obtained the membership list from the CLUW state vice president. This pre-test resulted in a response rate of only 20%, which prompted me to revise the questionnaire considerably—I shortened it by dropping 30 of 80 questions and improved it graphically. Rather than mailing it to 500 members as originally planned, the questionnaire was mailed to 1,993[1] randomly selected CLUW members.

The questionnaire was mailed out on July 1, 1994. By the middle of July, 277 questionnaires had been returned. 110 questionnaires could not be delivered. At the end of July, I mailed a reminder postcard. By the middle of August 1994 (the designated end of the survey), 453 questionnaires had been returned. This resulted in a response rate of 25%, because a total of 182 questionnaires could not be delivered. At about the same time the survey was mentioned in the newsletter *CLUW News.* The article in the newsletter did not result in the return of more questionnaires. Due to this low response rate, I mailed the questionnaire a second time to half of the sample (686) and a reminder letter to the other half of the sample. In this reminder letter I encouraged recipients to call the CLUW Center and request a questionnaire in case the original questionnaire had been lost. In the reminder I emphasized that the participation in the survey was crucial for capturing the multicultural character of the organization.

These three reminders resulted in the questionnaire being returned by 524 members (a total response rate of 30%). Based on a comparison of the respondents with the sample regarding union affiliation and geographic location, the respondents were representative of the total population, though blue-collar workers were slightly underrepresented. Active members might have been overrepresented among the respondents. However, about 40% of the respondents said that they were currently not very active in CLUW while 25% reported having never been active in the organization. This means that even if inactive members were underrepresented this did not affect the results concerning the relationship between the level of activity and other variables.

Due to the low response of 30%, I mailed out another very short questionnaire to 128 (10%) of those who did not respond to the survey after three reminders, to find out why they did not participate in the study. This survey was translated into Spanish and Chinese, in order to learn if language barriers contributed to an underrepresentation of Spanish and Chinese members. This was not the case. The response rate of this survey was 29%: 34 returned the questionnaire, while 9 questionnaires could not be delivered. Four (12%) indicated that they had filled out and returned the questionnaire. Eight (23%) said that they never received a questionnaire. Sixteen (47%) indicated that they lost the questionnaire. Nine (26%) respondents reported that they supported CLUW with their dues and felt that the questions did not apply to them. Two respondents found the questionnaire too long and one respondent felt that the survey was not anonymous.

Of those to whom the questionnaire about not participating in the survey was sent, twenty-six (76%) of the respondents held a union office. Thirteen (38%) of the respondents had been active in CLUW in the past, six (18%) were currently active in CLUW. Compared to the respondents of the national survey, the respondents of the follow-up survey were more likely to have held a union office and somewhat less likely to have been active in CLUW.

The fact that several respondents indicated that they never received a questionnaire or that they had filled out and returned the questionnaire suggests that problems of mailing contributed to the low response rate. A few days after I mailed out the survey the *Washington Post* reported that Washington, D.C. has one of the worst postal services in the United States, with mail piling up at post offices and being delivered either several months late or not at all.

The Membership Types and the Survey

I coded the types the following way: I coded female respondents who joined CLUW before 1978 and did not participate in the SDS as founding mothers (N = 50). Female respondents who participated in the SDS were coded as rebellious daughters (N = 72). Female respondents who joined CLUW in 1978 or later, did not participate in the SDS, and were married were coded as political animals (N = 127). Female respondents who joined CLUW in 1978 or later, did not participate in the SDS, and were divorced were coded as fighting victims (N = 71).

NOTE

1. The sample of 2000 contained seven double-entries, which I dropped.

Bibliography

Ackelsberg, Martha, and Irene Diamond. Gender and Political Life. In *Analyzing Gender,* ed. by Beth B. Hess and Myra Marx Ferree. Newbury Park, CA. Sage, 1987, 504–525.

Acker, Joan. *Doing Comparable Worth: Gender, Class, and Pay Equity.* Philadelphia, PA. Temple University Press, 1989.

Adams, Larry. Transforming Unions and Building a Movement. In *A New Labor Movement for the New Century,* ed. by Gregory Mantsios. New York, NY. Garland, 1998, 233–247.

Adler, Patricia A., and Peter Adler. *Membership Roles in Field Research.* Newbury Park, CA. Sage, 1987.

Amott Teresa L., and Julie A. Matthaei. *Race, Gender and Work: A Multicultural Economic History of Women in the United States.* Boston, MA. South End Press, 1991.

Andrews, Molly. *Lifetimes of Commitment. Aging, Politics, and Psychology.* Cambridge, NY. Cambridge University Press, 1991.

Arnold, Gretchen. Dilemmas of Feminist Coalitions. Collective Identity and Strategic Effectiveness in the Battered Women's Movement. In *Feminist Organizations. Harvest of the New Women's Movement,* ed. by Myra Marx Ferree and Patricia Yancey Martin. Philadelphia, PA. Temple University Press, 1995, 276–290.

Baden, Naomi. Developing an Agenda. Expanding the Role of Women in Unions. *Labor Studies Journal,* vol. 10, 1986, 229–249.

Balser, Diane. *Sisterhood and Solidarity. Feminism and Labor in Modern Times.* Boston, MA. South End Press, 1987.

Barker, Colin. Fear, Laughter, and Collective Power: The Making of Solidarity at the Lenin Shipyard in Gdansk, Poland, August 1980. In *Passionate Politics Emotions and Social Movements,* ed. by Jeff Goodwin, James M. Jasper, and Francesca Polletta. Chicago, IL. University of Chicago Press, 2001, 175–194.

Barnett, Bernice McNair. Invisible Southern Black Women Leaders in the Civil Rights Movement. The Triple Constraints of Gender, Race, and Class. *Gender and Society*, vol. 7, 1993, 162–182.

Barnett, Bernice McNair. Black Women's Collectivist Movement Organizations. Their Struggle during the Doldrums. In *Feminist Organizations. Harvest of the New Women's Movement*, ed. by Myra Marx Ferree and Patricia Yancey Martin. Philadelphia, PA. Temple University Press, 1995, 199–219.

Bell, Deborah E. Unionized Workers, Feminism, and the Labor Movement. In *Women, Work and Protest. A Century of U.S. Women's Labor History*, ed. by Ruth Milkman. Boston, MA. Routledge and Kegan Paul, 1985, 300–322.

Blum, Linda. *Between Feminism and Labor. The Significance of the Comparable Worth Movement*. Berkeley, CA. University of California Press, 1991.

Blumberg, Rhoda Lois. White Mothers as Civil Rights Activists. The Interweave of Family and Movement Roles. In *Women and Social Protest,* ed. by Guida West and Rhoda Lois Blumberg. New York, NY. Oxford University Press, 1990, 166–179.

Bookman, Ann, and Sandra Morgan. *Women and the Politics of Empowerment.* Philadelphia, PA. Temple University Press, 1988.

Braungart, Richard G., and Margaret M. Braungart. Conceptual and Methodological Approaches to Studying Life Course and Generational Politics. *Research in Political Sociology,* vol. 1, 1985, 269–304.

Breines, Wini. *Community and Organization in the New Left.* New Brunswick, NJ. Rutgers University Press, 1982.

Bronfenbrenner, Kate, Sheldon Friedman, Richard W. Hurd, Rudolph A. Oswald, and Ronald L. Seeber (eds.). *Organizing to Win. New Research on Union Strategies.* Ithaca, NY. ILR Press, 1998.

Brownmiller, Susan, and Dolores Alexander. How We Got There: From Carmita Wood to Anita Hill. In *Sexual Harassment in America: A Documentary History*, ed. by Laura W. Stein. Westport, CT. Greenwood, 1999, 1-4.

Buechler, Steven. *Women's Movements in the United States. Woman Suffrage, Equal Rights, and Beyond.* New Brunswick, NJ. Rutgers University Press, 1990.

Bureau of the Census. *Current Population Survey.* Washington, DC. Bureau of the Census, 2001.

Bureau of Labor Statistics. *Directory of National Unions and Employee Associations.* Washington, DC. Bureau of Labor Statistics, 1971.

Bureau of Labor Statistics. *Directory of National Unions and Employee Associations.* Washington, DC. Bureau of Labor Statistics, 1975.

Bureau of Labor Statistics. *Directory of National Unions and Employee Associations.* Washington, DC. Bureau of Labor Statistics, 2002.

Callahan, Mary. Forty Years I'm Secretary Treasurer of the Local. In *Rocking the Boat. Union Women's Voices, 1915–1975,* ed. by Brigid O'Farrell and Joyce L. Kornbluh. New Brunswick, NJ. Rutgers University Press, 1996, 110–134.

Chen, May, and Kent Wong. The Challenge of Diversity and Inclusion in the AFL-CIO. In *A New Labor Movement for the New Century*, ed. by Gregory Mantsios. New York, NY. Garland, 1998, 213–232.

Clawson, Dan, and Mary Ann Clawson. What has Happened to the US Labor Movement? Union Decline and Renewal. *Annual Review of Sociology,* vol. 25, 1999, 95–119.

Clemens, Elisabeth S. Organizational Repertoires and Institutional Change. Women's Groups and the Transformation of U.S. Politics, 1820–1920. *American Journal of Sociology,* vol. 98, 1993, 755–798.

Clemens, Elisabeth S. *The People's Lobby. Organizational Innovation and the Rise of Interest Group Politics in the United States, 1890-1925.* Chicago, IL. University of Chicago Press, 1997.

Cobble, Dorothy Sue. Introduction. Remaking Unions for the New Majority. In *Women and Unions. Forging a Partnership,* ed. by Dorothy Sue Cobble. Ithaca, NY: ILR Press, 1993, 3–23.

Cobble, Dorothy Sue. Recapturing Working-Class Feminism. Union Women in the Postwar Era. In *Not June Cleaver. Women and Gender in Postwar America, 1945-1960,* ed. by Joanne Meyerowitz. Philadelphia, PA. Temple University Press, 1994, 57–82.

Collins, Patricia Hill. *Black Feminist Thought: Knowledge, Consciousness, and the Politics of Empowerment.* London. Routledge, 1991 [1990].

Conroy, Catherine. Somebody Has to Have the Guts. In *Rocking the Boat. Union Women's Voices, 1915-1975,* ed. by Brigid O'Farrell and Joyce L. Kornbluh. New Brunswick, NJ. Rutgers University Press, 1996, 231–256.

Cook, Alice. Women and American Trade Unions. *Annals of the American Academy of Political and Social Science,* vol. 375, 1968, 124–132.

Cook, Alice. Introduction. In *Women and Trade Unions in Eleven Industrialized Countries* ed. by Alice H. Cook, Val R. Lorwin, and Arlene Kaplan Daniels. Philadelphia, PA. Temple University Press, 1984, 3–36.

Cook, Alice, Val. R. Lorwin, and Arlene Kaplan Daniels. *The Most Difficult Revolution. Women and Trade Unions.* Ithaca, NY. Cornell University Press, 1992.

Cornfield, Daniel B., and Bill Fletcher. The U.S. Labor Movement. Toward a Sociology of Labor Revitalization. In *Sourcebook of Labor Markets: Evolving Structures and Processes* ed. by Ivar Berg and Arne L. Kalleberg. New York, NY. Kluwer Academic/Plenum Publisher, 2001, 61–82

Costain, Anne N. *Inviting Women's Rebellion. A Political Process Interpretation of the Women's Movement.* Baltimore, MD. Johns Hopkins University Press, 1992.

Davis, Flora. *Moving the Mountain. The Women's Movement in America since 1960.* New York, NY. Touchstone, 1991.

Della Porta, Donatella. Life Histories in the Analysis of Social Movement Activists. In *Studying Collective Action,* ed. by Mario Diani and Ron Eyerman. Sage Modern Politics Series, vol. 10. London. Sage, 1992, 168–193.

Diani, Mario. Analysing Social Movement Networks. In *Studying Collective Action,* ed. by Mario Diani and Ron Eyerman. London. Sage, 1992, 107–135.

DiMaggio, Paul J., and Walter W. Powell. The Iron Cage Revisited: Institutional Isomorphism and Collective Rationality in Organizational Fields. *American Sociological Review,* vol. 48, 1983, 147–160.

Downey, Gary L. Ideology and the Clamshell Identity. Organizational Dilemmas in the Anti-Nuclear Power Movement. *Social Problems,* vol. 33, 1986, 357–373.

Dye, Nancy Schrom. *As Equals and as Sisters. Feminism, the Labor Movement, and the Women's Trade Union League of New York.* Columbia. University of Missouri Press, 1980.

Eisenstein, Hester. The Australian Femocratic Experiment. A Feminist Case for Bureaucracy. In *Feminist Organizations. Harvest of the New Women's Movement,* ed. by Myra Marx Ferree and Patricia Yancey Martin. Philadelphia, PA. Temple University Press, 1995, 69–83.

Elkiss, Helen. Mentoring for Union Women. Critical On-the-Job Leadership Training. *Workplace Topics,* vol. 4, 1995, 45–57.

Evans, Sarah. *Personal Politics: The Roots of Women's Liberation in the Civil Rights Movement and the New Left.* New York, NY. Alfred A. Knopf, 1979.

Evans, Sara M., and Harry C. Boyte. *Free Spaces. The Sources of Democratic Change in America.* New York, NY. Harper and Row, 1986.

Fantasia, Rick. *Cultures of Solidarity.* Berkeley, CA. University of California Press, 1988.

Fantasia, Rick, and Eric L. Hirsch. Culture in Rebellion: The Appropriation and Transformation of the Veil in the Algerian Revolution. In *Social Movements and Culture,* ed. by Hank Johnston and Bert Klandermans. Minneapolis. University of Minnesota Press, 1995, 144–159.

Feldberg, Roslyn. Women and Trade Unions: Are We Asking the Right Questions? In *Hidden Aspects of Women's Work,* ed. by Christine Bose. New York, NY. Praeger, 1987.

Ferguson, Kathy E. *The Feminist Case against Bureaucracy.* Philadelphia, PA. Temple University Press, 1984.

Ferree, Myra Marx. Was bringt die Biografieforschung der Bewegungsforschung? In *Politische Biografien und sozialer Wandel,* ed. by Ingrid Miethe and Silke Roth. Giessen. Psychosozial, 2000, 111–128.

Ferree, Myra Marx, William Anthony Gamson, Jürgen Gerhards, and Dieter Rucht. *Shaping Abortion Discourse. Democracy and the Public Sphere in Germany and the United States.* New York, NY. Cambridge University Press, 2002.

Ferree, Myra Marx, and Beth Hess. *Controversy and Coalition. The New Feminist Movement across Three Decades of Change.* New York, NY. Routledge, 2000.

Ferree, Myra Marx, and Patricia Yancey Martin. Doing the Work of the Movement. Feminist Organizations. In *Feminist Organizations: Harvest of the New Women's Movement,* ed. by Myra Marx Ferree and Patricia Yancey Martin. Philadelphia, PA. Temple University Press, 1995, 3–23.

Ferree, Myra Marx, and Silke Roth. Gender, Class, and the Interaction between Social Movements: A Strike on West Berlin Day Care Workers. *Gender and Society,* vol. 12, no. 6, 1998, 626–648.

Ferree, Myra Marx, and Mangala Subramaniam. The International Women's Movement at Century's End. In *Gender Mosaics: Sociological Perspectives,* ed. by Dana Vannoy. Los Angeles. Roxbury Press, 2001, 496–506.

Fink, Leon, and Brian Greenberg. *Upheaval in the Quiet Zone: A History of Hospital Workers' Union, Local 1199.* Urbana. University of Illinois Press, 1989.

Flam, Helena. Nxiety and the Successful Oppositional Construction of Societal Reality: The Case of KOR. *Mobilization,* vol. 1, no. 1, 1996, 103–121.

Flammang, Janet A. Women Made a Difference. Comparable Worth in San Jose In *The Women's Movements of the United States and Western Europe: Consciousness, Political Opportunity, and Public Policy*, ed. by Mary Fainsod Katzenstein and Carol McClurg Mueller. Philadelphia, PA. Temple University Press, 1987, 290–309.

Fletcher, Bill Jr. Whose Democracy? Organized Labor and Member Control. In *A New Labor Movement for the New Century*, ed. by Gregory Mantsios. New York, NY. Garland, 1998.

Foerster, Amy. Confronting the Dilemmas of Organizing: Obstacles and Innovations at the AFL-CIO Organizing Institute. In *Rekindling the Movement: Labor's Quest for Relevance in the 21st Century*, ed. by Lowell Turner, Harry C. Katz, and Richard W. Hurd. Ithaca. ILR Press, 2001, 155–181.

Foner, Philip S. *Women and the American Labor Movement*. New York, NY. The Free Press, vol. 1,2, 1979, 1980.

Fonow, Mary Margaret. Occupation/Steelworker. Sex/Female. In *Feminist Frontiers III*, ed. by Laurel Richardson and Verta Taylor. New York, NY. McGraw-Hill, 1993, 217–222.

Fonow, Mary Margaret. *Union Women. Forging Feminism in the United Steelworkers of America*. Minneapolis. University of Minnesota Press, 2003.

Freeman, Jo. The Origins of the Women's Liberation Movement. *American Journal of Sociology*, vol. 78, 1973, 792–811.

Freeman, Jo. *The Politics of Women's Liberation*. New York, NY. David McKay, 1975.

Freeman, Jo. *The Tyranny of Structurelessness*. London. Dark Starr Press and Rebel Press, 1984.

Friedan, Betty. *The Feminine Mystique*. McCall, 1963.

Friedman, Debra, and Doug McAdam. Collective Identity and Activism. Networks, Choices, and the Life of a Social Movement. In *Frontiers in Social Movement Theory*, ed. by Aldon D. Morris and Carol McClurg Mueller. New Haven/London. Yale University Press, 1992, 156–173.

Gabin, Nancy. Women and the United Automobile Workers' Union in the 1950s. In *Women, Work and Protest: A Century of U.S. Women's Labor History*, ed. by Ruth Milkman. Boston, MA. Routledge and Kegan Paul, 1985, 259–279.

Gamson, Joshua. The Organizational Shaping of Collective Identity: The Case of Lesbian and Gay Film Festivals in New York. *Sociological Forum*, vol. 11, 1996, 231–262.

Gamson, Joshua. Messages of Exclusion. Gender, Movements, and Symbolic Boundaries. *Gender and Society*, vol. 11, 1997, 178–99.

Gamson, William. The Social Psychology of Collective Action. In *Frontiers in Social Movement Theory*, ed. by Aldon D. Morris and Carol McClurg Mueller. New Haven, CT. Yale University Press, 1992, 53–76.

Gamson, William A., Bruce Fireman, and Steven Rytina. *Encounters with Unjust Authority*. Homewood, IL. Dorsey Press, 1982.

Gerhards, Jürgen, and Dieter Rucht. Mesomobilization. Organizing and Framing in Two Protest Campaigns in West Germany. *American Journal of Sociology*, 98, 1992, 555–95.

Giele, Janet Zollinger. *Two Paths to Women's Equality. Temperance, Suffrage, and the Origins of Modern Feminism.* New York, NY. Twayne, 1995.

Gilkes, Cheryl Townsend. 'If It Wasn't for the Women': African American Women, Community Work, and Social Change. In *Women of Color in US Society,* ed. by Maxine Baca Zinn and Bonnie Thornton Dill. Philadelphia, PA. Temple University Press, 1994.

Glassberg Elyse, Naomi Baden, and Karin Gerstel. *Absent from the Agenda. A Report on the Role of Women in American Unions.* New York, NY. Coalition of Labor Union Women/Center for Education and Research, 1980.

Glick, Phyllis Sharon. *Bridging Feminism and Trade Unionism. A Study of Working Women's Organizing in the United States.* Brandeis University, Ph.D. dissertation, 1983.

Gluck, Sherna Berger, with Maylei Blackwell, Sharon Cotrell, and Karen S. Harper. Whose Feminism, Whose History? Reflections on Excavating the History of (the) US Women's Movement(s). In *Community Activism and Feminist Politics: Organizing Across Race, Class, and Gender,* ed. by Nancy A. Naples. New York, NY. Routledge, 1998, 31–56.

Gold, Michael Evan. *An Introduction to Labor Law.* ILR Bulletin 66. Ithaca, NY. ILR Press, 1989.

Gordon, Linda. Gender, State and Society: A Debate with Theda Skocpol. *Contention,* vol. 2, no. 3, 1993, 139–156.

Gray, Lois. The Route to the Top. Female Union Leaders and Union Policy. In *Women and Unions: Forging a Partnership,* ed. by Dorothy Sue Cobble. Ithaca, NY. ILR Press, 1993, 378–393.

Gwartney-Gibbs, Patricia A., and Denise H. Lach. Gender Differences in Grievance Processing and the Implications for Rethinking Shopfloor Practices. In *Women and Unions. Forging a Partnership,* ed. by Dorothy Sue Cobble. Ithaca, NY. ILR Press, 1993, 299–315.

Hansen, Karen V. Women's Unions and the Search for a Political Identity. *Socialist Review,* vol.14, 1986, 67–95.

Hartmann, Heidi. Capitalism, Patriarchy, and Job Segregation by Sex. In *Women and the Work-Place: The Implications of Occupational Segregation,* ed. by Martha Blaxall and Barbara Reagan. Chicago, IL. University of Chicago Press, 1976.

Hasse, Raimund, and Georg Krücken. *Neoinstitutionalismus.* Bielefeld. Transcript-Verlag, 1999.

Heckscher, Charles C. The New Unionism: Employee Involvement in the Changing Corporation. New York, NY. Basic Books, 1988.

Hirsch, Barry and Dave McPherson. Union Membership and Earnings Data Book: Compilation from the Current Population. Washington, DC. Bureau of National Affairs, 2002.

Hochschild, Arlie Russell. *The Managed Heart: Commercialization of Human Feeling.* Berkeley, CA. University of California Press, 1983.

Horowitz, Daniel. *Betty Friedan and the Making of the Feminine Mystique: The American Left, the Cold War, and Modern Feminism.* Amherst, MA. University of Massachusetts Press, 1998.

Hoyman, Michelle. Working Women. The Potential of Unionization and Collective Action in the United States. *Women's Studies International Forum*, vol. 12, 1979, 51–59.

James, Stanlie M. Mothering: A Possible Black Feminist Link to Social Transformations? In *Theorizing Black Feminisms: The Visionary Pragmatism of Black Women*, ed. by Stanlie M. James and Abena P.A. Busia. London. Routledge, 1993.

Jasper, James M. *The Art of Moral Protest: Culture, Biography, and Creativity in Social Movements*. Chicago, IL. University of Chicago Press, 1997.

Johnson, Gloria. Comments. In *Women and Unions. Forging a Partnership*, ed. by Dorothy Sue Cobble. Ithaca, NY. ILR Press, 1993, 93–99.

Johnston, Paul. *Success while Others Fail: Social Movement Unionism and the Public Workplace*. Ithaca, NY. ILR Press, 1994.

Johnston, Paul. Organize for What? The Resurgence of Labor as a Citizenship Movement. In *Rekindling the Movement: Labor's Quest for Relevance in the 21st Century*, ed. by Lowell Turner, Harry C. Katz, and Richard W. Hurd. Ithaca, NY. ILR Press, 2001, 27–58.

Jordan, Ruth. Like Old Times: 3000 Women Unionist from 58 Unions Form Coalition. In *Press Associates, Inc.* April 1, 1974.

Judis, John. The Pressure Elite: Inside the Narrow World of Advocacy Group Politics. *American Prospect*, vol. 9, 1992, 15–29.

Katzenstein, Mary Fainsod. Feminism within American Institutions. Unobtrusive Mobilization in the 1980s. *Signs*, vol. 16, 1990, 27–55.

Katzenstein, Mary Fainsod. Discursive Politics and Feminist Activism in the Catholic Church. In *Feminist Organizations: Harvest of the New Women's Movement*, ed. by Myra Marx Ferree and Patricia Yancey Martin. Philadelphia, PA. Temple University Press, 1995, 35–52.

Katzenstein, Mary Fainsod. *Faithful and Fearless: Moving Feminist Protest inside the Church and Military*. Princeton, NJ. Princeton University Press, 1998.

Keck, Margaret E. and Kathryn Sikkink. *Activists beyond Borders: Advocacy Networks in International Politics*. Ithaca, NY. Cornell University Press, 1998.

Kessler-Harris, Alice. Where Are the Organized Women's Workers? *Feminist Studies*, vol. 3, 1975, 92–110.

Kessler-Harris, Alice. *Out to Work: A History of Wage Earning Women in the United States*. Oxford. Oxford University Press, 1982.

Klandermans, Bert. Linking the "Old" and the "New" Movement Networks in the Netherlands. In *Challenging the Political Order: New Social and Political Movements in Western Democracies*, ed. by Russell J. Dalton and Manfred Küchler. New York, NY. Oxford University Press, 1990, 122–36.

Klandermans, Bert. The Social Construction of Protest and Multiorganizational Fields. In *Frontiers of Social Movement Research*, ed. by Aldon Morris and Carol McClurg Mueller. New Haven, CT. Yale University Press, 1992, 77–103.

Klandermans, Bert. Transient Identities? Membership Patterns in the Dutch Peace Movement. In *New Social Movements: From Ideology to Identity*, ed. by Enrique Larana, Hank Johnston and Joseph R. Gusfield. Philadelphia, PA. Temple University Press, 1994, 185–208.

Klandermans, Bert. *The Social Psychology of Protest.* Cambridge, MA. Blackwell
     Publishers, 1997.
Klein, Ethel. The Diffusion of Consciousness in the United States and Western Europe.
     In *The Women's Movements of the United States and Western Europe:
     Consciousness, Political Opportunity, and Public Policy*, ed. by Mary Fainsod
     Katzenstein and Carol McClurg Mueller. Philadelphia, PA. Temple University
     Press, 1987, 23–43.
Knoke, David, and Nancy Wisely. Social Movements. In *Political Networks: The
     Structural Perspective*, ed. by David Knoke. Cambridge, MA. Cambridge
     University Press, 1990, 57–84.
Kornbluh, Joyce L., and Mary Frederickson (eds.). *Sisterhood and Solidarity: Workers'
     Education for Women, 1914–1984*. Philadelphia, PA. Temple University Press,
     1984.
La Luz, Jose, and Paula Finn. Getting Serious about Inclusion: A Comprehensive
     Approach. In *A New Labor Movement for the New Century*, ed. by Gregory
     Mantsios. New York, NY. Garland, 1998, 213–232.
Leidner, Robin. Constituency, Accountability, and Deliberation: Reshaping Democracy
     in the National Women's Studies Association. *NWSA Journal*, vol. 5, 1993, 4–
     27.
Mannheim, Karl. The Problem of Generations. In *Essays on the Sociology of Knowledge*,
     ed. by Paul Kecskemeti. London. Routledge and Kegan Paul, 1952, 276–321.
Mansbridge, Jane. *Why We Lost the ERA.* Chicago, IL. University of Chicago Press,
     1986.
Mansbridge, Jane. What is the Feminist Movement? In *Feminist Organizations: Harvest
     of the New Women's Movement*, ed. by Myra Marx Ferree and Patricia Yancey
     Martin. Philadelphia, PA. Temple University Press, 1995, 27–34.
Mansbridge, Jane, and Aldon Morris. *Oppositional Consciousness. The Subjective Roots
     of Social Protest.* Chicago, IL. University of Chicago Press, 2001.
Martin, Patricia Yancey. Rethinking Feminist Organizations. *Gender and Society,* vol. 4,
     1990, 182–206.
Martin, Patricia Yancey, Sandra Seymour, Karolyn Godbey, Myrna Courage, and
     Richard Tate. Corporate, Union, Feminist, and Pro-Family Leaders' Views on
     Work-Family Relations. *Gender and Society,* vol. 2, 1988, 385–400.
Mazey, Sonia. *Gender Mainstreaming in the EU. Principles and Practice.* London.
     Kogan Page, 2001.
McAdam, Doug. *Political Process and the Development of Black Insurgency, 1930–
     1970.* Chicago, IL. University of Chicago Press, 1982.
McAdam, Doug. *Freedom Summer.* New York, NY. Oxford University Press, 1988a.
McAdam, Doug. Micromobilization Contexts and Recruitment to Activism. *International
     Social Movement Research*, vol. 1, 1988b, 125–154.
McAdam, Doug. The Biographical Consequences of Activism. *American Sociological
     Review*, vol. 54, 1989, 744–760.
McAdam, Doug. Gender as a Mediator of the Activist Experience: The Case of Freedom
     Summer. *American Journal of Sociology*, vol. 97, 1992, 1211–1240.

McAdam, Doug. Culture and Social Movements. In *New Social Movements: From Ideology to Identity*, ed. by Enrique Larana, Hank Johnston, and Joseph R. Gusfield. Philadelphia, PA. Temple University Press, 1994, 36–57.

McAdam, Doug and Dieter Rucht. The Cross-National Diffusion of Movement Ideas. *Annals of the American Academy of Political and Social Science*, vol. 528, 1993, 56–74.

McCarthy, John, and Mayer Zald. Resource Mobilization and Social Movements. A Partial Theory. *American Journal of Sociology*, vol. 82, 1977, 1212–1241.

Melucci, Alberto. *Nomads of the Present. Social Movements and Individual Needs in Contemporary Society.* Philadelphia, PA. Temple University Press, 1989.

Meyer, David S., and Nancy Whittier. Social Movement Spillover. *Social Problems*, vol. 41, 1994, 277–298.

Michels, Robert. *Political Parties: A Sociological Study of the Oligarchical Tendencies of Modern Democracy.* New York, NY. The Free Press, 1962.

Miethe, Ingrid. *Frauen in der DDR Opposition. Lebens- und kollektivgeschichtliche Verläufe in einer Frauenfriedensgruppe.* Opladen. Leske und Budrich, 1999.

Miethe, Ingrid, and Silke Roth. Einleitung: Biografische Ansätze und Paradigmen der Bewegungsforschung. In *Politische Biografien und sozialer Wandel*, ed. by Ingrid Miethe and Silke Roth. Giessen. Psychosozial, 2000, 7–24.

Milkman, Ruth. Women Workers, Feminism and the Labor Movement since the 1960s. In *Women, Work and Protest: A Century of U.S. Women's Labor History*, ed. by Ruth Milkman. Boston, MA. Routledge and Kegan Paul, 1985b, 300–322.

Milkman, Ruth. *Gender at Work: The Dynamics of Job Segregation by Sex during World War II.* Urbana, IL. University of Illinois Press, 1987.

Milkman, Ruth. Gender and Trade Unions in Historical Perspective. In *Women, Politics and Change*, ed. by Louise A. Tilly and Patricia Gurin. New York, NY. Russell Sage Foundation, 1990, 87–107.

Milkman, Ruth. Organizing Immigrant Women in New York's Chinatown: An Interview with Katie Quan. In *Women and Unions: Forging a Partnership*, ed. by Dorothy Sue Cobble. Ithaca, NY. ILR Press, 1993a, 281–298.

Milkman, Ruth. Union Responses to Workforce Feminization in the United States. In *The Challenge of Restructuring: North American Labor Movements Respond*, ed. by Jane Jenson and Rianne Mahon. Philadelphia, PA. Temple University Press, 1993b, 226–250.

Milkman, Ruth. Introduction. In *Organizing Immigrants. The Challenge for Unions IN Contemporary California*, ed. by Ruth Milkman. Ithaca, NY. ILR Press, 2000, 1–24.

Milkman, Ruth (ed.). *Women, Work and Protest: A Century of U.S. Women's Labor History.* Boston, MA. Routledge and Kegan Paul, 1985a.

Mills, C. Wright. *The Sociological Imagination.* Oxford. Oxford University Press, 1959.

Mische, Anne. Cross-Talk in Movements: Reconceiving the Culture-Network Link. In *Social Movements and Networks: Relational Approaches to Collective Action*, ed. by Mario Diani and Doug McAdam. Oxford. Oxford University Press, 2003, 258–280.

Moore, Kelly. *Doing Good while Doing Science: The Origins and Consequences of Public Interest Science Organizations in America, 1945–1990.* Unpublished dissertation, University of Arizona, 1993.

Morgan, Kimberly. Cash for Care: The Origins and Impacts of the Private Model of Child Care Provision in the U.S. Paper presented at the 2001 Annual Meeting of the American Political Science Association. San Francisco, 2001.

Morgen, Sandra, and Ann Bookman. Rethinking Women and Politics: An Introductory Essay. In *Women and the Politics of Empowerment*, ed. by Ann Bookman and Sandra Morgen. Philadelphia, PA. Temple University Press, 1988, 3–29.

Morris, Aldon D. *The Origins of the Civil Rights Movement. Black Communities Organizing for Change.* New York, NY. The Free Press, 1984.

Morris, Aldon D. Political Consciousness and Collective Action. In *Frontiers in Social Movement Theory*, ed. by Aldon D. Morris and Carol McClurg Mueller. New Haven, CT. Yale University Press, 1992, 351–374.

Morris, Aldon D., Shirley J. Hatchett, and Ronald E. Brown. The Civil Rights Movement and Black Political Socialization. In *Political Learning in Adulthood: Sourcebook of Theory and Research*, ed. by Roberta S. Sigel. Chicago, IL. University of Chicago Press, 1989, 272–305.

Myerson, Harold. A Second Chance: The New AFL–CIO and the Prospective Revival of American Labor. In *Not Your Father's Union Movement*, ed. by Jo-Ann Mort. London. Verso, 1998, 1–26.

Needleman, Ruth. Women Workers: Strategies for Inclusion and Rebuilding Unionism. In *A New Labor Movement for the New Century*, ed. by Gregory Mantsios. New York, NY. Garland, 1998, 213–232.

O'Farrell, Brigid, and Joyce L. Kornbluh (eds.). *Rocking the Boat: Union Women's Voices, 1915–1975,* ed. by New Brunswick, NJ. Rutgers, 1996.

O'Farrell, Brigid, and Suzanne Moore. Unions, Hard Hats, and Women Workers. In *Women and Unions: Forging a Partnership*, ed. by Dorothy Sue Cobble. Ithaca, NY. ILR Press, 1993, 69–84.

Oliver, Pamela. "If You Don't Do It, Nobody Else Will": Active and Token Contributors to Local Collective Action. *American Sociological Review*, vol. 49, 1984, 601–640.

Payne, Charles. Ella Baker and Models of Social Change. *Signs,* vol. 14, 1989, 885–889.

Payne, Charles. "Men Led, but Women Organized": Movement Participation of Women in the Mississippi Delta. In *Women and Social Protest*, ed. by Guida West and Rhoda Lois Blumberg. New York, NY. Oxford University Press, 1990, 156–165.

Piven, Francis Ford, and Richard A. Cloward. *Poor Peoples Movements: Why They Succeed, How They Fail.* New York, NY. Vintage Books, 1979.

Powell, Walter W., and Paul DiMaggio. Expanding the Scope of Institutional Analysis. In *The New Institutionalism in Organizational Analysis*, ed. by Walter Powell and Paul DiMaggio. London. University of Chicago Press, 1991, 183–203.

Ray, Raka. *Fields of Protest*. Minneapolis, MN. University of Minnesota Press, 1999.

Reinelt, Claire. Moving onto the Terrain of the State: The Battered Women's Movement and the Politics of Engagement. In *Feminist Organizations: Harvest of the New Women's Movement*, ed. by Myra Marx Ferree and Patricia Yancey Martin. Philadelphia, PA. Temple University Press, 1995, 84-104.

Reverby, Susan. An Epilogue or Prologue to CLUW? *Radical America*, vol. 9, 1975, 111–114.

Riccucci, Norma M. *Women, Minorities, and Unions in the Public Sector*. (Contributions in Labor Studies, Number 1928). Westport, CT. Greenwood Press, 1990.

Rinehart, Sue Tolleson. *Gender Consciousness and Politics*. New York, NY. Routledge, 1992.

Robinson, Ian. Economistic Unionism in Crisis: The Origins, Consequences, and Prospects of Divergence in Labour-Movement Characteristics. In *The Challenge of Restructuring: North American Labor Movements Respond*, ed. by Jane Jenson and Rianne Mahon. Philadelphia, PA. Temple University Press, 1993, 19–47.

Robnett, Belinda. *How Long? How Long? African-American Women in the Struggle for Civil Rights*. New York, NY. Oxford University Press. 1997.

Roby, Pamela. Becoming Shop Stewards. Perspectives on Gender and Race in Ten Trade Unions. *Labor Studies Journal*, vol. 20, 1995, 65–82.

Roby, Pamela, and Lynet Uttal. Putting It All Together: The Dilemmas of Rank-and-File Union Leaders. In *Women and Unions: Forging a Partnership*, ed. by Dorothy Sue Cobble. Ithaca, NY. ILR Press, 1993, 363–377.

Roediger, David R. *The Wages of Whiteness: Race and the Making of the American Working Class*. New York, NY. Verso, 1991.

Rose, Fred. *Coalitions across the Class Divide: Lessons from the Labor, Peace, and Environmental Movements*. Ithaca, NY. Cornell University Press, 2000.

Roth, Benita. *Race, Ethnicity and the Women's Movement in America: The Separate Roads of Black, Chicana, and White Feminism*. Cambridge, MA Cambridge University Press, 2004.

Roth, Silke. Developing Working Class Feminism: A Biographical Approach to Social Movement Participation. In *Self, Identity and Social Movements*, ed. by Sheldon Stryker, Timothy Owens, and Robert W. White. Minneapolis, MN. University of Minnesota Press, 2000, 300–323.

Rothschild-Whitt, Joyce. The Collectivist Organization. An Alternative to Rational-Bureaucratic Models. *American Sociological Review*, vol. 44, 1979, 509–527.

Rundblad, Georganne. Gender, Power, and Sexual Harassment. In *Gender Mosaics: Sociological Perspectives*, ed. by Dana Vannoy. Los Angeles, CA. Roxbury, 2001, 352–362.

Rupp, Leila J., and Verta Taylor. *Survival in the Doldrums. The American Women's Right's Movement, 1945 to the 1960s*. New York, NY. Oxford University Press, 1987.

Rushing, Beth. Choices and Contexts: The Social Construction of Reproduction. In *Gender Mosaics: Sociological Perspectives*, ed. by Dana Vannoy. Los Angeles, CA. Roxbury, 2001, 448–457.

Ryan, Barbara. *Feminism and the Women's Movement. Dynamics of Change in Social Movement Ideology and Activism*. London. Routledge, 1992.

Sapiro, Virginia. The Women's Movement and the Creation of Gender Consciousness. Social Movements As Socialization Agents. In *Political Socialization, Citizenship Education, and Democracy*, ed. by Orit Ichilov. New York, NY. Teachers College, Columbia University, 1990, 266–280.

Sapiro, Virginia. Political Socialization during Adulthood. Clarifying the Political Time of Our Lives. *Research in Micropolitics*, vol. 4, 1994, 197–223.

Schlozman, Kay Lehman. Representing Women in Washington: Sisterhood and Pressure Politics. In *Women, Politics, and Change*, ed. by Louise A. Tilly and Patricia Gurin. New York, NY. Russell Sage Foundation, 1991, 339–382.

Schrecker, Ellen. *Many Are the Crimes: McCarthyism in America*. Boston, MA. Little, Brown, 1998.

Seifer, Nancy, and Barbara Wertheimer. New Approaches to Collective Action. In *Women Organizing: An Anthology*, ed. by Bernice Cummings and Victoria Schuck. New York, NY. Basic Books, 1979, 152–183.

Sexton, Patricia Cayo. Workers (Female) Arise! *Dissent*, vol. 21, no. 3, 1974, 380–95.

Skocpol, Theda. *Protecting Soldiers and Mothers. The Political Origins of Social Policy in the United States*. Cambridge, MA Belknap, 1992

Snow, David A., and Robert D. Benford. Master Frames and Cycles of Protest. In *Frontiers in Social Movement Theory*, ed. by Aldon D. Morris and Carol McClurg Mueller. New Haven/London. Yale University Press, 1992, 133–155.

Snow, David A., E. Burke Rochford Jr., Steven K. Worden, and Robert D. Benford. Frame Alignment Processes, Micromobilization, and Movement Participation. *American Sociological Review*, vol. 51, 1986, 464–481.

Spalter-Roth, Roberta, Heidi Hartmann, and Nancy Collins. What Do Unions Do for Women? In *Restoring the Promise of American Labor Law*, ed. by Sheldon Friedman, Richard W. Hurd, Rudolph A. Oswald, and Ronald L. Seeber. Ithaca, NY. ILR Press, 1994, 193–206.

Spalter-Roth, Roberta, and Ronnee Schreiber. Outsider Issues and Insider Tactics: Strategic Tensions in the Women's Policy Network during the 1980s. In *Feminist Organizations: Harvest of the New Women's Movement*, ed. by Myra Marx Ferree and Patricia Yancey Martin. Philadelphia, PA. Temple University Press, 1995, 105–127.

Staggenborg, Suzanne. The Consequences of Professionalization and Formalization in the Pro-Choice Movement. *American Sociological Review*, vol. 53, 1988, 585–606.

Staggenborg, Suzanne. Stability and Innovation in the Women's Movement: A Comparison of Two Movement Organizations. *Social Problems*, vol. 36, 1989, 75–92.

Staggenborg, Suzanne. Can Feminist Organizations Be Effective? In *Feminist Organizations. Harvest of the New Women's Movement*, ed. by Myra Marx Ferree and Patricia Yancey Martin. Philadelphia, PA. Temple University Press, 1995, 339–355.

Strauss, Anselm. *Mirrors and Masks: The Search for Identity*. Glencoe, IL. The Free Press, 1959.

Strobel, Margaret. Organizational Learning in the Chicago Women's Liberation Union. In *Feminist Organizations: Harvest of the New Women's Movement*, ed. by Myra Marx Ferree and Patricia Yancey Martin. Philadelphia, PA. Temple University Press, 1995, 145–164.

Strom, Sharon Hartman. 'We're No Kitty Foyles': Organizing Office Workers for the Congress of Industrial Organization, 1937–50. In *Women Work, and Protest: A Century of US Women's Labor History*, ed. by Ruth Milkman. New York, NY. Routledge, 1985, 206–234.

Tarrow, Sidney. *Power in Movement. Social Movements, Collective Action, and Politics.* Cambridge, MA. Cambridge University Press, 1994.

Tax, Meredith. *The Rising of the Women. Feminist Solidarity and Class Conflict, 1880–1917.* New York, NY. Monthly Review Press, 1980.

Taylor, Verta. Social Movement Continuity: The Women's Movement in Abeyance. *American Sociological Review*, vol. 54, 1989, 761–775.

Taylor, Verta, and Leila J. Rupp, Leila J. Loving Internationalism: The Emotion Culture of Transnational Women's Organizations, 1888-1945. *Mobilization*, vol. 7, 2002, 141-158.

Taylor, Verta, and Nancy E. Whittier. Collective Identity in Social Movement Communities: Lesbian Feminist Mobilization. In *Frontiers of Social Movement Research*, ed. by Aldon D. Morris and Carol McClurg Mueller. New Haven, CT. Yale University Press, 1992, 104–129.

Tilly, Charles. *From Mobilization to Revolution.* Reading, MA. Addison-Wesley, 1978.

Troger, Annemarie. Coalition of Labor Union Women: Strategic Hope, Tactical Despair. *Radical America*, vol. 9, 1975, 85–110.

Tuchman, Gaye. *Making News: A Study in the Construction of Reality.* New York, NY. The Free Press, 1978.

Tuchman, Gaye, and Harry Gene Levine. New York Jews and Chinese Food: The Social Construction of an Ethnic Pattern. *Journal of Contemporary Ethnography*, vol. 22, 1993, 382–407.

Turner, Lowell, Harry Katz, and Richard W. Hurd (eds.). *Rekindling the Movement: Labor's Quest for Relevance in the 21st Century.* Ithaca, NY. ILR Press, 2001.

Wallace, Phyllis A., and James W. Driscoll. Social Issues in Collective Bargaining. In *U.S. Industrial Relations 1950–1980: A Critical Appraisal. Industrial Relations Research Association*, ed. by Jack Stieber et al. Madison, WI. Industrial Relations Research Association. 1981, 199–254.

Wasburn, Philo C. A Life Course Model of Political Socialization. *Politics and the Individual,* Vol. 4, 1994, 1–26.

Weber, Max. *Economy and Society. An Outline of Interpretative Sociology.* 2 vols. Berkeley, CA. University of California Press, 1979.

Weigand, Kate. *Red Feminism: American Communism and the Making of Women's Liberation.* Baltimore. Johns Hopkins Press, 2001.

Wertheimer, Barbara. *We Were There.* New York, NY. Pantheon Books, 1977.

Wertheimer, Barbara M., and Anne H. Nelson. *Trade Union Women. A Study of Their Participation in New York City Locals.* New York, NY. Praeger, 1975.

Whalen, Jack and Richard Flacks. *Beyond the Barricades. The Sixties Generation Grows Up.* Philadelphia, PA. Temple University Press, 1989.

Whittier, Nancy. *Feminist Generations. The Persistence of the Radical Women's Movement*. Philadelphia, PA. Temple University Press, 1995.

Withorn, Ann. The Death of CLUW. *Radical America*, vol. 10, 1976, 48–54.

Zavella, Patricia. The Politics of Race and Gender: Organizing Chicana Cannery Workers in Northern California. In *Women and the Politics of Empowerment*, ed. by Ann Bookman and Sandra Morgen. Philadelphia, PA. Temple University Press, 1988, 202–224.

Zippel, Kathrin. *Policies against Sexual Harassment: Gender Equality Policies in Germany, the European Union, and the United States in Comparative Perspective*. Ph.D. dissertation. University of Wisconsin-Madison, 2000.

CLUW PUBLICATIONS

1975   *Women and Health Security*

1977   *Commitment to Child Care*

1979   *Effective Contract Language for Union Women, CLUW Health and Safety-Series*

1980   *Absent from the Agenda* (Glassberg, Baden and Gerstel 1980)

1981   *Lead. A New Perspective on an Old Problem*

1982   *A Handbook for Empowerment of Union Women, Color Me Union*

1985   *Bargaining for Child Care. A Union Parent's Guide*

1986   *Sexual Harassment. An Ongoing Barrier to Equal Opportunity*

1990   *Women and Children First. An Analysis of Trends in Federal Tax Policy*

1991   *Is Your Job Making You Sick? A CLUW Handbook on Workplace Hazards, Bargaining for Family Benefits: A Union Member's Guide*

1993   *Union Women Speak Out on Health Care Issues Including Abortion, Women Care About Health, Family Medical Leave Act. A Resource Guide*

1996   *Coalition of Labor Union Women Leadership Directory*

2000   *Sharing Our Stories*

1975–2002 *CLUW News* (newsletter)

Index

About the Author

SILKE ROTH is Visiting Assistant Professor of Sociology, University of Pennsylvania.